CONTENTS

INTRODUCTION

What's the difference between an air fryer and deep fryer?

Air fryers bake food at a high temperature with a high-powered fan, while deep fryers cook food in a vat of oil that has been heated up to a specific temperature. Both cook food quickly, but an air fryer requires practically zero preheat time while a deep fryer can take upwards of 10 minutes. Air fryers also require little to no oil and deep fryers require a lot that absorb into the food. Food comes out crispy and juicy in both appliances, but don't taste the same, usually because deep fried foods are coated in batter that cook differently in an air fryer vs a deep fryer. Battered foods needs to be sprayed with oil before cooking in an air fryer to help them color and get crispy, while the hot oil soaks into the batter in a deep fryer. Flour-based batters and wet batters don't cook well in an air fryer, but they come out very well in a deep fryer.

AIR FRYER
CHEAT SHEET

Master everything from juicy chicken breast to crispy Brussels sprouts, without fail. Most foods can be reheated in an air fryer in 5 to 8 minutes at 300°F without drying out or becoming rubbery.

INGREDIENT	TEMP	TIME	PREP
CHICKEN BREASTS, 6 oz each	380°F	10 TO 15 MIN.	Brush with oil, season and flip halfway through cooking.
CHICKEN WINGS, split, 1 lb	400°F	20 TO 25 MIN.	Toss with seasoning.
CHICKEN THIGHS, bone-in	400°F	15 TO 20 MIN.	Season and arrange skin side up.
PORK CHOPS, bone-in, 1 in. thick	400°F	10 TO 15 MIN.	Season and flip halfway through cooking.
STEAK, 1 in. thick	400°F	10 TO 15 MIN.	Season and flip halfway through cooking.
FISH FILLETS, 1 in. thick, 6 oz each	400°F	8 TO 10 MIN.	Brush with oil and season.
SWEET POTATOES, cut into 1-in. wedges	400°F	12 TO 15 MIN.	Toss with oil, season and shake basket halfway through cooking.
BRUSSELS SPROUTS, halved	400°F	10 TO 15 MIN.	Toss with oil, season and shake basket twice during cooking.
BUTTERNUT SQUASH, cut into 1-in. pieces	400°F	12 TO 15 MIN.	Toss with oil, season and shake basket halfway through cooking.
FROZEN FRIES, 1 lb.	400°F	15 TO 20 MIN.	Shake twice during cooking.

Air fryers are *fast*, and once you understand how they work, they can be used to heat **frozen foods or cook all sorts of fresh food** like chicken, steak, pork chops, salmon and veggies. Most meats require no added oil because they're already so juicy: just season them with salt and your favorite herbs and spices. Make sure you stick to dry seasonings — less moisture leads to crispier results. If you want to baste meats with barbecue sauce or honey, wait until the last couple minutes of cooking.

Lean cuts of meat, or foods with little or no fat, require oil to brown and crisp up. Brush boneless chicken breasts and pork chops with a bit of oil before seasoning. Vegetable oil or canola oil is usually recommended due to its higher smoke point, meaning it can stand up to the high heat in an air fryer.

Vegetables also need to be tossed in oil before air frying. We recommend sprinkling them with salt before air frying, but use a little less than you're used to: The crispy, air fried bits pack a lot of flavor. We love air frying broccoli florets, Brussels sprouts and baby potato halves. They come out so crispy! Butternut squash, sweet potatoes and beets all seem to get sweeter, and green beans and peppers take no time at all.

TRY IT!
9 FOODS YOU SHOULD AIR-FRY

Because of the unique way an air fryer cooks, it's one of the most versatile appliances we've tested. Trust it to perfectly melt cheese, cook delicate meats and more.

Grilled Cheese	S'mores	Burgers
Nachos	Lobster Tails	Pork Chops
Salmon	Veggie Tots	Cauliflower Gnocchi

Are air fryers worth it?

First off, consider whether you're in the market for another appliance. Many toaster ovens have air frying capabilities now, like the Cuisinart TOA-65 and the Breville Smart Oven Air, as do some pressure cookers, like the Ninja Foodi. If you do decide to spring for an air fryer, consider that salone air fryers range in price from $40 for small compact ones to $400 for large, air fryer toaster ovens. When shopping for an air fryer, consider how many people you're cooking for: The smallest air fryers (1.2 liters) are good for 1-2 people, while the medium sizes (3-4 liters) are good for 2-3 people, and the largest (6 liters or more) are good for 4-6. We prefer air fryers with baskets instead of shelves because they cook more evenly.

VEGETABLE & SIDE DISHES

1. Cauliflower Tots

Servings: 8
Cooking Time: 20 Minutes
Ingredients:
- 1 large head cauliflower
- ½ cup parmesan cheese, grated
- 1 cup mozzarella cheese, shredded
- 1 tsp. seasoned salt
- 1 egg

Directions:
1. Place a steamer basket over a pot of boiling water, ensuring the water is not high enough to enter the basket.
2. Cut up the cauliflower into florets and transfer to the steamer basket. Cover the pot with a lid and leave to steam for seven minutes, making sure the cauliflower softens.
3. Place the florets on a cheesecloth and leave to cool. Remove as much moisture as possible. This is crucial as it ensures the cauliflower will harden.
4. In a bowl, break up the cauliflower with a fork.
5. Stir in the parmesan, mozzarella, seasoned salt, and egg, incorporating the cauliflower well with all of the other ingredients. Make sure the mixture is firm enough to be moldable.
6. Using your hand, mold about two tablespoons of the mixture into tots and repeat until you have used up all of the mixture. Put each tot into your air fryer basket. They may need to be cooked in multiple batches.
7. Cook at 320°F for twelve minutes, turning them halfway through. Ensure they are brown in color before serving.

2. Garlic Mushrooms

Servings: 4
Cooking Time: 5 Minutes
Ingredients:
- 4 Portobello mushroom caps
- 4 teaspoons olive oil
- 1 teaspoon garlic, diced

Directions:
1. Trim the mushrooms if needed. Preheat the air fryer to 400F. In the mixing bowl mix up oil and garlic. Sprinkle the mushrooms with garlic mixture and put in the how air fryer. Cook the mushroom steaks for 5 minutes.

3. Rosemary Crispy Potatoes

Servings:4
Cooking Time: 35 Minutes
Ingredients:
- 2 tbsp olive oil
- 3 garlic cloves, grated
- 1 tbsp minced fresh rosemary
- 1 tsp salt
- ¼ tsp freshly ground black pepper

Directions:
1. In a bowl, mix potatoes, olive oil, garlic, rosemary, salt, and pepper, until they are well-coated. Arrange the potatoes in the air fryer and cook on 360 F for 25 minutes, shaking twice during the cooking. Cook until crispy on the outside and tender on the inside.

4. Roasted Mushrooms

Servings: 4

Cooking Time: 15 Minutes

Ingredients:

- 2 lbs mushrooms, clean and quarters
- 2 tbsp vermouth
- 2 tsp herb de Provence
- 1/2 tsp garlic powder
- 1 tbsp butter, melted

Directions:

1. Add mushrooms in a bowl with remaining ingredients and toss well.
2. Transfer mushrooms into the air fryer basket and cook at 320 F for 15 minutes. Toss halfway through.
3. Serve and enjoy.

5. Air-frier Baked Potatoes

Servings:4

Cooking Time: 45 Minutes

Ingredients:

- 2 tbsp olive oil
- Salt and ground black pepper to taste

Directions:

1. Rub potatoes with half tbsp of olive oil. Season with salt and pepper, and arrange them on the air fryer. Cook for 40 minutes at 400 F. Let cool slightly, then make a slit on top. Use a fork to fluff the insides of the potatoes. Fill the potato with cheese or garlic mayo.

6. Sweet Garlicky Chicken Wings

Servings:4

Cooking Time: 20 Minutes

Ingredients:

- ¼ cup butter
- ¼ cup honey
- ½ tbsp salt

- 4 garlic cloves, minced
- ¾ cup potato starch

Directions:

1. Preheat air fryer to 370 F. Mix chicken with starch. Place in the air fryer. Cook for 5 minutes. Whisk the rest of the ingredients in a bowl. Pour the sauce over the wings and cook for another 10 minutes.

7. Skinny Pumpkin Chips

Servings: 2

Cooking Time: 20 Minutes

Ingredients:

- 1 pound pumpkin, cut into sticks
- 1 tablespoon coconut oil
- 1/2 teaspoon rosemary
- 1/2 teaspoon basil
- Salt and ground black pepper, to taste

Directions:

1. Start by preheating the Air Fryer to 395 degrees F. Brush the pumpkin sticks with coconut oil; add the spices and toss to combine.
2. Cook for 13 minutes, shaking the basket halfway through the cooking time.
3. Serve with mayonnaise. Bon appétit!

8. Healthy Green Beans

Servings: 4

Cooking Time: 6 Minutes

Ingredients:

- 1 lb green beans, trimmed
- Pepper
- Salt

Directions:

1. Spray air fryer basket with cooking spray.
2. Preheat the air fryer to 400 F.

3. Add green beans in air fryer basket and season with pepper and salt.
4. Cook green beans for 6 minutes. Turn halfway through.
5. Serve and enjoy.

9. Corn-crusted Chicken Tenders

Servings:4
Cooking Time: 25 Minutes
Ingredients:
- Salt and black pepper to taste
- 1 egg
- 1 cup ground cornmeal

Directions:
1. Preheat the Air Fryer to 390 F.
2. In a bowl, mix ground cornmeal, salt, and pepper. In another bowl, beat egg; season with salt and pepper. Dip the chicken in the egg and then coat in cornmeal; shake off. Spray the prepared sticks with cooking spray and place them in the air fryer basket in a single layer. Cook for 6 minutes. Slide out the basket and flip; cook for another 6 minutes until golden brown. Serve with your favorite dip.

10. Air-fried Crispy Chicken Thighs

Servings:4
Cooking Time: 30 Minutes
Ingredients:
- ½ tsp salt
- ¼ tsp black pepper
- ¼ tsp garlic powder

Directions:

1. Season the thighs with salt, pepper, and garlic powder. Arrange thighs, skin side down, in the air fryer and cook until golden brown, for 20 minutes at 350 F.

11. Chili Rutabaga

Servings: 4
Cooking Time: 20 Minutes
Ingredients:
- 15 ounces rutabaga, cut into fries
- 4 tablespoons olive oil
- 1 teaspoon chili powder
- A pinch of salt and black pepper

Directions:
1. In a bowl, mix the rutabaga fries with all the other ingredients, toss and put them in your air fryer's basket. Cook at 400 degrees F for 20 minutes, divide between plates and serve as a side dish.

12. Rosemary Potato Chips

Servings:3
Cooking Time: 50 Minutes
Ingredients:
- ¼ cup olive oil
- 1 tbsp garlic
- ½ cup cream
- 2 tbsp rosemary

Directions:
1. Preheat your air fryer to 390 F.
2. In a bowl, add oil, garlic and salt to form a marinade.Add in potatoes and allow sitting for 30 minutes. Lay the potato slices onto your air fryer's cooking basket and cook for 20 minutes. After 10 minutes, give the chips a turn, sprinkle with rosemary and serve.

13. Homemade Peanut Corn Nuts

Servings: 4
Cooking Time: 30 Minutes
Ingredients:
- 3 tbsp peanut oil
- 2 tbsp old bay seasoning
- Salt to taste

Directions:
1. Preheat the Air Fryer to 390 F.
2. Pat dry hominy and season with salt and old bay seasoning. Drizzle with oil and toss to coat. Spread in the air fryer basket. Cook for 14 minutes. Slide out the basket and shake; cook for another 10 minutes until crispy. Remove to a towel-lined plate to soak up the excess fat. Leave to cool before serving.

14. Lemon Roasted Peppers

Servings: 4
Cooking Time: 8 Minutes
Ingredients:
- 4 shishito peppers
- 1 teaspoon lemon juice
- ½ teaspoon sesame oil

Directions:
1. Pierce the shishito peppers to make many small cuts and sprinkle them with lemon juice and sesame oil. Preheat the air fryer to 400F. Put the peppers in the air fryer basket and cook them for 4 minutes from each side.

15. Paprika Jicama

Servings: 5
Cooking Time: 7 Minutes
Ingredients:

- 15 oz jicama, peeled
- ½ teaspoon salt
- ½ teaspoon ground paprika
- ½ teaspoon chili flakes
- 1 teaspoon sesame oil

Directions:
1. Preheat the air fryer to 400F. Cut Jicama into the small sticks and sprinkle with salt, ground paprika, and chili flakes. Then put the Jicama stick in the air fryer and sprinkle with sesame oil. Cook the vegetables for 4 minutes. Then shake them well and cook for 3 minutes.

16. Not-so-plain Grilled Plantains

Servings: 2
Cooking Time: 8 Minutes
Ingredients:
- 2 ripe plantains, sliced
- A pinch of salt to taste
- Oil for brushing

Directions:
1. Place the grill pan accessory in the air fryer.
2. Arrange the plantain slices on the grill pan.
3. Sprinkle with salt and brush with oil on both sides.
4. Close the air fryer and cook for 8 minutes at 300°F.

17. Mustard Greens Mix

Servings: 6
Cooking Time: 12 Minutes
Ingredients:
- 1 pound collard greens, trimmed

- ¼ pound bacon, cooked and chopped
- A drizzle of olive oil
- Salt and black pepper to taste
- ½ cup veggie stock

Directions:
1. Place all ingredients in a pan that fits your air fryer and mix well.
2. Put the pan in the fryer and cook at 260 degrees F for 12 minutes.
3. Divide everything between plates and serve.

18. Breaded Mushrooms

Servings:4
Cooking Time: 55 Minutes
Ingredients:
- 2 cups breadcrumbs
- 2 eggs, beaten
- Salt and pepper to taste
- 2 cups Parmigiano Reggiano cheese, grated

Directions:
1. Preheat air fryer to 360 F. Pour breadcrumbs in a bowl, add salt and pepper and mix well. Pour cheese in a separate bowl. Dip each mushroom in the eggs, then in the crumbs, and then in the cheese. Slide-out the fryer basket and add 6 to 10 mushrooms. Cook for 20 minutes. Serve with cheese dip.

19. Bacon Green Beans Mix

Servings: 4
Cooking Time: 13 Minutes
Ingredients:
- 1 cup green beans, trimmed
- 4 oz bacon, sliced
- ¼ teaspoon salt
- 1 tablespoon avocado oil

Directions:
1. Wrap the green beans in the sliced bacon. After this, sprinkle the vegetables with salt and avocado oil. Preheat the air fryer to 385F. Carefully arrange the green beans in the air fryer in one layer and cook them for 5 minutes. Then flip the green beans on another side and cook for 8 minutes more.

20. Zucchini Parmesan Chips

Servings:3
Cooking Time: 15 Minutes
Ingredients:
- 1 cup breadcrumbs
- 2 eggs, beaten
- 1 cup grated Parmesan cheese
- Salt and pepper to taste
- 1 tsp smoked paprika

Directions:
1. In a bowl, add breadcrumbs, salt, pepper, cheese, and paprika. Mix well. Dip zucchini slices in eggs and then in the cheese mix while pressing to coat them well. Spray the coated slices with cooking spray and put the in the fryer basket. Cook at 350 F for 8 minutes. Serve with salt spicy dip.

21. Kabocha Fries

Servings: 2
Cooking Time: 11 Minutes
Ingredients:
- 6 oz Kabocha squash, peeled
- ½ teaspoon olive oil
- ½ teaspoon salt

Directions:

1. Cut the Kabocha squash into the shape of the French fries and sprinkle with olive oil. Preheat the air fryer to 390F. Put the Kabocha squash fries in the air fryer basket and cook them for 5 minutes. Then shake them well and cook for 6 minutes more. Sprinkle the cooked Kabocha fries with salt and mix up well.

22. Cajun Peppers

Servings: 4
Cooking Time: 12 Minutes
Ingredients:
- 1 tablespoon olive oil
- ½ pound mixed bell peppers, sliced
- 1 cup black olives, pitted and halved
- ½ tablespoon Cajun seasoning

Directions:
1. In a pan that fits the air fryer, combine all the ingredients. Put the pan it in your air fryer and cook at 390 degrees F for 12 minutes. Divide the mix between plates and serve.

23. Rosemary Green Beans

Servings: 1
Cooking Time: 10 Minutes
Ingredients:
- 1 tbsp. butter, melted
- 2 tbsp. rosemary
- ½ tsp. salt
- 3 cloves garlic, minced
- ¾ cup green beans, chopped

Directions:
1. Pre-heat your fryer at 390°F.
2. Combine the melted butter with the rosemary, salt, and minced garlic. Toss

in the green beans, making sure to coat them well.
3. Cook in the fryer for five minutes.

24. Simple Cheesy Melty Mushrooms

Servings:2
Cooking Time: 20 Minutes
Ingredients:
- Salt and pepper to taste
- 10 button mushromm caps
- 2 cups mozzarella cheese, chopped
- 2 cups cheddar cheese, chopped
- 3 tbsp mixture of Italian herbs

Directions:
1. Preheat your air fryer to 340 F. In a bowl, mix oil, salt, pepper, and herbs to form a marinade. Add button mushrooms to the marinade and toss to coat well. In a separate bowl, mix both kinds of cheese. Stuff mushrooms with the cheese mixture. Place in air fryer's cooking basket and cook for 10 minutes.

25. Elegant Carrot Cookies

Servings:8
Cooking Time: 30 Minutes
Ingredients:
- Salt and pepper to taste
- 1 tbsp parsley
- 1¼ oz oats
- 1 whole egg, beaten
- 1 tbsp thyme

Directions:
1. Preheat your air fryer to 360 F.
2. In a bowl, combine carrots with salt, pepper, beaten egg, oats, thyme , and

parsley and mix well. Form the batter into cookie shapes. Place in air fryer's basket and cook for 15 minutes.

26. Green Beans And Tomato Sauce

Servings: 4
Cooking Time: 15 Minutes
Ingredients:
- ½ pound green beans, trimmed and halved
- 1 cup black olives, pitted and halved
- ¼ cup bacon, cooked and crumbled
- 1 tablespoon olive oil
- ¼ cup keto tomato sauce

Directions:
1. In a pan that fits the air fryer, combine all the ingredients, toss, put the pan in the air fryer and cook at 380 degrees F for 15 minutes. Divide between plates and serve.

27. Spicy Olives And Tomato Mix

Servings: 4
Cooking Time: 15 Minutes
Ingredients:
- 2 cups kalamata olives, pitted
- 2 small avocados, pitted, peeled and sliced
- ¼ cup cherry tomatoes, halved
- Juice of 1 lime
- 1 tablespoon coconut oil, melted

Directions:
1. In a pan that fits the air fryer, combine the olives with the other ingredients, toss, put the pan in your air fryer and cook at 370 degrees F for 15 minutes.

Divide the mix between plates and serve.

28. Lemon Cabbage

Servings: 4
Cooking Time: 25 Minutes
Ingredients:
- 1 green cabbage head, shredded and cut into large wedges
- 2 tablespoons olive oil
- 1 tablespoon cilantro, chopped
- 1 tablespoon lemon juice
- A pinch of salt and black pepper

Directions:
1. Preheat your air fryer at 370 degrees F, add the cabbage wedges mixed with all the ingredients in the basket and cook for 25 minutes. Divide between plates and serve as a side dish.

29. Grilled Cheese

Servings: 2
Cooking Time: 25 Minutes
Ingredients:
- 4 slices bread
- ½ cup sharp cheddar cheese
- ¼ cup butter, melted

Directions:
1. Pre-heat the Air Fryer at 360°F.
2. Put cheese and butter in separate bowls.
3. Apply the butter to each side of the bread slices with a brush.
4. Spread the cheese across two of the slices of bread and make two sandwiches. Transfer both to the fryer.
5. Cook for 5 – 7 minutes or until a golden brown color is achieved and the cheese is melted.

30. Mozzarella Green Beans

Servings: 4
Cooking Time: 6 Minutes
Ingredients:
- 1 cup green beans, trimmed
- 2 oz Mozzarella, shredded
- 1 teaspoon butter
- ½ teaspoon chili flakes
- ¼ cup beef broth

Directions:
1. Sprinkle the green beans with chili flakes and put in the air fryer baking pan. Add beef broth and butter. Then top the vegetables with shredded Mozzarella. Preheat the air fryer to 400F. Put the pan with green beans in the air fryer and cook the meal for 6 minutes.

31. Perfect Crispy Tofu

Servings: 4
Cooking Time: 20 Minutes
Ingredients:
- 1 block firm tofu, pressed and cut into 1-inch cubes
- 1 tbsp arrowroot flour
- 2 tsp sesame oil
- 1 tsp vinegar
- 2 tbsp soy sauce

Directions:
1. In a bowl, toss tofu with oil, vinegar, and soy sauce and let sit for 15 minutes.
2. Toss marinated tofu with arrowroot flour.
3. Spray air fryer basket with cooking spray.
4. Add tofu in air fryer basket and cook for 20 minutes at 370 F. Shake basket halfway through.

5. Serve and enjoy.

32. Dill Tomato

Servings: 2
Cooking Time: 8 Minutes
Ingredients:
- 1 oz Parmesan, sliced
- 1 tomato
- 1 teaspoon fresh dill, chopped
- 1 teaspoon olive oil
- ¼ teaspoon dried thyme

Directions:
1. Trim the tomato and slice it on 2 pieces. Then preheat the air fryer to 350F. Top the tomato slices with sliced Parmesan, chopped fresh dill, and thyme. Sprinkle the tomatoes with olive oil and put in the air fryer. Cook the meal for 8 minutes. Remove cooked tomato parm from the air fryer with the help of the spatula.

33. Balsamic Okra

Servings: 2
Cooking Time: 6 Minutes
Ingredients:
- 1 teaspoon balsamic vinegar
- 1 teaspoon avocado oil
- 8 oz okra, sliced
- ½ teaspoon salt
- ½ teaspoon white pepper

Directions:
1. Sprinkle the sliced okra with avocado oil, salt, and white pepper. Then preheat the air fryer to 360F. Put the okra in the air fryer basket and cook it for 3 minutes. Then shake the sliced vegetables well and cook for 3 minutes more. Transfer the cooked okra in the

serving bowl and sprinkle with balsamic vinegar.

34. Hot Chicken Wingettes

Servings:3
Cooking Time: 30 Minutes
Ingredients:
- Salt and pepper to taste
- ⅓ cup hot sauce
- ½ tbsp vinegar

Directions:
1. Preheat air fryer to 360 F. Season the chicken with pepper and salt. Add to the air fryer and cook for 25 minutes. Toss every 5 minutes. Mix vinegar and hot sauce. Pour the sauce over the chicken to serve.

35. Butter Endives

Servings: 4
Cooking Time: 10 Minutes
Ingredients:
- 4 endives, trimmed and halved
- Salt and black pepper to taste
- 1 tablespoon lime juice
- 1 tablespoon butter, melted

Directions:
1. Put the endives in your air fryer, and add the salt, pepper, lemon juice, and butter.
2. Cook at 360 degrees F for 10 minutes.
3. Divide between plates and serve.

36. Bacon-wrapped Avocados

Servings:6
Cooking Time: 40 Minutes
Ingredients:
- 3 large avocados, sliced

- ⅓ tsp salt
- ⅓ tsp chili powder
- ⅓ tsp cumin powder

Directions:
1. Stretch the bacon strips to elongate and cut in half to make 24 pieces. Wrap each bacon piece around a slice of avocado. Tuck the end of bacon into the wrap. Season with salt, chili and cumin.
2. Arrange wrapped pieces on the fryer and cook at 350 F for 8 minutes, flipping halfway through to cook evenly. Remove onto a wire rack and repeat the process for the remaining avocado pieces.

37. Endives And Bacon

Servings: 4
Cooking Time: 10 Minutes
Ingredients:
- 4 endives, trimmed and halved
- Salt and black pepper to taste
- 1 tablespoon olive oil
- 2 tablespoons bacon, cooked and crumbled
- ½ teaspoon nutmeg, ground

Directions:
1. Put the endives in your air fryer's basket, and add the salt, pepper, oil, and nutmeg; toss gently.
2. Cook at 360 degrees F for 10 minutes.
3. Divide the endives between plates, sprinkle the bacon on top, and serve.

38. Carrot Crisps

Servings:2
Cooking Time: 20 Minutes
Ingredients:
- Salt to taste

Directions:

1. Put the carrot strips in a bowl and season with salt to taste. Grease the fryer basket lightly with cooking spray, and add the carrot strips. Cook at 350 F for 10 minutes, stirring once halfway through.

39. Green Beans And Tomatoes Recipe

Servings: 4
Cooking Time:25 Minutes
Ingredients:

- 1-pint cherry tomatoes
- 2 tbsp. olive oil
- 1 lb. green beans
- Salt and black pepper to the taste

Directions:

1. In a bowl; mix cherry tomatoes with green beans, olive oil, salt and pepper, toss, transfer to your air fryer and cook at 400 °F, for 15 minutes. Divide among plates and serve right away

40. Parmesan Crusted Pickles

Servings:4
Cooking Time: 35 Minutes
Ingredients:

- 2 eggs
- 2 tsp water
- 1 cup grated Parmesan cheese
- 1 ½ cups breadcrumbs, smooth
- Black pepper to taste

Directions:

1. Add breadcrumbs and pepper to a bowl and mix well. In another bowl, beat eggs with water. Add cheese to a separate bowl. Spray fryer basket and spray with cooking spray.

2. Preheat the air fryer to 400 F. Dredge the pickle slices in the egg mixture, then in breadcrumbs and then in cheese. Place them in the fryer. Cook for 4 minutes. Turn and cook for further for 5 minutes.

41. Lemon And Butter Artichokes

Servings: 4
Cooking Time: 15 Minutes
Ingredients:

- 12 ounces artichoke hearts
- Juice of ½ lemon
- 4 tablespoons butter, melted
- 2 tablespoons tarragon, chopped
- Salt and black pepper to the taste

Directions:

1. In a bowl, mix all the ingredients, toss, transfer the artichokes to your air fryer's basket and cook at 370 degrees F for 15 minutes. Divide between plates and serve as a side dish.

42. Macadamia And Cauliflower Rice

Servings: 4
Cooking Time: 8 Minutes
Ingredients:

- 9 oz cauliflower
- 1 tablespoon butter
- 1 oz macadamia nuts, grinded
- 3 tablespoons chicken broth

Directions:

1. Cut the cauliflower on the florets. Then grate the cauliflower with the help of the grater. Grease the air fryer pan with butter and put the cauliflower rice

inside. Add grinded macadamia nuts and chicken broth. Gently stir the vegetable mixture. Cook the cauliflower rice at 365F for 8 minutes. Stir the vegetables after 4 minutes of cooking.

43. Roasted Eggplant

Servings: 1
Cooking Time: 20 Minutes
Ingredients:
- 1 large eggplant
- 2 tbsp. olive oil
- ¼ tsp. salt
- ½ tsp. garlic powder

Directions:
1. Prepare the eggplant by slicing off the top and bottom and cutting it into slices around a quarter-inch thick.
2. Apply olive oil to the slices with a brush, coating both sides. Season each side with sprinklings of salt and garlic powder.
3. Place the slices in the fryer and cook for fifteen minutes at 390°F.
4. Serve right away.

44. Roasted Coconut Carrots

Servings: 4
Cooking Time: 15 Minutes
Ingredients:
- 1 pound horse carrots, sliced
- Salt and black pepper to taste
- ½ tsp chili powder

Directions:
1. Preheat the Air fryer to 400 F.
2. In a bowl, mix the carrots with coconut oil, chili powder, salt, and pepper. Place in the air fryer and cook for 7 minutes. Slide out the basket and shake;

cook for another 5 minutes until golden brown.

45. Cheesy Cheddar Biscuits

Servings: 8
Cooking Time: 35 Minutes
Ingredients:
- 2 tbsp sugar
- 3 cups flour
- 1 ⅓ cups buttermilk
- ½ cup Cheddar, grated

Directions:
1. Preheat your air fryer to 380 F. Lay a parchment paper on a baking plate. In a bowl, mix sugar, flour, ½ cup butter, cheese and buttermilk to form a batter. Make 8 balls from the batter and roll in flour.
2. Place the balls in your air fryer's cooking basket and flatten into biscuit shapes. Sprinkle cheese and the remaining butter on top. Cook for 30 minutes, tossing every 10 minutes. Serve warm.

46. Cheese Zucchini Rolls

Servings: 2
Cooking Time: 10 Minutes
Ingredients:
- 1 large zucchini, trimmed
- 1 teaspoon keto tomato sauce
- 3 oz Mozzarella, sliced
- 1 teaspoon olive oil

Directions:
1. Slice the zucchini on the long thin slices. Then sprinkle every zucchini slice with marinara sauce and top with sliced Mozzarella. Roll the zucchini and secure it with toothpicks. Preheat the

air fryer to 385F. Put the zucchini rolls in the air fryer and sprinkle them with olive oil. Cook the zucchini rolls for 10 minutes.

47. Gluten-free Beans

Servings: 2
Cooking Time: 10 Minutes
Ingredients:
- 8 oz green beans, cut ends and cut beans in half
- 1 tsp sesame oil
- 1 tbsp tamari

Directions:
1. Add all ingredients into the zip-lock bag and shake well.
2. Place green beans into the air fryer basket and cook at 400 F for 10 minutes. Turn halfway through.
3. Serve and enjoy.

48. Hot Broccoli

Servings: 4
Cooking Time: 5 Minutes
Ingredients:
- 11 oz broccoli stems
- 1 tablespoon olive oil
- ¼ teaspoon chili powder

Directions:
1. Preheat the air fryer to 400F. Then chop the broccoli stems roughly and sprinkle with chili powder and olive oil. Transfer the greens in the preheated air fryer and cook them for 5 minutes.

49. Ghee Savoy Cabbage

Servings: 4
Cooking Time: 15 Minutes

Ingredients:
- 1 Savoy cabbage head, shredded
- Salt and black pepper to the taste
- 1 and ½ tablespoons ghee, melted
- ¼ cup coconut cream
- 1 tablespoon dill, chopped

Directions:
1. In a pan that fits the air fryer, combine all the ingredients except the coconut cream, toss, put the pan in the air fryer and cook at 390 degrees F for 10 minutes. Add the cream, toss, cook for 5 minutes more, divide between plates and serve.

50. Simple Cauliflower Bars

Servings: 12
Cooking Time: 35 Minutes
Ingredients:
- 1 big cauliflower head; florets separated
- 1 tsp. Italian seasoning
- 1/2 cup mozzarella; shredded
- 1/4 cup egg whites
- Salt and black pepper to the taste

Directions:
1. Put cauliflower florets in your food processor; pulse well, spread on a lined baking sheet that fits your air fryer, introduce in the fryer and cook at 360 °F, for 10 minutes.
2. Transfer cauliflower to a bowl; add salt, pepper, cheese, egg whites and Italian seasoning; stir really well, spread this into a rectangle pan that fits your air fryer; press well, introduce in the fryer and cook at 360 °F, for 15 minutes more. Cut into 12 bars, arrange them on a platter and serve as a snack

51. Roasted Broccoli

Servings: 4
Cooking Time: 7 Minutes
Ingredients:
- 4 cups broccoli florets
- 1/4 cup water
- 1 tbsp olive oil
- 1/4 tsp pepper
- 1/8 tsp kosher salt

Directions:
1. Add broccoli, oil, pepper, and salt in a bowl and toss well.
2. Add 1/4 cup of water into the bottom of air fryer (under the basket).
3. Transfer broccoli into the air fryer basket and cook for 7 minutes at 400 F.
4. Serve and enjoy.

52. Ghee Lemony Endives

Servings: 4
Cooking Time: 15 Minutes
Ingredients:
- 3 tablespoons ghee, melted
- 12 endives, trimmed
- A pinch of salt and black pepper
- 1 tablespoon lemon juice

Directions:
1. In a bowl, mix the endives with the ghee, salt, pepper and lemon juice and toss. Put the endives in the fryer's basket and cook at 350 degrees F for 15 minutes. Divide between plates and serve.

53. Lime Green Beans And Sauce

Servings: 4
Cooking Time: 8 Minutes

Ingredients:
- 1 pound green beans, trimmed
- 1 tablespoon lime juice
- A pinch of salt and black pepper
- 2 tablespoons ghee, melted
- 1 teaspoon chili powder

Directions:
1. In a bowl, mix the ghee with the rest of the ingredients except the green beans and whisk really well. Mix the green beans with the lime sauce, toss, put them in your air fryer's basket and cook at 400 degrees F for 8 minutes. Serve right away.

54. Cheese-crusted Brussels Sprouts

Servings:4
Cooking Time: 20 Minutes
Ingredients:
- 2 tbsp canola oil
- 3 tbsp breadcrumbs
- 1 tbsp paprika
- 2 tbsp Grana Padano cheese, grated
- 2 tbsp sage, chopped

Directions:
1. Preheat the Air fryer to 400 F. Line the air fryer basket with parchment paper.
2. In a bowl, mix breadcrumbs and paprika with Grana Padano cheese. Drizzle the Brussels sprouts with the canola oil and pour in the breadcrumb/cheese mixture; toss to coat. Place in the air fryer basket and cook for 15 minutes, shaking it every 4-5 minutes. Serve sprinkled with chopped sage.

55. Zucchini Parmesan Crisps

Servings: 4
Cooking Time: 20 Minutes
Ingredients:
- 1 pound zucchini, peeled and sliced
- 1 egg, lightly beaten
- 1 cup parmesan cheese, preferably freshly grated

Directions:
1. Pat the zucchini dry with a kitchen towel.
2. In a mixing dish, thoroughly combine the egg and cheese. Then, coat the zucchini slices with the breadcrumb mixture.
3. Cook in the preheated Air Fryer at 400 degrees F for 9 minutes, shaking the basket halfway through the cooking time.
4. Work in batches until the chips is golden brown. Bon appétit!

56. Spicy Cheese Lings

Servings:3
Cooking Time: 25 Minutes
Ingredients:
- 1 cup flour + extra for kneading
- ¼ tsp chili powder
- ½ tsp baking powder
- 3 tsp butter
- A pinch of salt

Directions:
1. In a bowl, mix cheese, flour, baking powder, chili powder, butter, and salt. Add some water and mix well to get a dough. Remove the dough on a flat floured surface. Using a rolling pin, roll the dough out into a thin sheet. Cut the dough into lings' shape. Add the cheese

lings to the basket, and cook for 6 minutes at 350 F, flipping once halfway through.

57. Crispy Squash

Servings:4
Cooking Time: 25 Minutes
Ingredients:
- 1 tbsp olive oil
- ¼ tsp salt
- ¼ tsp black pepper
- ¼ tsp dried thyme
- 1 tbsp finely chopped fresh parsley

Directions:
1. In a bowl, add squash, oil, salt, pepper, and thyme, and toss until squash is well-coated. Place squash in the air fryer and cook for 14 minutes at 360 F. Sprinkle with chopped parsley and serve chilled.

58. Platter Of French Fries

Servings:6
Cooking Time: 35 Minutes
Ingredients:
- 2 tbsp olive oil

Directions:
1. Preheat your air fryer to 360 F. Drizzle oil on the dried potatoes and toss to coat. Place the potatoes in your air fryer's cooking basket and cook for 30 minutes. Serve.

59. Swiss Chard Mix

Servings: 5
Cooking Time: 15 Minutes
Ingredients:
- 7 oz Swiss chard, chopped

- 4 oz Swiss cheese, grated
- 4 teaspoons almond flour
- ½ cup heavy cream
- ½ teaspoon ground black pepper

Directions:
1. Mix up Swiss chard and Swiss cheese. Add almond flour, heavy cream, and ground black pepper. Stir the mixture until homogenous. After this, transfer it in 5 small ramekins. Preheat the air fryer to 365F. Place the ramekins with gratin in the air fryer basket and cook them for 15 minutes.

60. Avocado And Green Beans

Servings: 4
Cooking Time: 15 Minutes
Ingredients:
- 1 pint mixed cherry tomatoes, halved
- 1 avocado, peeled, pitted and cubed
- ¼ pound green beans, trimmed and halved
- 2 tablespoons olive oil

Directions:
1. In a pan that fits your air fryer, mix the tomatoes with the rest of the ingredients, toss, put the pan in the machine and cook at 360 degrees F for 15 minutes. Transfer to bowls and serve.

61. Sesame Fennel

Servings: 2
Cooking Time: 15 Minutes
Ingredients:
- 8 oz fennel bulb
- 1 teaspoon sesame oil
- ½ teaspoon salt
- 1 teaspoon white pepper

Directions:

1. Trim the fennel bulb and cut it into halves. Then sprinkle the fennel bulb with salt, white pepper, and sesame oil. Preheat the air fryer to 370F. Put the fennel bulb halves in the air fryer and cook them for 15 minutes.

62. Sriracha Chili Chicken Wings

Servings:4
Cooking Time: 30 Minutes
Ingredients:
- Salt to taste
- ¼ cup sriracha chili sauce
- 1 tsp garlic powder

Directions:
1. Preheat the Air fryer to 370 F.
2. Season chicken with salt and garlic powder. Spray with cooking spray and place in the air fryer basket. Cook for 25 minutes, flipping once halfway through. When ready, coat in the sriracha sauce and serve.

63. Classic French Fries

Servings:2
Cooking Time: 25 Minutes
Ingredients:
- 2 russet potatoes, washed, dried, cut strips
- 2 tbsp olive oil
- Salt and black pepper to taste

Directions:
1. Spray air fryer basket with cooking spray. In a bowl, toss the strips with olive oil, and season with salt and pepper. Arrange in the air fryer and cook for 18 minutes at 400 F, turning once halfway through. Check for

crispiness and serve immediately, with garlic aioli, ketchup or crumbled cheese.

64. Awesome Cheese Sticks

Servings:6
Cooking Time: 15 Minutes
Ingredients:
- 12 sticks mozzarella cheese
- ¼ cup flour
- 2 cups breadcrumbs
- 2 whole eggs
- ¼ cup Parmesan cheese, grated

Directions:
1. Preheat air fryer to 350 F. Pour breadcrumbs in a bowl. Beat the eggs in a separate bowl. In a third bowl, mix Parmesan and flour. Dip each cheese stick the in flour mixture, then in eggs and finally in breadcrumbs. Put in air fryer's basket and cook for 7 minutes, turning once.

65. Easy Celery Root Mix

Servings: 4
Cooking Time: 15 Minutes
Ingredients:
- 2 cups celery root, roughly cubed
- A pinch of salt and black pepper
- ½ tablespoon butter, melted

Directions:
1. Put all of the ingredients in your air fryer and toss.
2. Cook at 350 degrees F for 15 minutes.
3. Divide between plates and serve.

66. Bacon Cabbage

Servings: 2
Cooking Time: 12 Minutes

Ingredients:
- 8 oz Chinese cabbage, roughly chopped
- 2 oz bacon, chopped
- 1 tablespoon sunflower oil
- ½ teaspoon onion powder
- ½ teaspoon salt

Directions:
1. Cook the bacon at 400F for 10 minutes. Stir it from time to time. Then sprinkle it with onion powder and salt. Add Chinese cabbage and shake the mixture well. Cook it for 2 minutes. Then add sunflower oil, stir the meal and place in the serving plates.

67. Super Cabbage Canapes

Servings:2
Cooking Time: 15 Minutes
Ingredients:
- 1 cube Amul cheese
- ½ carrot, cubed
- ¼ onion, cubed
- ¼ capsicum, cubed
- Fresh basil to garnish

Directions:
1. Preheat your air fryer to 360 F. Using a bowl, mix onion, carrot, capsicum and cheese. Toss to coat everything evenly. Add cabbage rounds to the air fryer's cooking basket. Top with the veggie mixture and cook for 5 minutes. Serve with a garnish of fresh basil.

68. Chicken Wings With Alfredo Sauce

Servings:4
Cooking Time: 60 Minutes
Ingredients:

- Salt to taste
- ½ cup Alfredo sauce

Directions:
1. Preheat the air fryer to 370°F.
2. Season the wings with salt. Arrange them in the air fryer, without touching. Cook in batches if needed, for 20 minutes, until no longer pink in the center. Increase the temperature to 390 F and cook for 5 minutes more. Remove to a big bowl and coat well with the sauce to serve.

69. Air Fryer Mushrooms

Servings: 1
Cooking Time: 8 Minutes
Ingredients:
- 12 button mushrooms, cleaned
- 1 tsp olive oil
- 1/4 tsp garlic salt
- Pepper
- Salt

Directions:
1. Add all ingredients into the bowl and toss well.
2. Spray air fryer basket with cooking spray.
3. Transfer mushrooms into the air fryer basket and cook at 380 F for 8 minutes. Toss halfway through.
4. Serve and enjoy.

70. Flatbread

Servings: 1
Cooking Time: 20 Minutes
Ingredients:
- 1 cup mozzarella cheese, shredded
- ¼ cup blanched finely ground flour
- 1 oz. full-fat cream cheese, softened

Directions:
1. Microwave the mozzarella for half a minute until melted. Combine with the flour to achieve a smooth consistency, before adding the cream cheese. Keep mixing to create a dough, microwaving the mixture again if the cheese begins to harden.
2. Divide the dough into two equal pieces. Between two sheets of parchment paper, roll out the dough until it is about a quarter-inch thick. Cover the bottom of your fryer with another sheet of parchment.
3. Transfer the dough into the fryer and cook at 320°F for seven minutes. You may need to complete this step in two batches. Make sure to turn the flatbread halfway through cooking. Take care when removing it from the fryer and serve warm.

71. Bacon & Asparagus Spears

Servings:4
Cooking Time: 25 Minutes
Ingredients:
- 4 bacon slices
- 1 tbsp olive oil
- 1 tbsp sesame oil
- 1 tbsp brown sugar
- 1 garlic clove, crushed

Directions:
1. Preheat your air fryer to 380 F. In a bowl, mix the oils, sugar and crushed garlic. Separate the asparagus into 4 bunches (5 spears in 1 bunch) and wrap each bunch with a bacon slice. Coat the bunches with the sugar and oil mix. Place the bunches in your air fryer's cooking basket and cook for 8 minutes.

72. Bacon-wrapped Onion Rings

Servings: 8
Cooking Time: 15 Minutes
Ingredients:
- 1 large onion, peeled
- 8 slices sugar-free bacon
- 1 tbsp. sriracha

Directions:
1. Chop up the onion into slices a quarter-inch thick. Gently pull apart the rings. Take a slice of bacon and wrap it around an onion ring. Repeat with the rest of the ingredients. Place each onion ring in your fryer.
2. Cut the onion rings at 350°F for ten minutes, turning them halfway through to ensure the bacon crisps up.
3. Serve hot with the sriracha.

73. Italian-style Broccoli

Servings: 4
Cooking Time: 25 Minutes
Ingredients:
- 1/3 cup Asiago cheese
- 1 large-sized head broccoli, stemmed and cut small florets
- 2 1/2 tablespoons canola oil
- 1 tablespoon Italian seasoning blend
- Salt and ground black pepper, to taste

Directions:
1. Bring a medium pan filled with a lightly salted water to a boil. Then, boil the broccoli florets for about 3 minutes.
2. Then, drain the broccoli florets well; toss them with the canola oil, rosemary, basil, salt and black pepper.

3. Set your Air Fryer to 390 degrees F; arrange the seasoned broccoli in the cooking basket; set the timer for 17 minutes. Toss the broccoli halfway through the cooking process.
4. Serve warm topped with grated cheese and enjoy!

74. Parsley Savoy Cabbage Mix

Servings: 4
Cooking Time: 15 Minutes
Ingredients:
- 1 Savoy cabbage, shredded
- 2 spring onions, chopped
- 2 tablespoons keto tomato sauce
- Salt and black pepper to the taste
- 1 tablespoon parsley, chopped

Directions:
1. In a pan that fits your air fryer, mix the cabbage the rest of the ingredients except the parsley, toss, put the pan in the fryer and cook at 360 degrees F for 15 minutes. Divide between plates and serve with parsley sprinkled on top.

75. Paprika Green Beans

Servings: 4
Cooking Time: 20 Minutes
Ingredients:
- 6 cups green beans, trimmed
- 2 tablespoons olive oil
- 1 tablespoon hot paprika
- A pinch of salt and black pepper

Directions:
1. In a bowl, mix the green beans with the other ingredients, toss, put them in the air fryer's basket and cook at 370 degrees F for 20 minutes. Divide between plates and serve as a side dish.

76. Dill Corn

Servings: 4
Cooking Time: 6 Minutes
Ingredients:
- 4 ears of corn
- Salt and black pepper to taste
- 2 tablespoons butter, melted
- 2 tablespoon dill, chopped

Directions:
1. In a bowl, combine the salt, pepper, and the butter.
2. Rub the corn with the butter mixture, and then put it in your air fryer.
3. Cook at 390 degrees F for 6 minutes.
4. Divide the corn between plates, sprinkle the dill on top, and serve.

77. Roasted Almond Delight

Servings:12
Cooking Time: 20 Minutes
Ingredients:
- 3 tbsp liquid smoke
- 2 tsp salt
- 2 tbsp molasses

Directions:
1. Preheat your air fryer to 360 F. In a bowl, add salt, liquid, molasses, and cashews; toss to coat. Place in your air fryer's cooking basket and cook for 10 minutes, shaking the basket every 5 minutes.

78. Roasted Rhubarb

Servings: 4
Cooking Time: 15 Minutes
Ingredients:
- 1 pound rhubarb, cut in chunks
- 2 teaspoons olive oil
- 2 tablespoons orange zest
- ½ cup walnuts, chopped
- ½ teaspoon sugar

Directions:
1. In your air fryer, mix all the listed ingredients, and toss.
2. Cook at 380 degrees F for 15 minutes.
3. Divide the rhubarb between plates and serve as a side dish.

79. Green Bean Crisps

Servings:4
Cooking Time: 15 Minutes
Ingredients:
- 1 tbsp olive oil
- 1 tsp garlic powder
- 1 tsp onion powder
- 1 tsp paprika
- Salt and black pepper to taste

Directions:
1. Preheat the Air fryer to 390 F. Grease the air fryer basket with cooking spray.
2. In a bowl, mix olive oil, garlic and onion powder, paprika, salt, and pepper. Coat green beans in the mixture. Place in air fryer basket; cook for 10 minutes, shaking once. Allow to cool before serving.

80. Juicy Pickled Chips

Servings:3
Cooking Time: 20 Minutes
Ingredients:
- 3 tbsp smoked paprika
- 2 cups flour
- ¼ cup cornmeal
- Salt and black pepper to taste

Directions:

1. Preheat air fryer to 400 F. Mix flour, paprika, pepper, salt, cornmeal and powder. Dip the pickles in the spice mixture and place them in the air fryer's cooking basket. Cook for 10 minutes.

81. Cheesy Sticks With Sweet Thai Sauce

Servings:4
Cooking Time: 20 Minutes + Freezing Time
Ingredients:
- 2 cups breadcrumbs
- 3 eggs
- 1 cup sweet Thai sauce
- 4 tbsp skimmed milk

Directions:
1. Pour crumbs in a bowl. Beat eggs into another bowl with milk. One after the other, dip sticks in the egg mixture, in the crumbs, then egg mixture again and then in the crumbs again. Freeze for 1 hour.
2. Preheat air fryer to 380 F. Arrange the sticks on the fryer. Cook for 5 minutes, flipping them halfway through cooking to brown evenly. Cook in batches. Serve with a sweet Thai sauce.

82. Simple Taro Fries

Servings: 2
Cooking Time: 20 Minutes
Ingredients:
- 8 small taro, peel and cut into fries shape
- 1 tbsp olive oil
- 1/2 tsp salt

Directions:

1. Add taro slice in a bowl and toss well with olive oil and salt.
2. Transfer taro slices into the air fryer basket.
3. Cook at 360 F for 20 minutes. Toss halfway through.
4. Serve and enjoy.

83. Garlic Tomatoes Recipe

Servings: 4
Cooking Time:25 Minutes
Ingredients:
- 4 garlic cloves; crushed
- 1 lb. mixed cherry tomatoes
- 3 thyme springs; chopped.
- 1/4 cup olive oil
- Salt and black pepper to the taste

Directions:
1. In a bowl; mix tomatoes with salt, black pepper, garlic, olive oil and thyme, toss to coat, introduce in your air fryer and cook at 360 °F, for 15 minutes. Divide tomatoes mix on plates and serve

84. Crusted Coconut Shrimp

Servings:5
Cooking Time: 30 Minutes
Ingredients:
- ¾ cup shredded coconut
- 1 tbsp maple syrup
- ½ cup breadcrumbs
- ⅓ cup cornstarch
- ½ cup milk

Directions:
1. Pour the cornstarch and shrimp in a zipper bag and shake vigorously to coat. Mix the syrup and milk in a bowl and set aside. In a separate bowl, mix the breadcrumbs and shredded coconut.

Open the zipper bag and remove shrimp while shaking off excess starch.
2. Dip shrimp in the milk mixture and then in the crumb mixture. Place in the fryer. Cook 12 minutes at 350 F, flipping once halfway through. Cook until golden brown. Serve with a coconut-based dip.

85. Spicy Fries

Servings:4
Cooking Time: 20 Minutes
Ingredients:
- 2 tsp olive oil
- 2 tsp cayenne pepper
- 1 tsp paprika
- Salt and black pepper

Directions:
1. Place the fries into a bowl and sprinkle with oil, cayenne, paprika, salt, and black pepper. Toss and place them in the fryer. Cook for 7 minutes at 360 F, until golden and crispy. Give it a toss after 7-8 minutes and continue cooking for another 8 minutes. Serve.

86. Crispy Chicken Nuggets

Servings:4
Cooking Time: 25 Minutes
Ingredients:
- Salt and black pepper to taste
- 2 tbsp olive oil
- 5 tbsp plain breadcrumbs
- 2 tbsp panko breadcrumbs
- 2 tbsp grated Parmesan cheese

Directions:
1. Preheat air fryer to 380 F. and grease. Season the chicken with pepper and salt. In a bowl, pour olive oil. In a

separate bowl, add crumb, and Parmesan cheese. Place the chicken pieces in the oil to coat, then dip into breadcrumb mixture, and transfer to the air fryer. Work in batches if needed. Lightly spray chicken with cooking spray. Cook for 10 minutes, flipping once halfway through.

87. Turmeric Cauliflower

Servings: 4
Cooking Time: 8 Minutes
Ingredients:
- 1-pound cauliflower head
- 1 tablespoon ground turmeric
- 1 tablespoon coconut oil
- ½ teaspoon dried cilantro
- ¼ teaspoon salt

Directions:
1. Slice the cauliflower head on 4 steaks. Then rub every cauliflower steak with dried cilantro, salt, and ground turmeric. Sprinkle the steaks with coconut oil. Preheat the air fryer to 400F. Place the cauliflower steaks in the air fryer basket and cook for 4 minutes from each side.

88. Beet Wedges Dish

Servings: 4
Cooking Time:25 Minutes
Ingredients:
- 4 beets; washed, peeled and cut into large wedges
- 1 tbsp. olive oil
- 2 garlic cloves; minced
- 1 tsp. lemon juice
- Salt and black to the taste

Directions:

1. In a bowl; mix beets with oil, salt, pepper, garlic and lemon juice; toss well, transfer to your air fryer's basket and cook them at 400 °F, for 15 minutes. Divide beets wedges on plates and serve as a side dish.

89. Lemony Artichokes Side Dish

Servings: 4
Cooking Time:25 Minutes
Ingredients:
- 2 medium artichokes; trimmed and halved
- 2 tbsp. lemon juice
- Cooking spray
- Salt and black pepper to the taste

Directions:
1. Grease your air fryer with cooking spray, add artichokes; drizzle lemon juice and sprinkle salt and black pepper and cook them at 380 °F, for 15 minutes. Divide them on plates and serve as a side dish.

90. Air-fried Cheesy Broccoli With Garlic

Servings:2
Cooking Time: 25 Minutes
Ingredients:
- 1 egg white
- 1 garlic clove, grated
- Salt and black pepper to taste
- ½ lb broccoli florets
- ⅓ cup grated Parmesan cheese

Directions:
1. In a bowl, whisk together the butter, egg, garlic, salt, and black pepper. Toss in broccoli to coat well. Top with Parmesan cheese and; toss to coat. Arrange broccoli in a single layer in the air fryer, without overcrowding. Cook for 10 minutes at 360 F. Remove to a plate and sprinkle with Parmesan cheese.

POULTRY RECIPES

91. Cinnamon Balsamic Duck

Servings: 2
Cooking Time: 20 Minutes
Ingredients:
- 2 duck breasts, boneless and skin scored
- A pinch of salt and black pepper
- ¼ teaspoon cinnamon powder
- 4 tablespoons stevia
- 3 tablespoons balsamic vinegar

Directions:
1. In a bowl, mix the duck breasts with the rest of the ingredients and rub well. Put the duck breasts in your air fryer's basket and cook at 380 degrees F for 10 minutes on each side. Divide everything between plates and serve.

92. Jalapeno Chicken Breasts

Servings: 2
Cooking Time: 25 Minutes
Ingredients:
- 2 oz. full-fat cream cheese, softened
- 4 slices sugar-free bacon, cooked and crumbled
- ¼ cup pickled jalapenos, sliced
- ½ cup sharp cheddar cheese, shredded and divided
- 2 x 6-oz. boneless skinless chicken breasts

Directions:
1. In a bowl, mix the cream cheese, bacon, jalapeno slices, and half of the cheddar cheese until well-combined.
2. Cut parallel slits in the chicken breasts of about ¾ the length – make sure not to cut all the way down. You should be able to make between six and eight slices, depending on the size of the chicken breast.
3. Insert evenly sized dollops of the cheese mixture into the slits of the chicken breasts. Top the chicken with sprinkles of the rest of the cheddar cheese. Place the chicken in the basket of your air fryer.
4. Set the fryer to 350°F and cook the chicken breasts for twenty minutes.
5. Test with a meat thermometer. The chicken should be at 165°F when fully cooked. Serve hot and enjoy!

93. Lemon Pepper Chicken Legs

Servings: 4
Cooking Time: 30 Minutes
Ingredients:
- ½ tsp. garlic powder
- 2 tsp. baking powder
- 8 chicken legs
- 4 tbsp. salted butter, melted
- 1 tbsp. lemon pepper seasoning

Directions:
1. In a small bowl combine the garlic powder and baking powder, then use this mixture to coat the chicken legs. Lay the chicken in the basket of your fryer.
2. Cook the chicken legs at 375°F for twenty-five minutes. Halfway through, turn them over and allow to cook on the other side.
3. When the chicken has turned golden brown, test with a thermometer to ensure it has reached an ideal temperature of 165°F. Remove from the fryer.

4. Mix together the melted butter and lemon pepper seasoning and toss with the chicken legs until the chicken is coated all over. Serve hot.

94. Green Curry Hot Chicken Drumsticks

Servings:4
Cooking Time: 25 Minutes
Ingredients:
- 2 tbsp green curry paste
- 3 tbsp coconut cream
- Salt and black pepper
- ½ fresh jalapeno chili, finely chopped
- A handful of fresh parsley, roughly chopped

Directions:
1. In a bowl, add drumsticks, paste, cream, salt, black pepper and jalapeno; coat the chicken well. Arrange the drumsticks in the air fryer and cook for 6 minutes at 400 F, flipping once halfway through. Serve with fresh cilantro.

95. Chicken Wrapped In Bacon

Servings: 6
Cooking Time: 25 Minutes
Ingredients:
- 6 rashers unsmoked back bacon
- 1 small chicken breast
- 1 tbsp. garlic soft cheese

Directions:
1. Cut the chicken breast into six bite-sized pieces.
2. Spread the soft cheese across one side of each slice of bacon.

3. Put the chicken on top of the cheese and wrap the bacon around it, holding it in place with a toothpick.
4. Transfer the wrapped chicken pieces to the Air Fryer and cook for 15 minutes at 350°F.

96. Grandma's Chicken

Servings: 4
Cooking Time: 20 Minutes
Ingredients:
- 12 oz. chicken breast, diced
- 6 oz. general Tso sauce
- ½ tsp. white pepper
- ¼ cup milk
- 1 cup cornstarch

Directions:
1. Place the chicken and milk in a bowl.
2. Separate the milk from the chicken and coat the chicken with cornstarch.
3. Put the chicken in the Air Fryer basket and air fry at 350°F for 12 minutes.
4. Plate up the chicken and season with the white pepper.
5. Pour the Tso sauce over the chicken before serving.

97. Bacon-wrapped Chicken

Servings: 6
Cooking Time: 20 Minutes
Ingredients:
- 1 chicken breast, cut into 6 pieces
- 6 rashers back bacon
- 1 tbsp. soft cheese

Directions:
1. Put the bacon rashers on a flat surface and cover one side with the soft cheese.
2. Lay the chicken pieces on each bacon rasher. Wrap the bacon around the

chicken and use a toothpick stick to hold each one in place. Put them in Air Fryer basket.

3. Air fry at 350°F for 15 minutes.

98. Fried Herbed Chicken Wings

Servings: 4
Cooking Time: 11 Minutes
Ingredients:
- 1 tablespoon Emperor herbs chicken spices
- 8 chicken wings
- Cooking spray

Directions:
1. Generously sprinkle the chicken wings with Emperor herbs chicken spices and place in the preheated to 400F air fryer. Cook the chicken wings for 6 minutes from each side.

99. Chicken & Prawn Paste

Servings: 2
Cooking Time: 30 Minutes
Ingredients:
- 2 tbsp cornflour
- ½ tbsp wine
- 1 tbsp shrimp paste
- 1 tbsp ginger
- ½ tbsp olive oil

Directions:
1. Preheat your air fryer to 360 F. In a bowl, mix oil, ginger, and wine. Cover the chicken wings with the prepared marinade and top with flour. Add the floured chicken to shrimp paste and coat it. Place the chicken in your air fryer's cooking basket and cook for 20 minutes, until crispy on the outside.

100. Almond Coconut Chicken Tenders

Servings: 4
Cooking Time: 20 Minutes
Ingredients:
- 4 chicken breasts, skinless, boneless and cut into tenders
- A pinch of salt and black pepper
- 1/3 cup almond flour
- 2 eggs, whisked
- 9 ounces coconut flakes

Directions:
1. Season the chicken tenders with salt and pepper, dredge them in almond flour, then dip in eggs and roll in coconut flakes. Put the chicken tenders in your air fryer's basket and cook at 400 degrees F for 10 minutes on each side. Divide between plates and serve with a side salad.

101. Rotisserie Chicken With Herbes De Provence

Servings: 6
Cooking Time: 1 Hour
Ingredients:
- 3 pounds chicken, whole
- 2 tablespoons dried herbes de Provence
- 1 tablespoon salt

Directions:
1. Season the whole chicken with dried herbes de Provence and salt. Rub all the seasoning on the chicken including the cavity.
2. Preheat the air fryer at 375°F.
3. Place the grill pan accessory in the air fryer.

4. Place the chicken and grill for 1 hour.

102. Fried Chicken Legs

Servings:5
Cooking Time: 50 Minutes
Ingredients:
- 2 lemons, halved
- 5 tbsp garlic powder
- 5 tbsp oregano, dried
- ⅓ cup olive oil
- Salt and black pepper

Directions:
1. Set air fryer to 350 F. Brush the chicken legs with some olive oil.
2. Sprinkle with the lemon juice and arrange on the air fryer basket. In another bowl, combine, oregano, garlic powder, salt and pepper. Sprinkle the seasoning mixture over the chicken. Cook in the air fryer for 20 minutes, shaking every 5 minutes.

103. Cheese Herb Chicken Wings

Servings: 4
Cooking Time: 15 Minutes
Ingredients:
- 2 lbs chicken wings
- 1 tsp herb de Provence
- ½ cup parmesan cheese, grated
- 1 tsp paprika
- Salt

Directions:
1. Preheat the air fryer to 350 F.
2. In a small bowl, mix together cheese, herb de Provence, paprika, and salt.
3. Spray air fryer basket with cooking spray.

4. Toss chicken wings with cheese mixture and place into the air fryer basket and cook for 15 minutes. Turn halfway through.
5. Serve and enjoy.

104. Lemon Pepper Chicken

Servings:2
Cooking Time: 20 Minutes
Ingredients:
- 2 lemon, juiced and rind reserved
- 1 tbsp chicken seasoning
- 1 tbsp garlic puree
- A handful of peppercorns
- Salt and pepper to taste

Directions:
1. Preheat your fryer to 350 F. Place a silver foil sheet on a flat surface. Add all seasonings alongside the lemon rind.
2. Lay the chicken breast onto a chopping board and trim any fat and little bones. Season each side with the pepper and salt. Rub the chicken seasoning on both sides well. Place on your silver foil sheet and rub. Seal and flatten with a rolling pin. Place the breast in the basket and cook for 15 minutes. Serve.

105. Gyro Seasoned Chicken

Servings:4
Cooking Time:30 Minutes
Ingredients:
- 2 pounds chicken thighs
- 1 tablespoon avocado oil
- 2 tablespoons primal palate super gyro seasoning
- 2 tablespoons primal palate new bae seasoning
- 1 tablespoon Himalayan pink salt

Directions:
1. Preheat the Air fryer to 350 °F and grease an Air fryer basket.
2. Rub the chicken with avocado oil and half of the spices.
3. Arrange the chicken thighs in the Air fryer basket and cook for about 25 minutes, flipping once in between.
4. Sprinkle the remaining seasoning and cook for 5 more minutes.
5. Dish out and serve warm.

106. Fennel Chicken

Servings: 4
Cooking Time: 40 Minutes
Ingredients:
- 1 ½ cup coconut milk
- 2 tbsp. garam masala
- 1 ½ lb. chicken thighs
- ¾ tbsp. coconut oil, melted

Directions:
1. Combine the coconut oil and garam masala together in a bowl. Pour the mixture over the chicken thighs and leave to marinate for a half hour.
2. Pre-heat your fryer at 375°F .
3. Cook the chicken into the fryer for fifteen minutes.
4. Add in the coconut milk, giving it a good stir, then cook for an additional ten minutes.
5. Remove the chicken and place on a serving dish. Make sure to pour all of the coconut "gravy" over it and serve immediately.

107. Creamy Onion Chicken

Servings:4
Cooking Time: 20 Minutes

Ingredients:
- 1 ½ cup onion soup mix
- 1 cup mushroom soup
- ½ cup cream

Directions:
1. Preheat Fryer to 400 F. Add mushrooms, onion mix and cream in a frying pan. Heat on low heat for 1 minute. Pour the warm mixture over chicken slices and allow to sit for 25 minutes. Place the marinated chicken in the air fryer cooking basket and cook for 15 minutes. Serve with the remaining cream.

108. Greek Chicken Meatballs

Servings: 1
Cooking Time: 15 Minutes
Ingredients:
- ½ oz. finely ground pork rinds
- 1 lb. ground chicken
- 1 tsp. Greek seasoning
- 1/3 cup feta, crumbled
- 1/3 cup frozen spinach, drained and thawed

Directions:
1. Place all the ingredients in a large bowl and combine using your hands. Take equal-sized portions of this mixture and roll each into a 2-inch ball. Place the balls in your fryer.
2. Cook the meatballs at 350°F for twelve minutes, in several batches if necessary.
3. Once they are golden, ensure they have reached an ideal temperature of 165°F and remove from the fryer. Keep each batch warm while you move on to the next one. Serve with Tzatziki if desired.

109. Buffalo Chicken Strips

Servings: 1
Cooking Time: 30 Minutes
Ingredients:
- ¼ cup hot sauce
- 1 lb. boneless skinless chicken tenders
- 1 tsp. garlic powder
- 1 ½ oz. pork rinds, finely ground
- 1 tsp chili powder

Directions:
1. Toss the hot sauce and chicken tenders together in a bowl, ensuring the chicken is completely coated.
2. In another bowl, combine the garlic powder, ground pork rinds, and chili powder. Use this mixture to coat the tenders, covering them well. Place the chicken into your fryer, taking care not to layer pieces on top of one another.
3. Cook the chicken at 375°F for twenty minutes until cooked all the way through and golden. Serve warm with your favorite dips and sides.

110. Mesmerizing Honey Chicken Drumsticks

Servings:3
Cooking Time: 20 Minutes
Ingredients:
- 2 tbsp olive oil
- 2 tbsp honey
- ½ tbsp garlic, minced

Directions:
1. Preheat your air fryer to 400 F. Add garlic, oil and honey to a sealable zip bag. Add chicken and toss to coat; set aside for 30 minutes. Add the coated chicken to the air fryer basket, and cook for 15 minutes.

111. Chicken Sausage In Dijon Sauce

Servings: 4
Cooking Time: 20 Minutes
Ingredients:
- 4 chicken sausages
- 1/4 cup mayonnaise
- 2 tablespoons Dijon mustard
- 1 tablespoon balsamic vinegar
- 1/2 teaspoon dried rosemary

Directions:
1. Arrange the sausages on the grill pan and transfer it to the preheated Air Fryer.
2. Grill the sausages at 350 degrees F for approximately 13 minutes. Turn them halfway through cooking.
3. Meanwhile, prepare the sauce by mixing the remaining ingredients with a wire whisk. Serve the warm sausages with chilled Dijon sauce. Enjoy!

112. Chicken Enchiladas

Servings:6
Cooking Time: 65 Minutes
Ingredients:
- 2 cups cheese, grated
- ½ cup salsa
- 1 can green chilies, chopped
- 12 flour tortillas
- 2 cans enchilada sauce

Directions:
1. Preheat your Fryer to 400 F. In a bowl, mix salsa and enchilada sauce. Toss in the chopped chicken to coat. Place the chicken on the tortillas and roll; top with cheese. Place the prepared

tortillas in the air fryer cooking basket and cook for 60 minutes. Serve with guacamole

113. Caprese Chicken With Balsamic Sauce

Servings:6
Cooking Time: 25 Minutes
Ingredients:
- 6 basil leaves
- ¼ cup balsamic vinegar
- 6 slices tomato
- 1 tbsp butter
- 6 slices mozzarella cheese

Directions:
1. Preheat your Fryer to 400 F and heat butter and balsamic vinegar in a frying pan over medium heat. Cover the chicken meat with the marinade. Place the chicken in the cooking basket and cook for 20 minutes. Cover the chicken with basil, tomato slices and cheese. Serve and enjoy!

114. Poppin' Pop Corn Chicken

Servings: 1
Cooking Time: 20 Minutes
Ingredients:
- 1 lb. skinless, boneless chicken breast
- 1 tsp. chili flakes
- 1 tsp. garlic powder
- ½ cup flour
- 1 tbsp. olive oil cooking spray

Directions:
1. Pre-heat your fryer at 365°F. Spray with olive oil.
2. Cut the chicken breasts into cubes and place in a bowl. Toss with the chili

flakes, garlic powder, and additional seasonings to taste and make sure to coat entirely.
3. Add the coconut flour and toss once more.
4. Cook the chicken in the fryer for ten minutes. Turnover and cook for a further five minutes before serving.

115. Crusted Chicken

Servings: 2
Cooking Time: 30 Minutes
Ingredients:
- ¼ cup slivered s
- 2x 6-oz. boneless skinless chicken breasts
- 2 tbsp. full-fat mayonnaise
- 1 tbsp. Dijon mustard

Directions:
1. Pulse the s in a food processor until they are finely chopped. Spread the s on a plate and set aside.
2. Cut each chicken breast in half lengthwise.
3. Mix the mayonnaise and mustard together and then spread evenly on top of the chicken slices.
4. Place the chicken into the plate of chopped s to coat completely, laying each coated slice into the basket of your fryer.
5. Cook for 25 minutes at 350°F until golden. Test the temperature, making sure the chicken has reached 165°F. Serve hot.

116. Stuffed Chicken

Servings: 2
Cooking Time: 11 Minutes

Ingredients:
- 8 oz chicken fillet
- 3 oz Blue cheese
- ½ teaspoon salt
- ½ teaspoon thyme
- 1 teaspoon sesame oil

Directions:
1. Cut the fillet into halves and beat them gently with the help of the kitchen hammer. After this, make the horizontal cut in every fillet. Sprinkle the chicken with salt and thyme. Then fill it with Blue cheese and secure the cut with the help of the toothpick. Sprinkle the stuffed chicken fillets with sesame oil. Preheat the air fryer to 385F. Put the chicken fillets in the air fryer and cook them for 7 minutes. Then carefully flip the chicken fillets on another side and cook for 4 minutes more.

117. Buttermilk Brined Turkey Breast

Servings:8
Cooking Time:20 Minutes
Ingredients:
- ¾ cup brine from a can of olives
- 3½ pounds boneless, skinless turkey breast
- 2 fresh thyme sprigs
- 1 fresh rosemary sprig
- ½ cup buttermilk

Directions:
1. Preheat the Air fryer to 350 °F and grease an Air fryer basket.
2. Mix olive brine and buttermilk in a bowl until well combined.

3. Place the turkey breast, buttermilk mixture and herb sprigs in a resealable plastic bag.
4. Seal the bag and refrigerate for about 12 hours.
5. Remove the turkey breast from bag and arrange the turkey breast into the Air fryer basket.
6. Cook for about 20 minutes, flipping once in between.
7. Dish out the turkey breast onto a cutting board and cut into desired size slices to serve.

118. Celery Chicken Mix

Servings: 4
Cooking Time: 9 Minutes
Ingredients:
- 1 teaspoon fennel seeds
- ½ teaspoon ground celery
- ½ teaspoon salt
- 1 tablespoon olive oil
- 12 oz chicken fillet

Directions:
1. Cut the chicken fillets on 4 chicken chops. In the shallow bowl mix up fennel seeds and olive oil. Rub the chicken chops with salt and ground celery. Preheat the air fryer to 365F. Brush the chicken chops with the fennel oil and place it in the air fryer basket. Cook them for 9 minutes.

119. Deliciously Crisp Chicken

Servings:4
Cooking Time:12 Minutes
Ingredients:
- 1 egg, beaten
- ½ cup breadcrumbs

- 8 skinless, boneless chicken tenderloins
- 2 tablespoons vegetable oil

Directions:

1. Preheat the Air fryer to 355 °F and grease an Air fryer basket.
2. Whisk the egg in a shallow dish and mix vegetable oil and breadcrumbs in another shallow dish.
3. Dip the chicken tenderloins in egg and then coat in the breadcrumb mixture.
4. Arrange the chicken tenderloins in the Air fryer basket and cook for about 12 minutes.
5. Dish out and serve warm.

120. Thyme Turkey Nuggets

Servings:2
Cooking Time: 20 Minutes

Ingredients:

- 1 egg, beaten
- 1 cup breadcrumbs
- 1 tbsp dried thyme
- ½ tbsp dried parsley
- Salt and pepper, to taste

Directions:

1. Preheat air fryer to 350 F. In a bowl, mix ground chicken, thyme, parsley, salt and pepper. Shape the mixture into balls. Dip in the breadcrumbs, then egg, then in the breadcrumbs again. Place the nuggets in the air fryer basket, spray with cooking spray cook for 10 minutes, shaking once.

121. Chicken & Jalapeño Pepper Quesadilla

Servings:4
Cooking Time: 20 Minutes
Ingredients:

- 2 cups shredded Monterey Jack cheese
- ½ cup shredded and cooked chicken
- 1 cup canned fire-roasted jalapeño peppers, chopped

Directions:

1. Preheat the Air Fryer to 390 F. Divide chicken, cheese, and jalapeño peppers between 4 tortillas. Top each one with the remaining tortillas. Grease with cooking spray. In batches, place in the air fryer basket and cook for 12 minutes, turning once halfway through. Serve with green salsa.

122. Chicken And Potatoes

Servings: 4
Cooking Time: 20 Minutes
Ingredients:

- 4 gold potatoes, cut into medium chunks
- 1 yellow onion, thinly sliced
- 1 pound chicken thighs, boneless
- ½ cup chicken stock
- Salt and black pepper to taste

Directions:

1. In a pan that fits your air fryer, mix the chicken with the salt, pepper, onions, and the stock.
2. Place the pan in the fryer and cook at 380 degrees F for 10 minutes.
3. Add the potatoes, put the pan in the fryer again, and cook at 400 degrees F for 10 minutes more.
4. Divide between plates and serve.

123. Sweet Lime 'n Chili Chicken Barbecue

Servings:2
Cooking Time: 40 Minutes

Ingredients:
- ¼ cup soy sauce
- 1 cup sweet chili sauce
- 1-pound chicken breasts
- Juice from 2 limes, freshly squeezed

Directions:
1. In a Ziploc bag, combine all Ingredients and give a good shake. Allow to marinate for at least 2 hours in the fridge.
2. Preheat the air fryer to 390°F.
3. Place the grill pan accessory in the air fryer.
4. Place chicken on the grill and cook for 30 to 40 minutes. Make sure to flip the chicken every 10 minutes to cook evenly.
5. Meanwhile, use the remaining marinade and put it in a saucepan. Simmer until the sauce thickens.
6. Once the chicken is cooked, brush with the thickened marinade.

124. Sweet Turmeric Chicken Wings

Servings: 8
Cooking Time: 15 Minutes
Ingredients:
- 8 chicken wings
- 1 teaspoon Splenda
- 1 teaspoon ground turmeric
- ½ teaspoon cayenne pepper
- 1 tablespoon avocado oil

Directions:
1. Mix up Splenda and avocado oil and stir the mixture until Splenda is dissolved. Then rub the chicken wings with ground turmeric and cayenne pepper. Brush the chicken wings with sweet avocado oil from both sides. Preheat the air fryer to 390F. Place the chicken wings in the air fryer and cook them for 15 minutes.

125. Cajun Seasoned Chicken

Servings: 2
Cooking Time: 15 Minutes
Ingredients:
- 2 boneless chicken breasts
- 3 tbsp. Cajun spice

Directions:
1. Coat both sides of the chicken breasts with Cajun spice. Put the seasoned chicken in Air Fryer basket.
2. Air fry at 350°F for 10 minutes, ensuring they are cooked through before slicing up and serving.

126. Creamy Duck Strips

Servings: 5
Cooking Time: 17 Minutes
Ingredients:
- 12 oz duck breast, skinless, boneless
- ½ cup coconut flour
- 1/3 cup heavy cream
- 1 teaspoon salt
- 1 teaspoon white pepper

Directions:
1. Cut the duck breast on the small strips (fingers) and sprinkle with salt and white pepper. Then dip the duck fingers in the heavy cream and coat in the coconut flour. Preheat the air fryer to 375F. Put the duck fingers in the air fryer basket in one layer and cook them for 10 minutes. Then flip the duck fingers on another side and cook them for 7 minutes more.

127. Easy How-to Hard Boil Egg In Air Fryer

Servings:6
Cooking Time: 15 Minutes
Ingredients:

- 6 eggs

Directions:

1. Preheat the air fryer for 5 minutes.
2. Place the eggs in the air fryer basket.
3. Cook for 15 minutes at 360°F.
4. Remove from the air fryer basket and place in cold water.

128. Creamy Chicken Tenders

Servings:8
Cooking Time:20 Minutes
Ingredients:

- 2 pounds chicken tenders
- 1 cup feta cheese
- 4 tablespoons olive oil
- 1 cup cream
- Salt and black pepper, to taste

Directions:

1. Preheat the Air fryer to 340 °F and grease an Air fryer basket.
2. Season the chicken tenders with salt and black pepper.
3. Arrange the chicken tenderloins in the Air fryer basket and drizzle with olive oil.
4. Cook for about 15 minutes and set the Air fryer to 390 °F.
5. Cook for about 5 more minutes and dish out to serve warm.
6. Repeat with the remaining mixture and dish out to serve hot.

129. Chicken Pizza Crusts

Servings: 1
Cooking Time: 35 Minutes
Ingredients:

- ½ cup mozzarella, shredded
- ¼ cup parmesan cheese, grated
- 1 lb. ground chicken

Directions:

1. In a large bowl, combine all the ingredients and then spread the mixture out, dividing it into four parts of equal size.
2. Cut a sheet of parchment paper into four circles, roughly six inches in diameter, and put some of the chicken mixture onto the center of each piece, flattening the mixture to fill out the circle.
3. Depending on the size of your fryer, cook either one or two circles at a time at 375°F for 25 minutes. Halfway through, turn the crust over to cook on the other side. Keep each batch warm while you move onto the next one.
4. Once all the crusts are cooked, top with cheese and the toppings of your choice. If desired, cook the topped crusts for an additional five minutes.
5. Serve hot, or freeze and save for later!

130. Chicken Breast With Prosciutto And Brie

Servings:2
Cooking Time: 25 Minutes
Ingredients:

- 1 tbsp olive oil
- Salt and pepper to season
- 1 cup semi-dried tomatoes, sliced
- ½ cup brie cheese, halved

- 4 slices thin prosciutto

Directions:

1. Preheat the air fryer to 365 F. Put the chicken on a chopping board, and cut a small incision deep enough to make stuffing on both. Insert one slice of cheese and 4 to 5 tomato slices into each chicken.
2. Lay the prosciutto on the chopping board. Put the chicken on one side and roll the prosciutto over the chicken making sure that both ends of the prosciutto meet under the chicken.
3. Drizzle olive oil and sprinkle with salt and pepper. Place the chicken in the basket and cook for 10 minutes. Turn the breasts over and cook for another 5 minutes. Slice each chicken breast in half and serve with tomato salad.

131. Delightful Turkey Wings

Servings:4
Cooking Time:26 Minutes

Ingredients:

- 2 pounds turkey wings
- 4 tablespoons chicken rub
- 3 tablespoons olive oil

Directions:

1. Preheat the Air fryer to 380 °F and grease an Air fryer basket.
2. Mix the turkey wings, chicken rub, and olive oil in a bowl until well combined.
3. Arrange the turkey wings into the Air fryer basket and cook for about 26 minutes, flipping once in between.
4. Dish out the turkey wings in a platter and serve hot.

132. Shishito Pepper Rubbed Wings

Servings:6
Cooking Time: 30 Minutes

Ingredients:

- 1 ½ cups shishito peppers, pureed
- 2 tablespoons sesame oil
- 3 pounds chicken wings
- Salt and pepper to taste

Directions:

1. Place all Ingredients in a Ziploc bowl and allow to marinate for at least 2 hours in the fridge.
2. Preheat the air fryer to 390°F.
3. Place the grill pan accessory in the air fryer.
4. Grill for at least 30 minutes flipping the chicken every 5 minutes and basting with the remaining sauce.

133. Spinach 'n Bacon Egg Cups

Servings:4
Cooking Time: 10 Minutes

Ingredients:

- ¼ cup spinach, chopped finely
- 1 bacon strip, fried and crumbled
- 3 tablespoons butter
- 4 eggs, beaten
- Salt and pepper to taste

Directions:

1. Preheat the air fryer for 5 minutes.
2. In a mixing bowl, combine the eggs, butter, and spinach. Season with salt and pepper to taste.
3. Grease a ramekin with cooking spray and pour the egg mixture inside.
4. Sprinkle with bacon bits.
5. Place the ramekin in the air fryer.
6. Cook for 10 minutes at 350°F.

134. Cheddar Garlic Turkey

Servings: 4
Cooking Time: 20 Minutes
Ingredients:

- 1 big turkey breast, skinless, boneless and cubed
- Salt and black pepper to the taste
- ¼ cup cheddar cheese, grated
- ¼ teaspoon garlic powder
- 1 tablespoon olive oil

Directions:

1. Rub the turkey cubes with the oil, season with salt, pepper and garlic powder and dredge in cheddar cheese. Put the turkey bits in your air fryer's basket and cook at 380 degrees F for 20 minutes. Divide between plates and serve with a side salad.

135. Honey Chicken Drumsticks

Servings:2
Cooking Time: 20 Minutes
Ingredients:

- 2 tbsp olive oil
- 2 tbsp honey
- ½ tbsp garlic, minced

Directions:

1. Add the ingredients to a resealable bag; massage until well-coated. Allow the chicken to marinate for 30 minutes. Preheat your air fryer to 400 F. Add the chicken to the cooking basket and cook for 15 minutes, shaking once.

136. Simple Turkey Breast

Servings:10

Cooking Time:40 Minutes
Ingredients:

- 1 (8-pounds) bone-in turkey breast
- Salt and black pepper, as required
- 2 tablespoons olive oil

Directions:

1. Preheat the Air fryer to 360 °F and grease an Air fryer basket.
2. Season the turkey breast with salt and black pepper and drizzle with oil.
3. Arrange the turkey breast into the Air Fryer basket, skin side down and cook for about 20 minutes.
4. Flip the side and cook for another 20 minutes.
5. Dish out in a platter and cut into desired size slices to serve.

137. Sausage Stuffed Chicken

Servings:4
Cooking Time:15 Minutes
Ingredients:

- 4 (4-ounce) skinless, boneless chicken breasts
- 4 sausages, casing removed
- 2 tablespoons mustard sauce

Directions:

1. Preheat the Air fryer to 375 °F and grease an Air fryer basket.
2. Roll each chicken breast with a rolling pin for about 1 minute.
3. Arrange 1 sausage over each chicken breast and roll up.
4. Secure with toothpicks and transfer into the Air fryer basket.
5. Cook for about 15 minutes and dish out to serve warm.

138. Spicy Buffalo Chicken Wings

Servings:4
Cooking Time: 35 Minutes
Ingredients:
- ½ cup cayenne pepper sauce
- ½ cup coconut oil
- 1 tbsp Worcestershire sauce
- 1 tbsp kosher salt

Directions:
1. In a mixing cup, combine cayenne pepper sauce, coconut oil, Worcestershire sauce and salt; set aside. Pat the chicken dry and place in the air fryer cooking basket. Cook for 15 minutes at 380 F. Transfer to a plate and drizzle with the prepared sauce. Serve with celery sticks and enjoy!

139. Chicken Quarters With Broccoli And Rice

Servings:3
Cooking Time: 30 Minutes
Ingredients:
- 1 package instant long grain rice
- 1 cup chopped broccoli
- 2 cups water
- 1 can condensed cream chicken soup
- 1 tbsp minced garlic

Directions:
1. Preheat air fryer to 390 F, and place chicken in the air fryer. Season with salt, pepper and one tbsp oil; cook for 10 minutes. In a bowl, mix rice, water, garlic, soup and broccoli. Combine well. Remove the chicken from the air fryer and place it on a platter to drain. Spread the rice mixture on the bottom of the dish and place the chicken on top of the rice. Cook again for 10 minutes.

140. Fennel Duck Legs

Servings: 4
Cooking Time: 30 Minutes
Ingredients:
- 4 duck legs
- A pinch of salt and black pepper
- 3 teaspoons fennel seeds, crushed
- 4 teaspoons thyme, dried
- 2 tablespoons olive oil

Directions:
1. In a bowl, mix the duck legs with all the other ingredients and toss well. Put the duck legs in your air fryer's basket and cook at 380 degrees F for 15 minutes on each side. Divide between plates and serve

141. Spicy Chicken Wings

Servings:2
Cooking Time: 20 Minutes
Ingredients:
- 2 tbsp hot chili sauce
- ½ tbsp lime juice
- ½ tbsp honey
- ½ tbsp kosher salt
- ½ tbsp black pepper

Directions:
1. Preheat the air fryer to 350 F. Mix the lime juice, honey and chili sauce. Toss the mixture over the chicken wings. Put the chicken in the air fryer basket and cook for 15 minutes.

142. Breaded Chicken Tenderloins

Servings:4
Cooking Time:12 Minutes
Ingredients:
- 1 egg, beaten
- ½ cup breadcrumbs
- 8 skinless, boneless chicken tenderloins
- 2 tablespoons vegetable oil

Directions:
1. Preheat the Air fryer to 355 °F and grease an Air fryer basket.
2. Whisk the egg in a bowl and mix vegetable oil and breadcrumbs in another bowl.
3. Dip the chicken tenderloins into the whisked egg and then coat with the breadcrumb mixture.
4. Arrange the chicken tenderloins into the Air Fryer basket and cook for about 12 minutes.
5. Dish out the chicken tenderloins into a platter and serve hot.

143. Chicken With Mushrooms

Servings: 4
Cooking Time: 24 Minutes
Ingredients:
- 2 lbs chicken breasts, halved
- 1/3 cup sun-dried tomatoes
- 8 oz mushrooms, sliced
- 1/2 cup mayonnaise
- 1 tsp salt

Directions:
1. Preheat the air fryer to 370 F.
2. Spray air fryer baking dish with cooking spray.
3. Place chicken breasts into the baking dish and top with sun-dried tomatoes, mushrooms, mayonnaise, and salt. Mix well.
4. Place dish in the air fryer and cook for 24 minutes.
5. Serve and enjoy.

144. Chili And Paprika Chicken Wings

Servings:5
Cooking Time: 12 Minutes
Ingredients:
- 1-pound chicken wings
- 1 teaspoon ground paprika
- 1 teaspoon chili powder
- ½ teaspoon salt
- 1 tablespoon sunflower oil

Directions:
1. Pour the sunflower oil in the shallow bowl. Add chili powder and ground paprika. Gently stir the mixture. Sprinkle the chicken wings with red chili mixture and salt. Preheat the air fryer to 400F. Place the chicken wings in the preheated air fryer in one layer and cook for 6 minutes. Then flip the wings on another side and cook for 6 minutes more.

145. Turkey Strips With Cranberry Glaze

Servings:4
Cooking Time: 20 Minutes
Ingredients:
- 1 tbsp Chicken seasoning
- Salt and black pepper to taste
- ½ cup cranberry sauce

Directions:

1. Preheat your Air Fryer to 390 F. Spray the air fryer basket with cooking spray.
2. Cut the turkey into strips and season with chicken seasoning, salt, and black pepper. Spray with cooking spray and transfer to the cooking basket. Cook for 10 minutes, flipping once halfway through.
3. Meanwhile, put a saucepan over low heat, and add the cranberry sauce and ¼ cup of water. Simmer for 5 minutes, stirring continuously. Serve the turkey topped with the sauce.

146. Yummy Stuffed Chicken Breast

Servings:4
Cooking Time:15 Minutes
Ingredients:
- 2 (8-ounce) chicken fillets, skinless and boneless, each cut into 2 pieces
- 4 brie cheese slices
- 1 tablespoon chive, minced
- 4 cured ham slices
- Salt and black pepper, to taste

Directions:
1. Preheat the Air fryer to 355 °F and grease an Air fryer basket.
2. Make a slit in each chicken piece horizontally and season with the salt and black pepper.
3. Insert cheese slice in the slits and sprinkle with chives.
4. Wrap each chicken piece with one ham slice and transfer into the Air fryer basket.
5. Cook for about 15 minutes and dish out to serve warm.

147. Crispy Chicken With Parmesan

Servings:4
Cooking Time: 30 Minutes
Ingredients:
- 2 tablespoons grated Parmesan cheese
- 1 tablespoon butter, melted
- 4 chicken thighs
- ½ cup marinara sauce
- ½ cup shredded Monterrey jack cheese

Directions:
1. Spray the air fryer basket with cooking spray. In a bowl, mix the crumbs and Parmesan cheese. Pour the butter into another bowl. Brush the thighs with butter. Dip each one into the crumbs mixture, until well-coated.
2. Arrange chicken thighs in the air fryer, and spray with cooking oil. Cook for 5 minutes at 380 F. Flip over, top with marinara sauce and shredded Monterrey Jack cheese. Cook until no longer pink in the center, for 4 minutes. Ser.

148. Quick And Crispy Chicken

Servings:4
Cooking Time: 15 Minutes
Ingredients:
- 2 tbsp butter
- 2 oz breadcrumbs
- 1 large egg, whisked

Directions:
1. Preheat air fryer to 380 F. Combine butter the breadcrumbs in a bowl. Keep mixing and stirring until the mixture gets crumbly. Dip the chicken in the egg wash. Then dip the chicken in the

crumbs mix. Cook for 10 minutes. Serve.

149. Ricotta And Thyme Chicken

Servings: 3
Cooking Time: 18 Minutes
Ingredients:
- 3 chicken thighs, boneless
- 2 teaspoons adobo sauce
- 1 teaspoon ricotta cheese
- 1 teaspoon dried thyme
- Cooking spray

Directions:
1. In the mixing bowl mix up adobo sauce and ricotta cheese, Add dried thyme and churn the mixture. Then brush the chicken thighs with adobo sauce mixture and leave for 10 minutes to marinate. Preheat the air fryer to 385F. Spray the air fryer basket with cooking spray and put the chicken thighs inside. Cook them for 18 minutes.

150. Peppery Lemon-chicken Breast

Servings:1
Cooking Time:
Ingredients:
- 1 chicken breast
- 1 teaspoon minced garlic
- 2 lemons, rinds and juice reserved
- Salt and pepper to taste

Directions:
1. Preheat the air fryer.
2. Place all ingredients in a baking dish that will fit in the air fryer.
3. Place in the air fryer basket.

4. Close and cook for 20 minutes at 400°F.

151. Chicken Satay

Servings: 4
Cooking Time: 14 Minutes
Ingredients:
- 4 chicken wings
- 1 teaspoon olive oil
- 1 teaspoon keto tomato sauce
- 1 teaspoon dried cilantro
- ½ teaspoon salt

Directions:
1. String the chicken wings on the wooden skewers. Then in the shallow bowl mix up olive oil, tomato sauce, dried cilantro, and salt. Spread the chicken skewers with the tomato mixture. Preheat the air fryer to 390F. Arrange the chicken satay in the air fryer and cook the meal for 10 minutes. Then flip the chicken satay on another side and cook it for 4 minutes more.

152. Crispy Chicken

Servings: 2
Cooking Time: 10 Minutes
Ingredients:
- 1 lb. chicken skin
- 1 tsp. butter
- ½ tsp. chili flakes
- 1 tsp. dill

Directions:
1. Pre-heat the fryer at 360°F.
2. Cut the chicken skin into slices.
3. Heat the butter until melted and pour it over the chicken skin. Toss with chili flakes, dill, and any additional seasonings to taste, making sure to coat well.

4. Cook the skins in the fryer for three minutes. Turn them over and cook on the other side for another three minutes.
5. Serve immediately or save them for later – they can be eaten hot or at room temperature.

153. Air Fried Chicken Tenderloin

Servings:8
Cooking Time: 15 Minutes
Ingredients:
- ½ cup almond flour
- 1 egg, beaten
- 2 tablespoons coconut oil
- 8 chicken tenderloins
- Salt and pepper to taste

Directions:
1. Preheat the air fryer for 5 minutes.
2. Season the chicken tenderloin with salt and pepper to taste.
3. Soak in beaten eggs then dredge in almond flour.
4. Place in the air fryer and brush with coconut oil.
5. Cook for 15 minutes at 375°F.
6. Halfway through the cooking time, give the fryer basket a shake to cook evenly.

154. Turkey And Butter Sauce

Servings: 4
Cooking Time: 24 Minutes
Ingredients:
- 1 turkey breast, skinless, boneless and cut into 4 pieces
- A pinch of salt and black pepper
- Juice of 1 lemon
- 2 tablespoons rosemary, chopped
- 2 tablespoons butter, melted

Directions:
1. In a bowl, mix the butter with the rosemary, lemon juice, salt and pepper and whisk really well. Brush the turkey pieces with the rosemary butter, put them your air fryer's basket, cook at 380 degrees F for 12 minutes on each side. Divide between plates and serve with a side salad.

155. Chicken & Potatoes

Servings: 6
Cooking Time: 45 Minutes
Ingredients:
- 1 lb. potatoes
- 2 lb. chicken
- 2 tbsp. olive oil
- Pepper and salt to taste

Directions:
1. Pre-heat the Air Fryer to 350°F.
2. Place the chicken in Air Fryer basket along with the potatoes. Sprinkle on the pepper and salt.
3. Add a drizzling of the olive oil, making sure to cover the chicken and potatoes well.
4. Cook for 40 minutes.

156. Fried Chicken Thighs

Servings: 4
Cooking Time: 35 Minutes
Ingredients:
- 4 chicken thighs
- 1 ½ tbsp. Cajun seasoning
- 1 egg, beaten
- ½ cup flour
- 1 tsp. seasoning salt

Directions:

1. Pre-heat the Air Fryer to 350°F.
2. In a bowl combine the flour, Cajun seasoning, and seasoning salt.
3. Place the beaten egg in another bowl.
4. Coat the chicken with the flour before dredging it in the egg. Roll once more in the flour.
5. Put the chicken in the Air Fryer and cook for 25 minutes. Serve hot.

157. Grilled Chicken Recipe From Jamaica

Servings:2
Cooking Time: 30 Minutes
Ingredients:
- ¼ cup pineapple chunks
- 1 tablespoon vegetable oil
- 2 whole chicken thighs
- 3 teaspoons lime juice
- 4 tablespoons jerk seasoning

Directions:
1. In a shallow dish, mix well all Ingredients. Marinate in the ref for 3 hours.
2. Thread chicken pieces and pineapples in skewers. Place on skewer rack in air fryer.
3. For 30 minutes, cook on 360°F. Halfway through cooking time, turnover skewers.
4. Serve and enjoy.

158. Crumbed Sage Chicken Scallopini4

Servings:4
Cooking Time: 12 Minutes
Ingredients:
- 3 oz breadcrumbs

- 2 tbsp grated Parmesan cheese
- 2 oz flour
- 2 eggs, beaten
- 1 tbsp fresh, chopped sage

Directions:
1. Preheat the air fryer to 370 F. Place some plastic wrap underneath and on top of the chicken breasts. Using a rolling pin, beat the meat until it becomes really thin. In a bowl, combine the Parmesan cheese, sage and breadcrumbs.
2. Dip the chicken in the egg first, and then in the sage mixture. Spray with cooking oil and arrange the meat in the air fryer. Cook for 7 minutes.

159. Cheese Stuffed Chicken Breasts

Servings:4
Cooking Time: 15 Minutes
Ingredients:
- 2 (8-ounces) skinless, boneless chicken breast fillets
- Salt and ground black pepper, as required
- 4 Brie cheese slices
- 1 tablespoon fresh chive, minced
- 4 cured ham slices

Directions:
1. Cut each chicken fillet in 2 equal-sized pieces.
2. Carefully, make a slit in each chicken piece horizontally about ¼-inch from the edge.
3. Open each chicken piece and season with the salt and black pepper.
4. Place 1 cheese slice in the open area of each chicken piece and sprinkle with chives.

5. Close the chicken pieces and wrap each one with a ham slice.
6. Set the temperature of Air Fryer to 355 degrees F. Grease an Air Fryer basket.
7. Arrange the wrapped chicken pieces into the prepared Air Fryer basket.
8. Air Fry for about 15 minutes.
9. Remove from Air Fryer and transfer the chicken fillets onto a serving platter.
10. Serve hot.

160. Spinach Loaded Chicken Breasts

Servings:4
Cooking Time: 15 Minutes
Ingredients:
- 4 tbsp cottage cheese
- 2 boneless, skinless chicken breasts
- Juice of ½ lime
- 2 tbsp Italian seasoning
- 2 tbsp olive oil

Directions:
1. Preheat your Air Fryer to 390 F. Spray the air fryer basket with cooking spray.
2. Mix the spinach with the cottage cheese in a bowl. Halve the chicken breasts with a knife and flatten them with a meat mallet. Season with Italian seasoning. Divide the spinach/cheese mixture between the four chicken pieces. Roll up to form cylinders and use toothpicks to secure them.
3. Brush with olive oil and transfer to the air fryer basket. Cook for 6 minutes, flip, and cook for another 6 minutes.Serve with salad.

161. Goulash

Servings: 2

Cooking Time: 20 Minutes
Ingredients:
- 2 chopped bell peppers
- 2 diced tomatoes
- 1 lb. ground chicken
- ½ cup chicken broth
- Salt and pepper

Directions:
1. Pre-heat your fryer at 365°F and spray with cooking spray.
2. Cook the bell pepper for five minutes.
3. Add in the diced tomatoes and ground chicken. Combine well, then allow to cook for a further six minutes.
4. Pour in chicken broth, and season to taste with salt and pepper. Cook for another six minutes before serving.

162. Chili Chicken Cutlets

Servings: 4
Cooking Time: 16 Minutes
Ingredients:
- 15 oz chicken fillet
- 1 teaspoon white pepper
- 1 teaspoon ghee, melted
- ½ teaspoon onion powder
- ¼ teaspoon chili flakes

Directions:
1. Chop the chicken fillet into the tiny pieces. Then sprinkle the chopped chicken with white pepper, onion powder, and chili flakes. Stir the mixture until homogenous. Make the medium-size cutlets from the mixture. Preheat the air fryer to 365F. Brush the air fryer basket with ghee and put the chicken cutlets inside. Cook them for 8 minutes and then flip on another side with the help of the spatula. Transfer

the cooked chicken cutlets on the serving plate.

163. Simple Panko Turkey

Servings:6
Cooking Time: 25 Minutes
Ingredients:
- 2 cups panko breadcrumbs
- ½ tsp cayenne pepper
- Salt and black pepper to taste
- 1 stick butter, melted

Directions:
1. In a bowl, combine panko and cayenne pepper. In another small bowl, combine butter with salt and pepper. Don't add salt if you use salted butter.Brush the butter mixture over the turkey breast. Coat the turkey with the panko mixture. Arrange them on a lined baking dish. Air fry for 15 minutes at 390 F.

164. Roasted Chicken

Servings: 6
Cooking Time: 90 Minutes
Ingredients:
- 6 lb. whole chicken
- 1 tsp. olive oil
- 1 tbsp. minced garlic
- 1 white onion, peeled and halved
- 3 tbsp. butter

Directions:
1. Pre-heat the fryer at 360°F.
2. Massage the chicken with the olive oil and the minced garlic.
3. Place the peeled and halved onion, as well as the butter, inside of the chicken.
4. Cook the chicken in the fryer for seventy-five minutes.

5. Take care when removing the chicken from the fryer, then carve and serve.

165. Lemon Grilled Chicken Breasts

Servings:6
Cooking Time: 40 Minutes
Ingredients:
- 3 tablespoons fresh lemon juice
- 2 tablespoons olive oil
- 2 cloves of garlic, minced
- 6 boneless chicken breasts, halved
- Salt and pepper to taste

Directions:
1. Place all ingredients in a Ziploc bag
2. Allow to marinate for at least 2 hours in the fridge.
3. Preheat the air fryer at 375°F.
4. Place the grill pan accessory in the air fryer.
5. Grill for 40 minutes and make sure to flip the chicken every 10 minutes for even cooking.

166. Creamy Chicken Breasts With Crumbled Bacon

Servings:4
Cooking Time: 25 Minutes
Ingredients:
- ¼ cup olive oil
- 1 block cream cheese
- 4 chicken breasts
- 8 slices of bacon, fried and crumbled
- Salt and pepper to taste

Directions:
1. Preheat the air fryer for 5 minutes.
2. Place the chicken breasts in a baking dish that will fit in the air fryer.

3. Add the olive oil and cream cheese. Season with salt and pepper to taste.
4. Place the baking dish with the chicken and cook for 25 minutes at 350°F.
5. Sprinkle crumbled bacon after.

167. Simple Turkey Breasts

Servings: 5
Cooking Time: 35 Minutes
Ingredients:
- 6 – 7 lb. skinless, boneless turkey breast
- 2 tsp. salt
- 1 tsp. black pepper
- ½ tsp. dried cumin
- 2 tbsp. olive oil

Directions:
1. Massage all of the other ingredients into the turkey breast.
2. Pre-heat the Air Fryer to 340°F,
3. Cook the turkey breast for 15 minutes. Turn it over and cook for an additional 10 – 15 minutes, until cooked through and crispy.
4. Slice and serve the turkey with rice or fresh vegetables.

168. Cinnamon Chicken Thighs

Servings: 4
Cooking Time: 30 Minutes
Ingredients:
- 2 pounds chicken thighs
- A pinch of salt and black pepper
- 2 tablespoons olive oil
- ½ teaspoon cinnamon, ground

Directions:
1. Season the chicken thighs with salt and pepper, and rub with the rest of the ingredients. Put the chicken thighs in air fryer's basket, cook at 360 degrees F

for 15 minutes on each side, divide between plates and serve.

169. Roasted Chicken With Potatoes

Servings:2
Cooking Time:1 Hour
Ingredients:
- 1 (1½-pounds) whole chicken
- ½ pound small potatoes
- Salt and black pepper, as required
- 1 tablespoon olive oil

Directions:
1. Preheat the Air fryer to 355 °F and grease an Air fryer basket.
2. Season the chicken and potatoes with salt and black pepper and drizzle with olive oil.
3. Transfer the chicken into the Air fryer basket and cook for about 45 minutes.
4. Dish out in a serving platter and transfer the potatoes in the Air fryer basket.
5. Cook for about 15 minutes and serve alongside the chicken.

170. Mustard And Garlic Turkey

Servings: 4
Cooking Time: 20 Minutes
Ingredients:
- 1 big turkey breast, skinless, boneless and cubed
- 4 garlic cloves, minced
- Salt and black pepper to the taste
- 1 and ½ tablespoon olive oil
- 1 tablespoon mustard

Directions:

1. In a bowl, mix the chicken with the garlic and the other ingredients and toss. Put the turkey in your air fryer's basket, cook at 360 degrees F for 20 minutes, divide between plates and serve with a side salad.

171. Hot Chicken Skin

Servings: 4
Cooking Time: 30 Minutes
Ingredients:
- ½ teaspoon chili paste
- 8 oz chicken skin
- 1 teaspoon sesame oil
- ½ teaspoon chili powder
- ½ teaspoon salt

Directions:
1. In the shallow bowl mix up chili paste, sesame oil, chili powder, and salt. Then brush the chicken skin with chili mixture well and leave for 10 minutes to marinate. Meanwhile, preheat the air fryer to 365F. Put the marinated chicken skin in the air fryer and cook it for 20 minutes. When the time is finished, flip the chicken skin on another side and cook it for 10 minutes more or until the chicken skin is crunchy.

172. Easy & Crispy Chicken Wings

Servings: 8
Cooking Time: 20 Minutes
Ingredients:
- 1 1/2 lbs chicken wings
- 2 tbsp olive oil
- Pepper
- Salt

Directions:
1. Toss chicken wings with oil and place in the air fryer basket.
2. Cook chicken wings at 370 F for 15 minutes.
3. Shake basket and cook at 400 F for 5 minutes more.
4. Season chicken wings with pepper and salt.
5. Serve and enjoy.

173. Chimichurri Turkey

Servings: 1
Cooking Time: 70 Minutes
Ingredients:
- 1 lb. turkey breast
- ½ cup chimichurri sauce
- ½ cup butter
- ¼ cup parmesan cheese, grated
- ¼ tsp. garlic powder

Directions:
1. Massage the chimichurri sauce into the turkey breast, then refrigerate in an airtight container for at least a half hour.
2. In the meantime, prepare the herbed butter. Mix together the butter, parmesan, and garlic powder, using a hand mixer if desired (this will make it extra creamy)
3. Preheat your fryer at 350°F and place a rack inside. Remove the turkey from the refrigerator and allow to return to room temperature for roughly twenty minutes while the fryer warms.
4. Place the turkey in the fryer and allow to cook for twenty minutes. Flip and cook on the other side for a further twenty minutes.

5. Take care when removing the turkey from the fryer. Place it on a serving dish and enjoy with the herbed butter.

174. Fajita Style Chicken Breast

Servings: 2
Cooking Time: 35 Minutes
Ingredients:
- 2 x 6-oz. boneless skinless chicken breasts
- 1 green bell pepper, sliced
- ¼ medium white onion, sliced
- 1 tbsp. coconut oil, melted
- 3 tsp. taco seasoning mix

Directions:
1. Cut each chicken breast in half and place each one between two sheets of cooking parchment. Using a mallet, pound the chicken to flatten to a quarter-inch thick.
2. Place the chicken on a flat surface, with the short end facing you. Place four slices of pepper and three slices of onion at the end of each piece of chicken. Roll up the chicken tightly, making sure not to let any veggies fall out. Secure with some toothpicks or with butcher's string.
3. Coat the chicken with coconut oil and then with taco seasoning. Place into your air fryer.
4. Turn the fryer to 350°F and cook the chicken for twenty-five minutes.
5. Serve the rolls immediately with your favorite dips and sides.

175. Turkey Wings

Servings:4

Cooking Time: 26 Minutes
Ingredients:
- 2 pounds turkey wings
- 4 tablespoons chicken rub
- 3 tablespoons olive oil

Directions:
1. In a large bowl, mix together the turkey wings, chicken rub, and oil using your hands.
2. Set the temperature of Air Fryer to 380 degrees F. Grease an Air Fryer basket.
3. Arrange turkey wings into the prepared Air Fryer basket.
4. Air Fry for about 26 minutes, flipping once halfway through.
5. Remove from Air Fryer and place the turkey wings onto the serving plates.
6. Serve hot.

176. Southern Fried Chicken

Servings: 2
Cooking Time: 30 Minutes
Ingredients:
- 2 x 6-oz. boneless skinless chicken breasts
- 2 tbsp. hot sauce
- ½ tsp. onion powder
- 1 tbsp. chili powder
- 2 oz. pork rinds, finely ground

Directions:
1. Cut the chicken breasts in half lengthwise and rub in the hot sauce. Combine the onion powder with the chili powder, then rub into the chicken. Leave to marinate for at least a half hour.
2. Use the ground pork rinds to coat the chicken breasts in the ground pork rinds, covering them thoroughly. Place the chicken in your fryer.

3. Set the fryer at 350°F and cook the chicken for 13 minutes. Flip the chicken and cook the other side for another 13 minutes or until golden.
4. Test the chicken with a meat thermometer. When fully cooked, it should reach 165°F. Serve hot, with the sides of your choice.

177. Chicken Wings

Servings: 4
Cooking Time: 55 Minutes
Ingredients:
- 3 lb. bone-in chicken wings
- ¾ cup flour
- 1 tbsp. old bay seasoning
- 4 tbsp. butter
- Couple fresh lemons

Directions:
1. In a bowl, combine the all-purpose flour and Old Bay seasoning.
2. Toss the chicken wings with the mixture to coat each one well.
3. Pre-heat the Air Fryer to 375°F.
4. Give the wings a shake to shed any excess flour and place each one in the Air Fryer. You may have to do this in multiple batches, so as to not overlap any.
5. Cook for 30 – 40 minutes, shaking the basket frequently, until the wings are cooked through and crispy.
6. In the meantime, melt the butter in a frying pan over a low heat. Squeeze one or two lemons and add the juice to the pan. Mix well.
7. Serve the wings topped with the sauce.

178. Whole Chicken

Servings: 2
Cooking Time: 30 Minutes
Ingredients:
- 1 lb. whole chicken
- 1 lemon, juiced
- 1 tsp. lemon zest
- 1 tbsp. soy sauce
- 1 ½ tbsp. honey

Directions:
1. Place all of the ingredients in a bowl and combine well. Refrigerate for 1 hour.
2. Put the marinated chicken in the Air Fryer baking pan. Air fry at 320°F for 18 minutes.
3. Raise the heat to 350°F and cook for another 10 minutes or until chicken has turned light brown.

179. Sweet Chili Chicken Wings

Servings:4
Cooking Time: 20 Minutes
Ingredients:
- 1 tsp garlic powder
- 1 tbsp tamarind powder
- ¼ cup sweet chili sauce

Directions:
1. Preheat your Air Fryer to 390 F. Spray the air fryer basket with cooking spray.
2. Rub the chicken wings with tamarind and garlic powders. Spray with cooking spray and place in the cooking basket. Cook for 6 minutes, Slide out the fryer basket and cover with sweet chili sauce; cook for 8 more minutes. Serve cooled.

180. Fried Chicken Halves

Servings: 4

Cooking Time: 75 Minutes
Ingredients:
- 16 oz whole chicken
- 1 tablespoon dried thyme
- 1 teaspoon ground cumin
- 1 teaspoon salt
- 1 tablespoon avocado oil

Directions:

1. Cut the chicken into halves and sprinkle it with dried thyme, cumin, and salt. Then brush the chicken halves with avocado oil. Preheat the air fryer to 365F. Put the chicken halves in the air fryer and cook them for 60 minutes. Then flip the chicken halves on another side and cook them for 15 minutes more.

FISH & SEAFOOD RECIPES

181. Sautéed Shrimp

Servings:4
Cooking Time: 10 Minutes
Ingredients:
- 1 tbsp olive oil
- ½ a tbsp old bay seasoning
- ¼ a tbsp cayenne pepper
- ¼ a tbsp smoked paprika
- A pinch of sea salt

Directions:
1. Preheat the air fryer to 380 F, and mix all ingredients in a large bowl. Coat the shrimp with a little bit of oil and spices. Place the shrimp in the air fryer's basket and fry for 6-7 minutes. Serve with rice or salad.

182. Air Fried Calamari

Servings:3
Cooking Time: 30 Minutes
Ingredients:
- ½ cup cornmeal or cornstarch
- 2 large eggs, beaten
- 2 mashed garlic cloves
- 1 cup breadcrumbs
- lemon juice

Directions:
1. Coat calamari with the cornmeal. The first mixture is prepared by mixing the eggs and garlic. Dip the calamari in the eggs' mixture. Then dip them in the breadcrumbs. Put the rings in the fridge for 2 hours.
2. Then, line them in the air fryer and add oil generously. Fry for 10 to 13 minutes at 390 F, shaking once halfway through.

Serve with garlic mayonnaise and top with lemon juice.

183. Lime, Oil 'n Leeks On Grilled Swordfish

Servings:4
Cooking Time: 20 Minutes
Ingredients:
- 2 tablespoons olive oil
- 3 tablespoons lime juice
- 4 medium leeks, cut into an inch long
- 4 swordfish steaks
- Salt and pepper to taste

Directions:
1. Preheat the air fryer to 390°F.
2. Place the grill pan accessory in the air fryer.
3. Season the swordfish with salt, pepper and lime juice.
4. Brush the fish with olive oil
5. Place fish fillets on grill pan and top with leeks.
6. Grill for 20 minutes.

184. Sesame Seeds Coated Tuna

Servings:2
Cooking Time:6 Minutes
Ingredients:
- ¼ cup white sesame seeds
- 1 tablespoon black sesame seeds
- 1 egg white
- 2 (6-ounces) tuna steaks
- Salt and black pepper, as required

Directions:

1. Preheat the Air fryer to 400 °F and grease an Air fryer basket.
2. Whisk the egg white in a shallow bowl.
3. Mix the sesame seeds, salt, and black pepper in another bowl.
4. Dip the tuna steaks into the whisked egg white and dredge into the sesame seeds mixture.
5. Arrange the tuna steaks into the Air fryer basket in a single layer and cook for about 6 minutes, flipping once in between.
6. Dish out the tuna steaks onto serving plates and serve hot.

185. Prawns

Servings: 4
Cooking Time: 30 Minutes
Ingredients:
- 1 lb. prawns, peeled
- 1 lb. bacon slices

Directions:
1. Pre-heat the Air Fryer to 400°F.
2. Wrap the bacon slices around the prawns and put them in fryer's basket.
3. Air fry for 5 minutes and serve hot.

186. Herbed Garlic Lobster

Servings:3
Cooking Time: 15 Minutes
Ingredients:
- 1 tsp garlic, minced
- 1 tbsp butter
- Salt and pepper to taste
- ½ tbsp lemon Juice

Directions:
1. Add all the ingredients to a food processor, except shrimp, and blend well. Clean the skin of the lobster and

cover with the marinade. Preheat your air fryer to 380 F. Place the lobster in your air fryer's cooking basket and cook for 10 minutes. Serve with fresh herbs and enjoy!

187. Cajun Spiced Salmon

Servings:2
Cooking Time:8 Minutes
Ingredients:
- 2 (7-ounces) (¾-inch thick) salmon fillets
- 1 tablespoon Cajun seasoning
- ½ teaspoon sugar
- 1 tablespoon fresh lemon juice

Directions:
1. Preheat the Air fryer to 365 °F and grease an Air fryer grill pan.
2. Season the salmon evenly with Cajun seasoning and sugar.
3. Arrange the salmon fillets into the Air fryer grill pan, skin-side up.
4. Cook for about 8 minutes and dish out the salmon fillets in the serving plates.
5. Drizzle with the lemon juice and serve hot.

188. Crab Legs

Servings: 3
Cooking Time: 20 Minutes
Ingredients:
- 3 lb. crab legs
- ¼ cup salted butter, melted and divided
- ½ lemon, juiced
- ¼ tsp. garlic powder

Directions:
1. In a bowl, toss the crab legs and two tablespoons of the melted butter

together. Place the crab legs in the basket of the fryer.

2. Cook at 400°F for fifteen minutes, giving the basket a good shake halfway through.
3. Combine the remaining butter with the lemon juice and garlic powder.
4. Crack open the cooked crab legs and remove the meat. Serve with the butter dip on the side and enjoy!

189. Cajun Lemon Salmon

Servings: 1
Cooking Time: 15 Minutes
Ingredients:
- 1 salmon fillet
- 1 tsp. Cajun seasoning
- ½ lemon, juiced
- ¼ tsp. sugar
- 2 lemon wedges, for serving

Directions:
1. 1 Pre-heat the Air Fryer to 350°F.
2. 2 Combine the lemon juice and sugar.
3. 3 Cover the salmon with the sugar mixture.
4. 4 Coat the salmon with the Cajun seasoning.
5. 5 Line the base of your fryer with a sheet of parchment paper.
6. 6 Transfer the salmon to the fryer and allow to cook for 7 minutes.

190. Avocado Shrimp

Servings: 2
Cooking Time: 20 Minutes
Ingredients:
- ½ cup onion, chopped
- 2 lb. shrimp
- 1 tbsp. seasoned salt
- 1 avocado
- ½ cup pecans, chopped

Directions:
1. Pre-heat the fryer at 400°F.
2. Put the chopped onion in the basket of the fryer and spritz with some cooking spray. Leave to cook for five minutes.
3. Add the shrimp and set the timer for a further five minutes. Sprinkle with some seasoned salt, then allow to cook for an additional five minutes.
4. During these last five minutes, halve your avocado and remove the pit. Cube each half, then scoop out the flesh.
5. Take care when removing the shrimp from the fryer. Place it on a dish and top with the avocado and the chopped pecans.

191. Rosemary-infused Butter Scallops

Servings: 4
Cooking Time: 1 Hour 10 Minutes
Ingredients:
- 2 pounds sea scallops
- 1/2 cup beer
- 4 tablespoons butter
- 2 sprigs rosemary, only leaves
- Sea salt and freshly cracked black pepper, to taste

Directions:
1. In a ceramic dish, mix the sea scallops with beer; let it marinate for 1 hour.
2. Meanwhile, preheat your Air Fryer to 400 degrees F. Melt the butter and add the rosemary leaves. Stir for a few minutes.
3. Discard the marinade and transfer the sea scallops to the Air Fryer basket. Season with salt and black pepper.

4. Cook the scallops in the preheated Air Fryer for 7 minutes, shaking the basket halfway through the cooking time. Work in batches.
5. Bon appétit!

192. Broiled Tilapia

Servings: 4
Cooking Time: 10 Minutes
Ingredients:
- 1 lb. tilapia fillets
- ½ tsp. lemon pepper
- Salt to taste

Directions:
1. Spritz the Air Fryer basket with some cooking spray.
2. Put the tilapia fillets in basket and sprinkle on the lemon pepper and salt.
3. Cook at 400°F for 7 minutes.
4. Serve with a side of vegetables.

193. Stevia Cod

Servings: 4
Cooking Time: 14 Minutes
Ingredients:
- 1/3 cup stevia
- 2 tablespoons coconut aminos
- 4 cod fillets, boneless
- A pinch of salt and black pepper

Directions:
1. In a pan that fits the air fryer, combine all the ingredients and toss gently. Introduce the pan in the fryer and cook at 350 degrees F for 14 minutes, flipping the fish halfway. Divide everything between plates and serve.

194. Citrusy Branzini On The Grill

Servings:2
Cooking Time: 15 Minutes
Ingredients:
- 2 branzini fillets
- Salt and pepper to taste
- 3 lemons, juice freshly squeezed
- 2 oranges, juice freshly squeezed

Directions:
1. Place all ingredients in a Ziploc bag. Allow to marinate in the fridge for 2 hours.
2. Preheat the air fryer at 390°F.
3. Place the grill pan accessory in the air fryer.
4. Place the fish on the grill pan and cook for 15 minutes until the fish is flaky.

195. Rice Flour Coated Shrimp

Servings:3
Cooking Time:20 Minutes
Ingredients:
- 3 tablespoons rice flour
- 1 pound shrimp, peeled and deveined
- 2 tablespoons olive oil
- 1 teaspoon powdered sugar
- Salt and black pepper, as required

Directions:
1. Preheat the Air fryer to 325 °F and grease an Air fryer basket.
2. Mix rice flour, olive oil, sugar, salt, and black pepper in a bowl.
3. Stir in the shrimp and transfer half of the shrimp to the Air fryer basket.
4. Cook for about 10 minutes, flipping once in between.
5. Dish out the mixture onto serving plates and repeat with the remaining mixture.

196. Fish Sticks

Servings: 4
Cooking Time: 20 Minutes
Ingredients:
- 1 lb. tilapia fillets, cut into strips
- 1 large egg, beaten
- 2 tsp. Old Bay seasoning
- 1 tbsp. olive oil
- 1 cup friendly bread crumbs

Directions:
1. Pre-heat the Air Fryer at 400°F.
2. In a shallow dish, combine together the bread crumbs, Old Bay, and oil. Put the egg in a small bowl.
3. Dredge the fish sticks in the egg. Cover them with bread crumbs and put them in the fryer's basket.
4. Cook the fish for 10 minutes or until they turn golden brown.
5. Serve hot.

197. Shrimp And Scallions

Servings: 4
Cooking Time: 10 Minutes
Ingredients:
- 1 pound shrimp, peeled and deveined
- 2 tablespoons olive oil
- 1 tablespoon scallions, chopped
- 1 cup chicken stock

Directions:
1. In a pan that fits your air fryer, mix the shrimp with the oil, onion and the stock, introduce the pan in the fryer and cook at 380 degrees F for 10 minutes. Divide into bowls and serve.

198. Breaded Hake

Servings:2
Cooking Time:12 Minutes
Ingredients:
- 1 egg
- 4 ounces breadcrumbs
- 4 (6-ounces) hake fillets
- 1 lemon, cut into wedges
- 2 tablespoons vegetable oil

Directions:
1. Preheat the Air fryer to 350 °F and grease an Air fryer basket.
2. Whisk the egg in a shallow bowl and mix breadcrumbs and oil in another bowl.
3. Dip hake fillets into the whisked egg and then, dredge in the breadcrumb mixture.
4. Arrange the hake fillets into the Air fryer basket in a single layer and cook for about 12 minutes.
5. Dish out the hake fillets onto serving plates and serve, garnished with lemon wedges.

199. Breaded Flounder

Servings:3
Cooking Time:12 Minutes
Ingredients:
- 1 egg
- 1 cup dry breadcrumbs
- 3 (6-ounces) flounder fillets
- 1 lemon, sliced
- ¼ cup vegetable oil

Directions:
1. Preheat the Air fryer to 360 °F and grease an Air fryer basket.

2. Whisk the egg in a shallow bowl and mix breadcrumbs and oil in another bowl.
3. Dip flounder fillets into the whisked egg and coat with the breadcrumb mixture.
4. Arrange flounder fillets into the Air fryer basket and cook for about 12 minutes.
5. Dish out the flounder fillets onto serving plates and garnish with the lemon slices to serve.

200. Air Fried Dilly Trout

Servings:3
Cooking Time: 30 Minutes
Ingredients:
- 3 tbsp olive oil
- Salt to taste
- ½ cup greek yogurt
- ½ cup sour cream
- 2 tbsp finely chopped dill

Directions:
1. Preheat the air fryer to 300 F. Drizzle the trout with oil and season with a pinch of salt. Place the seasoned trout into the air fryer's cooking basket. Cook for 20 minutes and top with the dill sauce before serving. For the dill sauce, in a large bowl, mix yogurt, sour cream, chopped dill and salt.

201. Golden Cod Fish Nuggets

Servings:4
Cooking Time: 20 Minutes
Ingredients:
- 2 tbsp olive oil
- 2 eggs, beaten
- 1 cup breadcrumbs
- A pinch of salt

- 1 cup flour

Directions:
1. Preheat air fryer to 390 F. Mix breadcrumbs, olive oil, and salt in a bowl until combined. In another bowl, place the eggs, and the flour into a third bowl. Toss the cod fillets in the flour, then in the eggs, and then in the breadcrumb mixture. Place in the fryer basket and cook for 9 minutes. At the 5-minute mark, quickly turn the chicken nuggets over. Once done, remove to a plate to serve.

202. Shrimp And Parsley Olives

Servings: 4
Cooking Time: 12 Minutes
Ingredients:
- 1 pound shrimp, peeled and deveined
- 4 garlic clove, minced
- 1 cup black olives, pitted and chopped
- 3 tablespoons parsley
- 1 tablespoon olive oil

Directions:
1. In a pan that fits the air fryer, combine all the ingredients, toss, put the pan in the machine and cook at 380 degrees F for 12 minutes. Divide between plates and serve.

203. Butter Lobster

Servings: 4
Cooking Time: 6 Minutes
Ingredients:
- 4 lobster tails, peeled
- 4 teaspoons almond butter
- ½ teaspoon salt

- ½ teaspoon dried thyme
- 1 tablespoon avocado oil

Directions:

1. Make the cut on the back of every lobster tail and sprinkle them with dried thyme and salt. After this, sprinkle the lobster tails with avocado oil. Preheat the air fryer to 380F. Place the lobster tails in the air fryer basket and cook them for 5 minutes. After this, gently spread the lobster tails with almond butter and cook for 1 minute more.

204. Orange Roughie With Caesar & Cheese Dressing

Servings:2
Cooking Time: 15 Minutes
Ingredients:

- 2 orange roughie fillets (4 ounces each)
- 1/2 cups crushed butter-flavored crackers
- 1/2 cup shredded cheddar cheese
- 1/4 cup creamy Caesar salad dressing

Directions:

1. Lightly grease baking pan of air fryer with cooking spray. Add filet on bottom of pan. Drizzle with dressing, sprinkle crumbled crackers.
2. For 10 minutes, cook on 390°F.
3. Sprinkle cheese and let it stand for 5 minutes.
4. Serve and enjoy.

205. Nutritious Salmon

Servings: 2
Cooking Time: 10 Minutes
Ingredients:

- 2 salmon fillets

- 1 tbsp olive oil
- 1/4 tsp ground cardamom
- 1/2 tsp paprika
- Salt

Directions:

1. Preheat the air fryer to 350 F.
2. Coat salmon fillets with olive oil and season with paprika, cardamom, and salt and place into the air fryer basket.
3. Cook salmon for 10-12 minutes. Turn halfway through.
4. Serve and enjoy.

206. Nacho Chips Crusted Prawns

Servings:2
Cooking Time: 8 Minutes
Ingredients:

- ¾ pound prawns, peeled and deveined
- 1 large egg
- 5 ounces Nacho flavored chips, finely crushed

Directions:

1. In a shallow bowl, beat the egg.
2. In another bowl, place the nacho chips
3. Dip each prawn into the beaten egg and then, coat with the crushed nacho chips.
4. Set the temperature of air fryer to 350 degrees F. Grease an air fryer basket.
5. Arrange prawns into the prepared air fryer basket.
6. Air fry for about 8 minutes.
7. Remove from air fryer and transfer the prawns onto serving plates.
8. Serve hot.

207. Simple Salmon Fillets

Servings: 2
Cooking Time: 7 Minutes

Ingredients:

- 2 salmon fillets
- 2 tsp olive oil
- 2 tsp paprika
- Pepper
- Salt

Directions:

1. Rub salmon fillet with oil, paprika, pepper, and salt.
2. Place salmon fillets in the air fryer basket and cook at 390 F for 7 minutes.
3. Serve and enjoy.

208. Almond Flour Coated Crispy Shrimps

Servings:4
Cooking Time: 10 Minutes
Ingredients:

- ½ cup almond flour
- 1 tablespoon yellow mustard
- 1-pound raw shrimps, peeled and deveined
- 3 tablespoons olive oil
- Salt and pepper to taste

Directions:

1. Place all ingredients in a Ziploc bag and give a good shake.
2. Place in the air fryer and cook for 10 minutes at 400°F.

209. Coconut Crusted Shrimp

Servings:3
Cooking Time:40 Minutes
Ingredients:

- 8 ounces coconut milk
- ½ cup sweetened coconut, shredded
- ½ cup panko breadcrumbs

- 1 pound large shrimp, peeled and deveined
- Salt and black pepper, to taste

Directions:

1. Preheat the Air fryer to 350 °F and grease an Air fryer basket.
2. Place the coconut milk in a shallow bowl.
3. Mix coconut, breadcrumbs, salt, and black pepper in another bowl.
4. Dip each shrimp into coconut milk and finally, dredge in the coconut mixture.
5. Arrange half of the shrimps into the Air fryer basket and cook for about 20 minutes.
6. Dish out the shrimps onto serving plates and repeat with the remaining mixture to serve.

210. Honey Glazed Salmon

Servings:2
Cooking Time:14 Minutes
Ingredients:

- 1 teaspoon water
- 2 (3½-ounce) salmon fillets
- 1/3 cup soy sauce
- 1/3 cup honey
- 3 teaspoons rice wine vinegar

Directions:

1. Preheat the Air fryer to 355 °F and grease an Air fryer grill pan.
2. Mix all the ingredients in a small bowl except salmon.
3. Reserve half of the mixture in a small bowl and coat the salmon in remaining mixture.
4. Refrigerate, covered for about 2 hours and place the salmon in the Air fryer grill pan.

5. Cook for about 13 minutes, flipping once in between and coat with reserved marinade.
6. Place the reserved marinade in a small pan and cook for about 1 minute.
7. Serve salmon with marinade sauce and enjoy.

211. Lemon Garlic Shrimp

Servings: 2
Cooking Time: 15 Minutes
Ingredients:
- 1 medium lemon
- ½ lb. medium shrimp, shelled and deveined
- ½ tsp. Old Bay seasoning
- 2 tbsp. unsalted butter, melted
- ½ tsp. minced garlic

Directions:
1. Grate the rind of the lemon into a bowl. Cut the lemon in half and juice it over the same bowl. Toss in the shrimp, Old Bay, and butter, mixing everything to make sure the shrimp is completely covered.
2. Transfer to a round baking dish roughly six inches wide, then place this dish in your fryer.
3. Cook at 400°F for six minutes. The shrimp is cooked when it turns a bright pink color.
4. Serve hot, drizzling any leftover sauce over the shrimp.

212. Amazing Salmon Fillets

Servings:2
Cooking Time:7 Minutes
Ingredients:

- 2 (7-ounce) (¾-inch thick) salmon fillets
- 1 tablespoon Italian seasoning
- 1 tablespoon fresh lemon juice

Directions:
1. Preheat the Air fryer to 355 °F and grease an Air fryer grill pan.
2. Rub the salmon evenly with Italian seasoning and transfer into the Air fryer grill pan, skin-side up.
3. Cook for about 7 minutes and squeeze lemon juice on it to serve.

213. Air Fried Tuna Sandwich

Servings:2
Cooking Time: 10 Minutes
Ingredients:
- 2 small tins of tuna, drained
- ½ onion, finely chopped
- 2 tbsp mayonnaise
- 1 cup mozzarella cheese, shredded
- Cooking spray

Directions:
1. Lay the bread on a cutting board. In a bowl, mix tuna, onion, mayonnaise. Spoon the mixture over two bread slices. Top with cheese and put the other piece of bread on top. Spray with oil and arrange the sandwiches on the air fryer basket. Cook at 360 F for 6 minutes, turning once halfway through cooking.

214. Chili Squid Rings

Servings: 2
Cooking Time: 10 Minutes
Ingredients:
- 8 oz squid tube, trimmed, washed
- 4 oz chorizo, chopped

- 1 teaspoon olive oil
- 1 teaspoon chili flakes
- 1 tablespoon keto mayonnaise

Directions:

1. Preheat the air fryer to 400F and put the chopped chorizo in the air fryer basket. Sprinkle it with chili flakes and olive oil and cook for 6 minutes. Then shake chorizo well. Slice the squid tube into the rings and add in the air fryer. Cook the meal for 4 minutes at 400F. Shake the cooked meal well and transfer it in the plates. Sprinkle the meal with keto mayonnaise.

215. Very Easy Lime-garlic Shrimps

Servings:1
Cooking Time: 6 Minutes
Ingredients:

- 1 clove of garlic, minced
- 1 cup raw shrimps
- 1 lime, juiced and zested
- Salt and pepper to taste

Directions:

1. In a mixing bowl, combine all Ingredients and give a good stir.
2. Preheat the air fryer to 390°F.
3. Skewer the shrimps onto the metal skewers that come with the double layer rack accessory.
4. Place on the rack and cook for 6 minutes.

216. Basil Scallops

Servings: 4
Cooking Time: 6 Minutes
Ingredients:

- 12 oz scallops

- 1 tablespoon dried basil
- ½ teaspoon salt
- 1 tablespoon coconut oil, melted

Directions:

1. Mix up salt, coconut oil, and dried basil. Brush the scallops with basil mixture and leave for 5 minutes to marinate. Meanwhile, preheat the air fryer to 400F. Put the marinated scallops in the air fryer and sprinkle them with remaining coconut oil and basil mixture. Cook the scallops for 4 minutes. Then flip them on another side and cook for 2 minutes more.

217. Quick & Easy Air Fried Salmon

Servings:1
Cooking Time: 13 Minutes
Ingredients:

- 1 tbsp soy sauce
- ¼ tsp garlic powder
- Salt and pepper

Directions:

1. Preheat air fryer to 350 F, and combine soy sauce, garlic powder, salt and pepper. Brush the mixture over salmon. Place salmon onto the air fryer; cook for 10 minutes, until crispy.

218. Grilled Shrimp With Chipotle-orange Seasoning

Servings:2
Cooking Time: 24 Minutes
Ingredients:

- 3 tablespoons minced chipotles in adobo sauce
- salt

- ½-pound large shrimps
- juice of 1/2 orange
- 1/4 cup barbecue sauce

Directions:
1. In a small shallow dish, mix well all Ingredients except for shrimp. Save ¼ of the mixture for basting.
2. Add shrimp in dish and toss well to coat. Marinate for at least 10 minutes.
3. Thread shrimps in skewers. Place on skewer rack in air fryer.
4. For 12 minutes, cook on 360°F. Halfway through cooking time, turnover skewers and baste with sauce. If needed, cook in batches.
5. Serve and enjoy.

219. Zesty Mahi Mahi

Servings:3
Cooking Time:8 Minutes
Ingredients:
- 1½ pounds Mahi Mahi fillets
- 1 lemon, cut into slices
- 1 tablespoon fresh dill, chopped
- ½ teaspoon red chili powder
- Salt and ground black pepper, as required

Directions:
1. Preheat the Air fryer to 375 °F and grease an Air fryer basket.
2. Season the Mahi Mahi fillets evenly with chili powder, salt, and black pepper.
3. Arrange the Mahi Mahi fillets into the Air fryer basket and top with the lemon slices.
4. Cook for about 8 minutes and dish out
5. Place the lemon slices over the salmon the salmon fillets in the serving plates.
6. Garnish with fresh dill and serve warm.

220. Cheese Crust Salmon

Servings: 5
Cooking Time: 20 Minutes
Ingredients:
- 2 lb. salmon fillet
- 2 garlic cloves, minced
- ¼ cup fresh parsley, chopped
- ½ cup parmesan cheese, grated
- Salt and pepper to taste

Directions:
1. Pre-heat the Air Fryer to 350°F.
2. Lay the salmon, skin-side-down, on a sheet of aluminum foil. Place another sheet of foil on top.
3. Transfer the salmon to the fryer and cook for 10 minutes.
4. Remove the salmon from the fryer. Take off the top layer of foil and add the minced garlic, parmesan cheese, pepper, salt and parsley on top of the fish.
5. Return the salmon to the Air Fryer and resume cooking for another minute.

221. Coconut Calamari

Servings: 2
Cooking Time: 6 Minutes
Ingredients:
- 6 oz calamari, trimmed
- 2 tablespoons coconut flakes
- 1 egg, beaten
- 1 teaspoon Italian seasonings
- Cooking spray

Directions:
1. Slice the calamari into the rings and sprinkle them with Italian seasonings. Then transfer the calamari rings in the bowl with a beaten egg and stir them gently. After this, sprinkle the calamari

rings with coconut flakes and shake well. Preheat the air fryer to 400F. Put the calamari rings in the air fryer basket and spray them with cooking spray. Cook the meal for 3 minutes. Then gently stir the calamari and cook them for 3 minutes more.

222. Crisped Flounder Filet With Crumb Tops

Servings:4
Cooking Time: 15 Minutes
Ingredients:
- 1 cup dry bread crumbs
- 1 egg beaten
- 1 lemon, sliced
- 4 pieces of flounder fillets
- 5 tablespoons vegetable oil

Directions:
1. Brush flounder fillets with vegetable oil before dredging in bread crumbs.
2. Preheat the air fryer to 390°F.
3. Place the fillets on the double layer rack.
4. Cook for 15 minutes.

223. Mustard Cod

Servings: 4
Cooking Time: 14 Minutes
Ingredients:
- 1 cup parmesan, grated
- 4 cod fillets, boneless
- Salt and black pepper to the taste
- 1 tablespoon mustard

Directions:
1. In a bowl, mix the parmesan with salt, pepper and the mustard and stir. Spread this over the cod, arrange the fish in the air fryer's basket and cook at 370 degrees F for 7 minutes on each

side. Divide between plates and serve with a side salad.

224. Soy-orange Flavored Squid

Servings:4
Cooking Time: 10 Minutes
Ingredients:
- ½ cup mirin
- 1 cup soy sauce
- 1/3 cup yuzu or orange juice, freshly squeezed
- 2 cups water
- 2 pounds squid body, cut into rings

Directions:
1. Place all ingredients in a Ziploc bag and allow the squid rings to marinate in the fridge for at least 2 hours.
2. Preheat the air fryer to 390°F.
3. Place the grill pan accessory in the air fryer.
4. Grill the squid rings for 10 minutes.
5. Meanwhile, pour the marinade over a sauce pan and allow to simmer for 10 minutes or until the sauce has reduced.
6. Baste the squid rings with the sauce before serving.

225. Italian Mackerel

Servings: 2
Cooking Time: 15 Minutes
Ingredients:
- 8 oz mackerel, trimmed
- 1 tablespoon Italian seasonings
- 1 teaspoon keto tomato sauce
- 2 tablespoons ghee, melted
- ½ teaspoon salt

Directions:

1. Rub the mackerel with Italian seasonings, and tomato sauce. After this, rub the fish with salt and leave for 15 minutes in the fridge to marinate. Meanwhile, preheat the air fryer to 390F. When the time of marinating is finished, brush the fish with ghee and wrap in the baking paper. Place the wrapped fish in the air fryer and cook it for 15 minutes.

226. Lovely & Slightly "blackened" Catfish

Servings:2
Cooking Time: 20 Minutes
Ingredients:
- 2 tsp blackening seasoning
- Juice of 1 lime
- 2 tbsp butter, melted
- 1 garlic clove, mashed
- 2 tbsp cilantro

Directions:
1. Preheat your air fryer to 360 F, and in a bowl, blend in garlic, lime juice, cilantro and butter. Divide the sauce into two parts, pour 1 part of the sauce over your fillets; cover the fillets with seasoning. Place the fillets in your air fryer's basket and cook for 15 minutes. Serve the fish with the remaining sauce.

227. 3-ingredients Catfish

Servings:4
Cooking Time: 23 Minutes
Ingredients:
- 4 (6-ounces) catfish fillets
- ¼ cup seasoned fish fry
- 1 tablespoon olive oil

Directions:

1. Set the temperature of air fryer to 400 degrees F. Grease an air fryer basket.
2. In a bowl, add the catfish fillets and seasoned fish fry. Toss to coat well.
3. Then, drizzle each fillet evenly with oil.
4. Arrange catfish fillets into the prepared air fryer basket in a single layer.
5. Air fry for about 10 minutes.
6. Flip the side and spray with the cooking spray.
7. Air fry for another 10 minutes.
8. Flip one last time and air fry for about 2-3 more minutes.
9. Remove from air fryer and transfer the catfish fillets onto serving plates.
10. Serve hot.

228. Lemon-pepper Red Mullet Fry

Servings:4
Cooking Time: 15 Minutes
Ingredients:
- 1 tablespoon olive oil
- 4 whole red mullets, gutted and scales removed
- Juice from 1 lemon
- Salt and pepper to taste

Directions:
1. Preheat the air fryer to 390°F.
2. Place the grill pan accessory in the air fryer.
3. Season the red mullet with salt, pepper, and lemon juice.
4. Brush with olive oil.
5. Grill for 15 minutes per batch.

229. Butter Flounder Fillets

Servings: 4
Cooking Time: 20 Minutes

Ingredients:
- 4 flounder fillets, boneless
- A pinch of salt and black pepper
- 1 cup parmesan, grated
- 4 tablespoons butter, melted
- 2 tablespoons olive oil

Directions:
1. In a bowl, mix the parmesan with salt, pepper, butter and the oil and stir well. Arrange the fish in a pan that fits the air fryer, spread the parmesan mix all over, introduce in the fryer and cook at 400 degrees F for 20 minutes. Divide between plates and serve with a side salad.

230. Easy Lobster Tail With Salted Butetr

Servings:4
Cooking Time: 6 Minutes
Ingredients:
- 2 tablespoons melted butter
- 4 lobster tails
- Salt and pepper to taste

Directions:
1. Preheat the air fryer to 390°F.
2. Place the grill pan accessory.
3. Cut the lobster through the tail section using a pair of kitchen scissors.
4. Brush the lobster tails with melted butter and season with salt and pepper to taste.
5. Place on the grill pan and cook for 6 minutes.

231. Bacon Wrapped Shrimp

Servings:4
Cooking Time: 14 Minutes
Ingredients:

- 1 pound bacon
- 1½ pounds tiger shrimp, peeled and deveined

Directions:
1. With a slice of bacon, wrap each shrimp.
2. Refrigerate for about 20 minutes.
3. Set the temperature of air fryer to 390 degrees F. Grease an air fryer basket.
4. Arrange shrimp into the prepared air fryer basket in 2 batches in a single layer.
5. Air fry for about 5-7 minutes.
6. Remove from air fryer and transfer the shrimp onto serving plates.
7. Serve hot.

232. Sesame Tuna Steak

Servings: 2
Cooking Time: 12 Minutes
Ingredients:
- 1 tbsp. coconut oil, melted
- 2 x 6-oz. tuna steaks
- ½ tsp. garlic powder
- 2 tsp. black sesame seeds
- 2 tsp. white sesame seeds

Directions:
1. Apply the coconut oil to the tuna steaks with a brunch, then season with garlic powder.
2. Combine the black and white sesame seeds. Embed them in the tuna steaks, covering the fish all over. Place the tuna into your air fryer.
3. Cook for eight minutes at 400°F, turning the fish halfway through.
4. The tuna steaks are ready when they have reached a temperature of 145°F. Serve straightaway.

233. Shrimp With Veggie

Servings: 4
Cooking Time: 20 Minutes
Ingredients:
- 50 small shrimp
- 1 tbsp Cajun seasoning
- 1 bag of frozen mix vegetables
- 1 tbsp olive oil

Directions:
1. Line air fryer basket with aluminum foil.
2. Add all ingredients into the large mixing bowl and toss well.
3. Transfer shrimp and vegetable mixture into the air fryer basket and cook at 350 F for 10 minutes.
4. Toss well and cook for 10 minutes more.
5. Serve and enjoy.

234. Foil Packet Salmon

Servings: 2
Cooking Time: 15 Minutes
Ingredients:
- 2 x 4-oz. skinless salmon fillets
- 2 tbsp. unsalted butter, melted
- ½ tsp. garlic powder
- 1 medium lemon
- ½ tsp. dried dill

Directions:
1. Take a sheet of aluminum foil and cut into two squares measuring roughly 5" x 5". Lay each of the salmon fillets at the center of each piece. Brush both fillets with a tablespoon of bullet and season with a quarter-teaspoon of garlic powder.
2. Halve the lemon and grate the skin of one half over the fish. Cut four half-slices of lemon, using two to top each fillet. Season each fillet with a quarter-teaspoon of dill.
3. Fold the tops and sides of the aluminum foil over the fish to create a kind of packet. Place each one in the fryer.
4. Cook for twelve minutes at 400°F.
5. The salmon is ready when it flakes easily. Serve hot.

235. Buttery Cod

Servings: 2
Cooking Time: 12 Minutes
Ingredients:
- 2 x 4-oz. cod fillets
- 2 tbsp. salted butter, melted
- 1 tsp. Old Bay seasoning
- ½ medium lemon, sliced

Directions:
1. Place the cod fillets in a baking dish.
2. Brush with melted butter, season with Old Bay, and top with some lemon slices.
3. Wrap the fish in aluminum foil and put into your fryer.
4. Cook for eight minutes at 350°F.
5. The cod is ready when it flakes easily. Serve hot.

236. Grilled Bacon 'n Scallops

Servings: 2
Cooking Time: 12 Minutes
Ingredients:
- 1 teaspoon smoked paprika
- 6 bacon strips
- 6 large scallops

Directions:
1. Wrap one bacon around one scallop and thread in a skewer ensuring that it will

not unravel. Repeat until all ingredients are used.
2. Season with paprika.
3. Place on skewer rack in air fryer.
4. For 12 minutes, cook on 390°F. Halfway through cooking time, turnover skewers.
5. Serve and enjoy.

237. Italian Shrimp

Servings: 4
Cooking Time: 12 Minutes
Ingredients:
- 1 pound shrimp, peeled and deveined
- A pinch of salt and black pepper
- 1 tablespoon sesame seeds, toasted
- ½ teaspoon Italian seasoning
- 1 tablespoon olive oil

Directions:
1. In a bowl, mix the shrimp with the rest of the ingredients and toss well. Put the shrimp in the air fryer's basket, cook at 370 degrees F for 12 minutes, divide into bowls and serve,

238. Lemon And Thyme Sea Bass

Servings: 3
Cooking Time: 15 Minutes
Ingredients:
- 8 oz sea bass, trimmed, peeled
- 4 lemon slices
- 1 tablespoon thyme
- 2 teaspoons sesame oil
- 1 teaspoon salt

Directions:
1. Fill the sea bass with lemon slices and rub with thyme, salt, and sesame oil.

Then preheat the air fryer to 385F and put the fish in the air fryer basket. Cook it for 12 minutes. Then flip the fish on another side and cook it for 3 minutes more.

239. Greek-style Salmon With Dill Sauce

Servings:4
Cooking Time: 25 Minutes
Ingredients:
- Salt and pepper to taste
- 2 tsp olive oil
- 3 tbsp chopped dill + extra for garnishing
- 1 cup sour cream
- 1 cup Greek yogurt

Directions:
1. For the dill sauce, in a bowl, mix well the sour cream, yogurt, dill, and salt. Preheat air fryer to 280 F.
2. Drizzle the olive oil over the salmon, and rub with salt and pepper. Arrange the salmon pieces in the fryer basket and cook them for 15 minutes. Remove salmon to a platter and top with the sauce. Serve.

240. Air Fried Cod With Basil Vinaigrette

Servings:4
Cooking Time: 15 Minutes
Ingredients:
- ¼ cup olive oil
- 4 cod fillets
- A bunch of basil, torn
- Juice from 1 lemon, freshly squeezed
- Salt and pepper to taste

Directions:

1. Preheat the air fryer for 5 minutes.
2. Season the cod fillets with salt and pepper to taste.
3. Place in the air fryer and cook for 15 minutes at 350°F.
4. Meanwhile, mix the rest of the ingredients in a bowl and toss to combine.
5. Serve the air fried cod with the basil vinaigrette.

241. Tortilla-crusted With Lemon Filets

Servings:4
Cooking Time: 15 Minutes
Ingredients:

- 1 cup tortilla chips, pulverized
- 1 egg, beaten
- 1 tablespoon lemon juice
- 4 fillets of white fish fillet
- Salt and pepper to taste

Directions:

1. Preheat the air fryer to 390°F.
2. Place a grill pan in the air fryer.
3. Season the fish fillet with salt, pepper, and lemon juice.
4. Soak in beaten eggs and dredge in tortilla chips.
5. Place on the grill pan.
6. Cook for 15 minutes.
7. Make sure to flip the fish halfway through the cooking time.

242. Lemon Butter Scallops

Servings: 1
Cooking Time: 30 Minutes
Ingredients:

- 1 lemon
- 1 lb. scallops
- ½ cup butter
- ¼ cup parsley, chopped

Directions:

1. Juice the lemon into a Ziploc bag.
2. Wash your scallops, dry them, and season to taste. Put them in the bag with the lemon juice. Refrigerate for an hour.
3. Remove the bag from the refrigerator and leave for about twenty minutes until it returns to room temperature. Transfer the scallops into a foil pan that is small enough to be placed inside the fryer.
4. Pre-heat the fryer at 400°F and put the rack inside.
5. Place the foil pan on the rack and cook for five minutes.
6. In the meantime, melt the butter in a saucepan over a medium heat. Zest the lemon over the saucepan, then add in the chopped parsley. Mix well.
7. Take care when removing the pan from the fryer. Transfer the contents to a plate and drizzle with the lemon-butter mixture. Serve hot.

243. Breaded Scallops

Servings:6
Cooking Time: 5 Minutes
Ingredients:

- 3 tbsp flour
- 4 salt and black pepper
- 1 egg, lightly beaten
- 1 cup breadcrumbs
- Cooking spray

Directions:

1. Coat the scallops with flour. Dip into the egg, then into the breadcrumbs. Spray

them with olive oil and arrange them in the air fryer. Cook for 6 minutes at 360 F, turning once halfway through cooking.

244. Foil Packet Lobster Tail

Servings: 2
Cooking Time: 15 Minutes
Ingredients:
- 2 x 6-oz. lobster tail halves
- 2 tbsp. salted butter, melted
- ½ medium lemon, juiced
- ½ tsp. Old Bay seasoning
- 1 tsp. dried parsley

Directions:
1. Lay each lobster on a sheet of aluminum foil. Pour a light drizzle of melted butter and lemon juice over each one, and season with Old Bay.
2. Fold down the sides and ends of the foil to seal the lobster. Place each one in the fryer.
3. Cook at 375°F for twelve minutes.
4. Just before serving, top the lobster with dried parsley.

245. Grilled Scallops With Pesto

Servings:3
Cooking Time: 15 Minutes
Ingredients:
- ½ cup prepared commercial pesto
- 12 large scallops, side muscles removed
- Salt and pepper to taste

Directions:
1. Place all ingredients in a Ziploc bag and allow the scallops to marinate in the fridge for at least 2 hours.
2. Preheat the air fryer to 390°F.

3. Place the grill pan accessory in the air fryer.
4. Grill the scallops for 15 minutes.
5. Serve on pasta or bread if desired.

246. Paprika Cod And Endives

Servings: 4
Cooking Time: 20 Minutes
Ingredients:
- 2 endives, shredded
- 2 tablespoons olive oil
- Salt and back pepper to the taste
- 4 salmon fillets, boneless
- ½ teaspoon sweet paprika

Directions:
1. In a pan that fits the air fryer, combine the fish with the rest of the ingredients, toss, introduce in the fryer and cook at 350 degrees F for 20 minutes, flipping the fish halfway. Divide between plates and serve right away.

247. Air Fried Catfish

Servings: 4
Cooking Time: 20 Minutes
Ingredients:
- 4 catfish fillets
- 1 tbsp olive oil
- 1/4 cup fish seasoning
- 1 tbsp fresh parsley, chopped

Directions:
1. Preheat the air fryer to 400 F.
2. Spray air fryer basket with cooking spray.
3. Seasoned fish with seasoning and place into the air fryer basket.
4. Drizzle fish fillets with oil and cook for 10 minutes.

5. Turn fish to another side and cook for 10 minutes more.
6. Garnish with parsley and serve.

248. Easy 'n Crispy Cod Nuggets

Servings:6
Cooking Time: 20 Minutes
Ingredients:
- ½ cup almond flour
- 1 ½ pound cod fillet cut into big chunks
- 1 egg, beaten
- 3 tablespoons olive oil
- Salt and pepper to taste

Directions:
1. Preheat the air fryer for 5 minutes.
2. Season the cod fillets with salt and pepper to taste.
3. Add the eggs and mix to combine.
4. Dredge individual cod chunks into the almond flour and set aside on a plate.
5. Brush all sides with olive oil.
6. Place in the fryer basket and cook for 20 minutes at 375°F.

249. Miso Fish

Servings: 2
Cooking Time: 10 Minutes
Ingredients:
- 2 cod fish fillets
- 1 tbsp garlic, chopped
- 2 tsp swerve
- 2 tbsp miso

Directions:
1. Add all ingredients to the zip-lock bag. Shake well place in the refrigerator for overnight.

2. Place marinated fish fillets into the air fryer basket and cook at 350 F for 10 minutes.
3. Serve and enjoy.

250. Breadcrumbed Fish

Servings: 2 – 4
Cooking Time: 25 Minutes
Ingredients:
- 4 tbsp. vegetable oil
- 5 oz. friendly bread crumbs
- 1 egg
- 4 medium fish fillets

Directions:
1. 1 Pre-heat your Air Fryer to 350°F.
2. 2 In a bowl, combine the bread crumbs and oil.
3. 3 In a separate bowl, stir the egg with a whisk. Dredge each fish fillet in the egg before coating it in the crumbs mixture. Put them in Air Fryer basket.
4. 4 Cook for 12 minutes and serve hot.

251. Cajun Spiced Veggie-shrimp Bake

Servings:4
Cooking Time: 20 Minutes
Ingredients:
- 1 Bag of Frozen Mixed Vegetables
- 1 Tbsp Gluten Free Cajun Seasoning
- Olive Oil Spray
- Season with salt and pepper
- Small Shrimp Peeled & Deveined (Regular Size Bag about 50-80 Small Shrimp)

Directions:
1. Lightly grease baking pan of air fryer with cooking spray. Add all Ingredients

and toss well to coat. Season with pepper and salt, generously.

2. For 10 minutes, cook on 330°F. Halfway through cooking time, stir.
3. Cook for 10 minutes at 330°F.
4. Serve and enjoy.

252. Easy Grilled Pesto Scallops

Servings:3
Cooking Time: 15 Minutes
Ingredients:
- 12 large scallops, side muscles removed
- Salt and pepper to taste
- ½ cup prepared commercial pesto

Directions:
1. Place all ingredients in a Ziploc bag and allow the scallops to marinate in the fridge for at least 2 hours.
2. Preheat the air fryer at 390°F.
3. Place the grill pan accessory in the air fryer.
4. Grill the scallops for 15 minutes.
5. Serve on pasta or bread if desired.

253. Fish Fillets

Servings: 4
Cooking Time: 25 Minutes
Ingredients:
- 4 fish fillets
- 1 egg, beaten
- 1 cup bread crumbs
- 4 tbsp. olive oil
- Pepper and salt to taste

Directions:
1. Pre-heat the Air Fryer at 350°F.
2. In a shallow dish, combine together the bread crumbs, oil, pepper, and salt.
3. Pour the beaten egg into a second dish.

4. Dredge each fish fillet in the egg before rolling them in the bread crumbs. Place in the Air Fryer basket.
5. Allow to cook in the Air Fryer for 12 minutes.

254. Thyme Scallops

Servings: 1
Cooking Time: 12 Minutes
Ingredients:
- 1 lb. scallops
- Salt and pepper
- ½ tbsp. butter
- ½ cup thyme, chopped

Directions:
1. Wash the scallops and dry them completely. Season with pepper and salt, then set aside while you prepare the pan.
2. Grease a foil pan in several spots with the butter and cover the bottom with the thyme. Place the scallops on top.
3. Pre-heat the fryer at 400°F and set the rack inside.
4. Place the foil pan on the rack and allow to cook for seven minutes.
5. Take care when removing the pan from the fryer and transfer the scallops to a serving dish. Spoon any remaining butter in the pan over the fish and enjoy.

255. Buttered Scallops

Servings:2
Cooking Time:4 Minutes
Ingredients:
- ¾ pound sea scallops, cleaned and patted very dry
- 1 tablespoon butter, melted

- ½ tablespoon fresh thyme, minced
- Salt and black pepper, as required

Directions:
1. Preheat the Air fryer to 390 °F and grease an Air fryer basket.
2. Mix scallops, butter, thyme, salt, and black pepper in a bowl.
3. Arrange scallops in the Air fryer basket and cook for about 4 minutes.
4. Dish out the scallops in a platter and serve hot.

256. Easy Bacon Shrimp

Servings: 4
Cooking Time: 7 Minutes
Ingredients:
- 16 shrimp, deveined
- 1/4 tsp pepper
- 16 bacon slices

Directions:
1. Preheat the air fryer to 390 F.
2. Spray air fryer basket with cooking spray.
3. Wrap shrimp with bacon slice and place into the air fryer basket and cook for 5 minutes.
4. Turn shrimp to another side and cook for 2 minutes more. Season shrimp with pepper.
5. Serve and enjoy.

257. Lime 'n Chat Masala Rubbed Snapper

Servings:2
Cooking Time: 25 Minutes
Ingredients:
- 1/3 cup chat masala
- 1-1/2 pounds whole fish, cut in half
- 2 tablespoons olive oil

- 3 tablespoons fresh lime juice
- Salt to taste

Directions:
1. Preheat the air fryer to 390°F.
2. Place the grill pan accessory in the air fryer.
3. Season the fish with salt, chat masala and lime juice.
4. Brush with oil
5. Place the fish on a foil basket and place inside the grill.
6. Cook for 25 minutes.

258. Crispy Prawn In Bacon Wraps

Servings:4
Cooking Time: 30 Minutes
Ingredients:
- 8 jumbo prawns, peeled and deveined
- Lemon Wedges for garnishing

Directions:
1. Wrap each prawn from head to tail with each bacon slice overlapping to keep the bacon in place. Secure the end of the bacon with a toothpick. It's ok not to cover the ends of the cheese with bacon. Refrigerate for 15 minutes.
2. Preheat air fryer to 400 F. Arrange the bacon-wrapped prawns on the fryer's basket, cook for 7 minutes or until the bacon is crispy. Transfer prawns to a paper towel to cool. Remove the toothpicks and serve the bacon-wrapped prawns with lemon wedges and a side of steamed green vegetables.

259. Grilled Squid With Aromatic Sesame Oil

Servings:3

Cooking Time: 10 Minutes

Ingredients:

- 1 ½ pounds squid, cleaned
- 2 tablespoon toasted sesame oil
- Salt and pepper to taste

Directions:

1. Preheat the air fryer to 390°F.
2. Place the grill pan accessory in the air fryer.
3. Season the squid with sesame oil, salt and pepper.
4. Grill the squid for 10 minutes.

260. Super-simple Scallops

Servings:2
Cooking Time:4 Minutes

Ingredients:

- ¾ pound sea scallops
- 1 tablespoon butter, melted
- ½ tablespoon fresh thyme, minced
- Salt and black pepper, to taste

Directions:

1. Preheat the Air fryer to 390 °F and grease an Air fryer basket.
2. Mix all the ingredients in a bowl and toss to coat well.
3. Arrange the scallops in the Air fryer basket and cook for about 4 minutes.
4. Dish out and serve warm.

261. Lemon-basil On Cod Filet

Servings:4
Cooking Time: 15 Minutes

Ingredients:

- ¼ cup olive oil
- 4 cod fillets
- A bunch of basil, torn
- Juice from 1 lemon, freshly squeezed
- Salt and pepper to taste

Directions:

1. Preheat the air fryer for 5 minutes.
2. Season the cod fillets with salt and pepper to taste. Place on lightly greased air fryer baking pan.
3. Mix the rest of the ingredients in a bowl and toss to combine. Pour over fish.
4. Cook for 15 minutes at 330°F.
5. Serve and enjoy.

262. Sweet And Sour Glazed Cod

Servings:2
Cooking Time:12 Minutes

Ingredients:

- 1 teaspoon water
- 4 (3½-ounces) cod fillets
- 1/3 cup soy sauce
- 1/3 cup honey
- 3 teaspoons rice wine vinegar

Directions:

1. Preheat the Air fryer to 355 °F and grease an Air fryer basket.
2. Mix the soy sauce, honey, vinegar and water in a small bowl.
3. Reserve about half of the mixture in another bowl.
4. Stir the cod fillets in the remaining mixture until well coated.
5. Cover and refrigerate to marinate for about 3 hours.
6. Arrange the cod fillets into the Air fryer basket and cook for about 12 minutes, flipping once in between.
7. Coat with the reserved marinade and dish out the cod to serve hot.

263. Japanese Citrus Soy Squid

Servings:4

Cooking Time: 10 Minutes

Ingredients:

- ½ cup mirin
- 1 cup soy sauce
- 1/3 cup yuzu or orange juice, freshly squeezed
- 2 cups water
- 2 pounds squid body, cut into rings

Directions:

1. Place all ingredients in a Ziploc bag and allow the squid rings to marinate in the fridge for at least 2 hours.
2. Preheat the air fryer at 390°F.
3. Place the grill pan accessory in the air fryer.
4. Grill the squid rings for 10 minutes.
5. Meanwhile, pour the marinade over a sauce pan and allow to simmer for 10 minutes or until the sauce has reduced.
6. Baste the squid rings with the sauce before serving.

264. Simple Sesame Squid On The Grill

Servings:3
Cooking Time: 10 Minutes

Ingredients:

- 1 ½ pounds squid, cleaned
- 2 tablespoon toasted sesame oil
- Salt and pepper to taste

Directions:

1. Preheat the air fryer at 390°F.
2. Place the grill pan accessory in the air fryer.
3. Season the squid with sesame oil, salt and pepper.
4. Grill the squid for 10 minutes.

265. Simple Air Fryer Salmon

Servings: 2
Cooking Time: 10 Minutes

Ingredients:

- 2 salmon fillets, skinless and boneless
- 1 tsp olive oil
- Pepper
- Salt

Directions:

1. Coat salmon fillets with olive oil and season with pepper and salt.
2. Place salmon fillets in air fryer basket and cook at 360 F for 8-10 minutes.
3. Serve and enjoy.

266. Paprika Shrimp

Servings:2
Cooking Time:10 Minutes

Ingredients:

- 1 pound tiger shrimp
- 2 tablespoons olive oil
- ½ teaspoon smoked paprika
- Salt, to taste

Directions:

1. Preheat the Air fryer to 390 °F and grease an Air fryer basket.
2. Mix all the ingredients in a large bowl until well combined.
3. Place the shrimp in the Air fryer basket and cook for about 10 minutes.
4. Dish out and serve warm.

267. Zesty Salmon

Servings:3
Cooking Time: 8 Minutes

Ingredients:

- 1½ pounds salmon
- ½ teaspoon red chili powder

- Salt and ground black pepper, as required
- 1 lemon, cut into slices
- 1 tablespoon fresh dill, chopped

Directions:

1. Set the temperature of air fryer to 375 degrees F. Grease an air fryer basket.
2. Season the salmon evenly with chili powder, salt, and black pepper.
3. Arrange salmon into the prepared air fryer basket.
4. Place the lemon slices over the salmon.
5. Air fry for about 8 minutes.
6. Remove from air fryer and place the salmon fillets onto serving plates.
7. Garnish with fresh dill and serve.

268. Fried Tilapia Bites

Servings:4
Cooking Time: 20 Minutes
Ingredients:

- ½ cup cornflakes
- 3 tbsp flour
- 1 egg, beaten
- Salt to taste
- Lemon wedges for serving

Directions:

1. Preheat your Air Fryer to 390 F. Spray the air fryer basket with cooking spray.
2. Put the flour, egg, and conflakes each into a different bowl, three bowls in total. Add salt egg bowl and mix well. Dip the tilapia first in the flour, then in the egg, and lastly, coat in the cornflakes. Lay on the air fryer basket. Spray with cooking spray and cook for 5 minutes. Slide out the fryer basket and shake the shrimp; cook further for 5 minutes. Serve with lemon wedges.

269. Baked Cod Fillet Recipe From Thailand

Servings:4
Cooking Time: 20 Minutes
Ingredients:

- ¼ cup coconut milk, freshly squeezed
- 1 tablespoon lime juice, freshly squeezed
- 1-pound cod fillet, cut into bite-sized pieces
- Salt and pepper to taste

Directions:

1. Preheat the air fryer for 5 minutes.
2. Place all ingredients in a baking dish that will fit in the air fryer.
3. Place in the air fryer.
4. Cook for 20 minutes at 325°F.

270. Cajun Salmon

Servings: 1
Cooking Time: 20 Minutes
Ingredients:

- 1 salmon fillet
- Cajun seasoning
- Light sprinkle of sugar
- ¼ lemon, juiced, to serve

Directions:

1. 1 Pre-heat Air Fryer to 355°F.
2. 2 Lightly cover all sides of the salmon with Cajun seasoning. Sprinkle conservatively with sugar.
3. 3 For a salmon fillet about three-quarters of an inch thick, cook in the fryer for 7 minutes, skin-side-up on the grill pan.
4. 4 Serve with the lemon juice.

BEEF,PORK & LAMB RECIPES

271. Almond Flour 'n Egg Crusted Beef

Servings:1
Cooking Time: 15 Minutes
Ingredients:
- ½ cup almond flour
- 1 egg, beaten
- 1 slice of lemon, to serve
- 1/2-pound beef schnitzel
- 2 tablespoons vegetable oil

Directions:
1. Preheat the air fryer for 5 minutes.
2. Mix the oil and almond flour together.
3. Dip the schnitzel into the egg and dredge in the almond flour mixture.
4. Press the almond flour so that it sticks on to the beef.
5. Place in the air fryer and cook for 15 minutes at 350°F.
6. Serve with a slice of lemon.

272. Super Simple Steaks

Servings:2
Cooking Time:14 Minutes
Ingredients:
- ½ pound quality cuts steak
- Salt and black pepper, to taste

Directions:
1. Preheat the Air fryer to 390 °F and grease an Air fryer basket.
2. Season the steaks evenly with salt and black pepper and transfer into the Air fryer basket.
3. Cook for about 14 minutes and dish out to serve.

273. Pork Chops Marinate In Honey-mustard

Servings:4
Cooking Time: 25 Minutes
Ingredients:
- 2 tablespoons honey
- 2 tablespoons minced garlic
- 4 pork chops
- 4 tablespoons mustard
- Salt and pepper to taste

Directions:
1. Preheat the air fryer to 330°F.
2. Place the air fryer basket.
3. Season the pork chops with the rest of the Ingredients.
4. Place inside the basket.
5. Cook for 20 to 25 minutes until golden.

274. Glazed Ham

Servings:4
Cooking Time:40 Minutes
Ingredients:
- 1 pound (10½ ounce) ham joint
- ¾ cup whiskey
- 2 tablespoons French mustard
- 2 tablespoons honey

Directions:
1. Preheat the Air fryer to 320 °F and grease an Air fryer pan.
2. Mix all the ingredients in a bowl except ham.
3. Keep ham joint for about 30 minutes at room temperature and place in the Air fryer pan.
4. Top with half of the whiskey mixture and transfer into the Air fryer.

5. Cook for about 15 minutes and flip the side.
6. Coat with the remaining whiskey mixture and cook for about 25 minutes.
7. Dish out in a platter and serve warm.

275. Buttered Striploin Steak

Servings:2
Cooking Time:12 Minutes
Ingredients:
- 2 (7-ounces) striploin steak
- 1½ tablespoons butter, softened
- Salt and black pepper, to taste

Directions:
1. Preheat the Air fryer to 390 °F and grease an Air fryer basket.
2. Rub the steak generously with salt and black pepper and coat with butter.
3. Transfer the steak in the Air fryer basket and cook for about 12 minutes, flipping once in between.
4. Dish out the steak and cut into desired size slices to serve.

276. Simple Beef Burgers

Servings:6
Cooking Time:12 Minutes
Ingredients:
- 2 pounds ground beef
- 12 cheddar cheese slices
- 12 dinner rolls
- 6 tablespoons tomato ketchup
- Salt and black pepper, to taste

Directions:
1. Preheat the Air fryer to 390 °F and grease an Air fryer basket.
2. Mix the beef, salt and black pepper in a bowl.

3. Make small equal-sized patties from the beef mixture and arrange half of patties in the Air fryer basket.
4. Cook for about 12 minutes and top each patty with 1 cheese slice.
5. Arrange the patties between rolls and drizzle with ketchup.
6. Repeat with the remaining batch and dish out to serve hot.

277. Bacon With Shallot And Greens

Servings: 2
Cooking Time: 10 Minutes
Ingredients:
- 7 ounces mixed greens
- 8 thick slices pork bacon
- 2 shallots, peeled and diced
- Nonstick cooking spray

Directions:
1. Begin by preheating the air fryer to 345 degrees F.
2. Now, add the shallot and bacon to the Air Fryer cooking basket; set the timer for 2 minutes. Spritz with a nonstick cooking spray.
3. After that, pause the Air Fryer; throw in the mixed greens; give it a good stir and cook an additional 5 minutes. Serve warm.

278. Bacon Wrapped Filet Mignon

Servings:2
Cooking Time:15 Minutes
Ingredients:
- 2 bacon slices
- 2 (6-ounces) filet mignon steaks

- Salt and black pepper, to taste
- 1 teaspoon avocado oil

Directions:
1. Preheat the Air fryer to 375 °F and grease an Air fryer basket.
2. Wrap each mignon steak with 1 bacon slice and secure with a toothpick.
3. Season the steak generously with salt and black pepper and coat with avocado oil.
4. Arrange the steaks in the Air fryer basket and cook for about 15 minutes, flipping once in between.
5. Dish out the steaks and cut into desired size slices to serve.

279. Simple Salt And Pepper Skirt Steak

Servings:3
Cooking Time: 30 Minutes
Ingredients:
- 1 ½ pounds skirt steak
- Salt and pepper to taste

Directions:
1. Preheat the air fryer to 390°F.
2. Place the grill pan accessory in the air fryer.
3. Season the skirt steak with salt and pepper.
4. Place on the grill pan and cook for 15 minutes per batch.
5. Flip the meat halfway through the cooking time.

280. Fried Steak

Servings: 1
Cooking Time: 15 Minutes
Ingredients:
- 3 cm-thick beef steak

- Pepper and salt to taste

Directions:
1. Pre-heat the Air Fryer 400°F for 5 minutes.
2. Place the beef steak in the baking tray and sprinkle on pepper and salt.
3. Spritz the steak with cooking spray.
4. Allow to cook for 3 minutes. Turn the steak over and cook on the other side for 3 more minutes. Serve hot.

281. Grilled Sausages With Bbq Sauce

Servings:3
Cooking Time: 30 Minutes
Ingredients:
- ½ cup prepared BBQ sauce
- 6 sausage links

Directions:
1. Preheat the air fryer to 390°F.
2. Place the grill pan accessory in the air fryer.
3. Place the sausage links and grill for 30 minutes.
4. Flip halfway through the cooking time.
5. Before serving brush with prepared BBQ sauce.

282. Glazed Pork Shoulder

Servings:5
Cooking Time: 18 Minutes
Ingredients:
- 1/3 cup soy sauce
- 2 tablespoons sugar
- 1 tablespoon honey
- 2 pounds pork shoulder, cut into 1½-inch thick slices

Directions:

1. In a bowl, mix together all the soy sauce, sugar, and honey.
2. Add the pork and generously coat with marinade.
3. Cover and refrigerate to marinate for about 4-6 hours.
4. Set the temperature of air fryer to 335 degrees F. Grease an air fryer basket.
5. Place pork shoulder into the prepared air fryer basket.
6. Air fry for about 10 minutes and then, another 6-8 minutes at 390 degrees F.
7. Remove from air fryer and transfer the pork shoulder onto a platter.
8. With a piece of foil, cover the pork for about 10 minutes before serving.
9. Enjoy!

283. Pork Tenderloin With Bacon And Veggies

Servings:3
Cooking Time:28 Minutes
Ingredients:
- 3 potatoes
- ¾ pound frozen green beans
- 6 bacon slices
- 3 (6-ounces) pork tenderloins
- 2 tablespoons olive oil
Directions:
1. Preheat the Air fryer to 390 °F and grease an Air fryer basket.
2. Wrap 4-6 green beans with one bacon slice and coat the pork tenderloins with olive oil.
3. Pierce the potatoes with a fork and arrange in the Air fryer basket.
4. Cook for about 15 minutes and add the pork tenderloins.
5. Cook for about 6 minutes and dish out in a bowl.

6. Arrange the bean rolls into the Air fryer basket and top with the pork tenderloins.
7. Cook for about 7 minutes and dish out in a platter.
8. Cut each tenderloin into desired size slices to serve alongside the potatoes and green beans rolls.

284. Salted Steak Pan Fried Steak

Servings:1
Cooking Time: 15 Minutes
Ingredients:
- 1-pound beef steak, bones removed
- 3 tablespoons coconut oil
- A dash of oregano
- Salt and pepper to taste
Directions:
1. Place all ingredients in a Ziploc bag and allow to marinate in the fridge for at least 2 hours.
2. Preheat the air fryer.
3. Place the steak in the air fryer and cook for 15 minutes at 400°F.

285. Buttered Filet Mignon

Servings:4
Cooking Time:14 Minutes
Ingredients:
- 2 (6-ounces) filet mignon steaks
- 1 tablespoon butter, softened
- Salt and black pepper, to taste
Directions:
1. Preheat the Air fryer to 390 °F and grease an Air fryer basket.
2. Rub the steak generously with salt and black pepper and coat with butter.

3. Arrange the steaks in the Air fryer basket and cook for about 14 minutes.
4. Dish out the steaks and cut into desired size slices to serve.

286. Beef And Spring Onions

Servings: 2
Cooking Time: 15 Minutes
Ingredients:
- 2 cups corned beef, cooked and shredded
- 2 garlic cloves, minced
- 1 pound radishes, quartered
- 2 spring onions, chopped
- A pinch of salt and black pepper

Directions:
1. In a pan that fits your air fryer, mix the beef with the rest of the ingredients, toss, put the pan in the fryer and cook at 390 degrees F for 15 minutes. Divide everything into bowls and serve.

287. Beef & Mushrooms

Servings: 1
Cooking Time: 3 Hours 15 Minutes
Ingredients:
- 6 oz. beef
- ¼ onion, diced
- ½ cup mushroom slices
- 2 tbsp. favorite marinade [preferably bulgogi]

Directions:
1. Slice or cube the beef and put it in a bowl.
2. Cover the meat with the marinade, place a layer of aluminum foil or saran wrap over the bowl, and place the bowl in the refrigerator for 3 hours.

3. Put the meat in a baking dish along with the onion and mushrooms
4. Air Fry at 350°F for 10 minutes. Serve hot.

288. Thyme And Turmeric Pork

Servings: 4
Cooking Time: 15 Minutes
Ingredients:
- 1-pound pork tenderloin
- ½ teaspoon salt
- ½ teaspoon ground turmeric
- 1 tablespoon dried thyme
- 1 tablespoon avocado oil

Directions:
1. Rub the pork tenderloin with salt, ground turmeric, and dried thyme. Then brush it with avocado oil. Preheat the air fryer to 370F. Place the pork tenderloin in the air fryer basket and cook it for 15 minutes. You can flip the meat on another side during cooking if desired.

289. Caramelized Pork

Servings:6
Cooking Time:17 Minutes
Ingredients:
- 2 pounds pork shoulder, cut into 1½-inch thick slices
- 1/3 cup soy sauce
- 2 tablespoons sugar
- 1 tablespoon honey

Directions:
1. Preheat the Air fryer to 335 °F and grease an Air fryer basket.
2. Mix all the ingredients in a large bowl and coat chops well.

3. Cover and refrigerate for about 8 hours.
4. Arrange the chops in the Air fryer basket and cook for about 10 minutes, flipping once in between.
5. Set the Air fryer to 390 °F and cook for 7 more minutes.
6. Dish out in a platter and serve hot.

290. Bacon Wrapped Pork Tenderloin

Servings:4
Cooking Time:30 Minutes
Ingredients:
- 1 (1½ pound) pork tenderloins
- 4 bacon strips
- 2 tablespoons Dijon mustard

Directions:
1. Preheat the Air fryer to 360 °F and grease an Air fryer basket.
2. Rub the tenderloin evenly with mustard and wrap the tenderloin with bacon strips.
3. Arrange the pork tenderloin in the Air fryer basket and cook for about 30 minutes, flipping once in between.
4. Dish out the steaks and cut into desired size slices to serve.

291. Burger Patties

Servings: 6
Cooking Time: 15 Minutes
Ingredients:
- 1 lb. ground beef
- 6 cheddar cheese slices
- Pepper and salt to taste

Directions:
1. Pre-heat the Air Fryer to 350°F.
2. Sprinkle the salt and pepper on the ground beef.

3. Shape six equal portions of the ground beef into patties and put each one in the Air Fryer basket.
4. Air fry the patties for 10 minutes.
5. Top the patties with the cheese slices and air fry for one more minute.
6. Serve the patties on top of dinner rolls.

292. Mustard'n Italian Dressing On Flank Steak

Servings:3
Cooking Time: 45 Minutes
Ingredients:
- ½ cup yellow mustard
- ½ teaspoon black pepper
- 1 ¼ pounds beef flank steak
- 1 cup Italian salad dressing
- Salt to taste

Directions:
1. Place all ingredients in a Ziploc bag and allow to marinate in the fridge for at least 2 hours.
2. Preheat the air fryer to 390°F.
3. Place the grill pan accessory in the air fryer.
4. Grill for 15 minutes per batch making sure to flip the meat halfway through the cooking time.

293. Another Easy Teriyaki Bbq Recipe

Servings:2
Cooking Time: 15 Minutes
Ingredients:
- 1 tbsp honey
- 1 tbsp mirin
- 1 tbsp soy sauce

- 1 thumb-sized piece of fresh ginger, grated
- 14 oz lean diced steak, with fat trimmed

Directions:
1. Mix all Ingredients in a bowl and marinate for at least an hour. Turning over halfway through marinating time.
2. Thread mead into skewers. Place on skewer rack.
3. Cook for 5 minutes at 390°F or to desired doneness.
4. Serve and enjoy.

294. Herbed Beef Roast

Servings:5
Cooking Time:45 Minutes
Ingredients:
- 2 pounds beef roast
- 1 tablespoon olive oil
- 1 teaspoon dried rosemary, crushed
- 1 teaspoon dried thyme, crushed
- Salt, to taste

Directions:
1. Preheat the Air fryer to 360 °F and grease an Air fryer basket.
2. Rub the roast generously with herb mixture and coat with olive oil.
3. Arrange the roast in the Air fryer basket and cook for about 45 minutes.
4. Dish out the roast and cover with foil for about 10 minutes.
5. Cut into desired size slices and serve.

295. Garlic Fillets

Servings: 4
Cooking Time: 15 Minutes
Ingredients:
- 1-pound beef filet mignon
- 1 teaspoon minced garlic

- 1 tablespoon peanut oil
- ½ teaspoon salt
- 1 teaspoon dried oregano

Directions:
1. Chop the beef into the medium size pieces and sprinkle with salt and dried oregano. Then add minced garlic and peanut oil and mix up the meat well. Place the bowl with meat in the fridge for 10 minutes to marinate. Meanwhile, preheat the air fryer to 400F. Put the marinated beef pieces in the air fryer and cook them for 10 minutes Then flip the beef on another side and cook for 5 minutes more.

296. Pork Tenderloin With Bacon & Veggies

Servings:3
Cooking Time: 28 Minutes
Ingredients:
- 3 potatoes
- ¾ pound frozen green beans
- 6 bacon slices
- 3 (6-ounces) pork tenderloins
- 2 tablespoons olive oil

Directions:
1. Set the temperature of air fryer to 390 degrees F. Grease an air fryer basket.
2. With a fork, pierce the potatoes.
3. Place potatoes into the prepared air fryer basket and air fry for about 15 minutes.
4. Wrap one bacon slice around 4-6 green beans.
5. Coat the pork tenderloins with oil
6. After 15 minutes, add the pork tenderloins into air fryer basket with potatoes and air fry for about 5-6 minutes.

7. Remove the pork tenderloins from basket.
8. Place bean rolls into the basket and top with the pork tenderloins.
9. Air fry for another 7 minutes.
10. Remove from air fryer and transfer the pork tenderloins onto a platter.
11. Cut each tenderloin into desired size slices.
12. Serve alongside the potatoes and green beans rolls.

297. Beer-braised Short Loin

Servings:4
Cooking Time:15 Minutes
Ingredients:
- 1 ½ pounds short loin
- 2 tablespoons olive oil
- 1 bottle beer
- 2-3 cloves garlic, finely minced
- 2 Turkish bay leaves

Directions:
1. Pat the beef dry; then, tenderize the beef with a meat mallet to soften the fibers. Place it in a large-sized mixing dish.
2. Add the remaining ingredients; toss to coat well and let it marinate for at least 1 hour.
3. Cook about 7 minutes at 395 degrees F; after that, pause the Air Fryer. Flip the meat over and cook for another 8 minutes, or until it's done.

298. Herbed Leg Of Lamb

Servings:5
Cooking Time: 75 Minutes
Ingredients:
- 2 pounds bone-in leg of lamb
- 2 tablespoons olive oil
- Salt and ground black pepper, as required
- 2 fresh rosemary sprigs
- 2 fresh thyme sprigs

Directions:
1. Coat the leg of lamb with oil and sprinkle with salt and black pepper.
2. Wrap the leg of lamb with herb sprigs.
3. Set the temperature of air fryer to 300 degrees F. Grease an air fryer basket.
4. Place leg of lamb into the prepared air fryer basket.
5. Air fry for about 75 minutes.
6. Remove from air fryer and transfer the leg of lamb onto a platter.
7. With a piece of foil, cover the leg of lamb for about 10 minutes before slicing.
8. Cut the leg of lamb into desired size pieces and serve.

299. Bjorn's Beef Steak

Servings: 1
Cooking Time: 15 Minutes
Ingredients:
- 1 steak, 1-inch thick
- 1 tbsp. olive oil
- Black pepper to taste
- Sea salt to taste

Directions:
1. Place the baking tray inside the Air Fryer and pre-heat for about 5 minutes at 390°F.
2. Brush or spray both sides of the steak with the oil.
3. Season both sides with salt and pepper.
4. Take care when placing the steak in the baking tray and allow to cook for 3 minutes. Flip the meat over, and cook for an additional 3 minutes.

5. Take it out of the fryer and allow to sit for roughly 3 minutes before serving.

300. Simple Garlic 'n Herb Meatballs

Servings:4
Cooking Time: 20 Minutes
Ingredients:
- 1 clove of garlic, minced
- 1 egg, beaten
- 1 tablespoon breadcrumbs or flour
- 1 teaspoon dried mixed herbs
- 1-pound lean ground beef

Directions:
1. Place all Ingredients in a mixing bowl and mix together using your hands.
2. Form small balls using your hands and set aside in the fridge to set.
3. Preheat the air fryer to 390°F.
4. Place the meatballs in the air fryer basket and cook for 20 minutes.
5. Halfway through the cooking time, give the meatballs a shake to cook evenly.

301. Easy & The Traditional Beef Roast Recipe

Servings:12
Cooking Time: 2 Hours
Ingredients:
- 1 cup organic beef broth
- 3 pounds beef round roast
- 4 tablespoons olive oil
- Salt and pepper to taste

Directions:
1. Place in a Ziploc bag all the ingredients and allow to marinate in the fridge for 2 hours.
2. Preheat the air fryer for 5 minutes.

3. Transfer all ingredients in a baking dish that will fit in the air fryer.
4. Place in the air fryer and cook for 2 hours for 400°F.

302. Beef Bulgogi

Servings:1
Cooking Time: 15 Minutes
Ingredients:
- ½ cup sliced mushrooms
- 2 tbsp bulgogi marinade
- 1 tbsp diced onion

Directions:
1. Cut the beef into small pieces and place them in a bowl. Add the bulgogi and mix to coat the beef completely. Cover the bowl and place in the fridge for 3 hours. Preheat the air fryer to 350 F.
2. Transfer the beef to a baking dish; stir in the mushroom and onion. Cook for 10 minutes, until nice and tender. Serve with some roasted potatoes and a green salad.

303. Air Fried Grilled Steak

Servings:2
Cooking Time: 45 Minutes
Ingredients:
- 2 top sirloin steaks
- 3 tablespoons butter, melted
- 3 tablespoons olive oil
- Salt and pepper to taste

Directions:
1. Preheat the air fryer for 5 minutes.
2. Season the sirloin steaks with olive oil, salt and pepper.
3. Place the beef in the air fryer basket.
4. Cook for 45 minutes at 350°F.
5. Once cooked, serve with butter.

304. Simple Herbs De Provence Pork Loin Roast

Servings:4
Cooking Time: 35 Minutes
Ingredients:

- 4 pounds pork loin
- A pinch of garlic salt
- A pinch of herbs de Provence

Directions:

1. Preheat the air fryer to 330°F.
2. Season pork with the garlic salt and herbs,
3. Place in the air fryer grill pan.
4. Cook for 30 to 35 minutes.

305. Garlic Dill Leg Of Lamb

Servings: 2
Cooking Time: 21 Minutes
Ingredients:

- 9 oz leg of lamb, boneless
- 1 teaspoon minced garlic
- 2 tablespoons butter, softened
- ½ teaspoon dried dill
- ½ teaspoon salt

Directions:

1. In the shallow bowl mix up minced garlic, butter, dried dill, and salt. Then rub the leg of lamb with butter mixture and place it in the air fryer. Cook it at 380F for 21 minutes.

306. Simple Lamb Chops

Servings:2
Cooking Time:6 Minutes
Ingredients:

- 4 (4-ounces) lamb chops
- Salt and black pepper, to taste
- 1 tablespoon olive oil

Directions:

1. Preheat the Air fryer to 390 °F and grease an Air fryer basket.
2. Mix the olive oil, salt, and black pepper in a large bowl and add chops.
3. Arrange the chops in the Air fryer basket and cook for about 6 minutes.
4. Dish out the lamb chops and serve hot.

307. Basil Pork

Servings: 4
Cooking Time: 25 Minutes
Ingredients:

- 4 pork chops
- A pinch of salt and black pepper
- 2 teaspoons basil, dried
- 2 tablespoons olive oil
- ½ teaspoon chili powder

Directions:

1. In a pan that fits your air fryer, mix all the ingredients, toss, introduce in the fryer and cook at 400 degrees F for 25 minutes. Divide everything between plates and serve.

308. Ribs And Chimichuri Mix

Servings: 4
Cooking Time: 35 Minutes
Ingredients:

- 1-pound pork baby back ribs, boneless
- 2 tablespoons chimichuri sauce
- ½ teaspoon salt

Directions:

1. Sprinkle the ribs with salt and brush with chimichuri sauce. Then preheat the air fryer to 365F. Put the pork ribs in the air fryer and cook for 35 minutes.

309. Pork Chops On The Grill Simple Recipe

Servings:6
Cooking Time: 50 Minutes
Ingredients:
- 1 cup salt
- 1 cup sugar
- 6 pork chops
- 8 cups water

Directions:
1. Place all ingredients in a deep bowl and allow to soak the pork chops in the brine solution for at least 2 days in the fridge.
2. Preheat the air fryer to 390°F.
3. Place the grill pan accessory in the air fryer.
4. Place the meat on the grill pan and cook for 50 minutes making sure to flip every 10 minutes for even grilling.

310. Salted Corned Beef With Onions

Servings:12
Cooking Time: 50 Minutes
Ingredients:
- 1 large onion, chopped
- 2 tablespoons Dijon mustard
- 3 pounds corned beef brisket, cut into chunks
- 4 cups water
- Salt and pepper to taste

Directions:
1. Preheat the air fryer for 5 minutes
2. Place all ingredients in a baking dish that will fit in the air fryer.
3. Cook for 50 minutes at 400°F.

311. Pureed Onion Marinated Beef

Servings:3
Cooking Time: 45 Minutes
Ingredients:
- 1 ½ pounds skirt steak
- 1 large red onion, grated or pureed
- 1 tablespoon vinegar
- 2 tablespoons brown sugar
- Salt and pepper to taste

Directions:
1. Place all ingredients in a Ziploc bag and allow to marinate in the fridge for at least 2 hours.
2. Preheat the air fryer to 390°F.
3. Place the grill pan accessory in the air fryer.
4. Grill for 15 minutes per batch.
5. Flip every 8 minutes for even grilling.

312. Sesame Lamb Chops

Servings: 6
Cooking Time: 11 Minutes
Ingredients:
- 6 lamb chops (3 oz each lamb chop)
- 1 tablespoon sesame oil
- 1 tablespoon za'atar seasonings

Directions:
1. Rub the lamb chops with za'atar seasonings and sprinkle with sesame oil. Preheat the air fryer to 400F. Then arrange the lamb chops in the air fryer in one layer and cook them for 5 minutes. Then flip the pork chops on another side and cook them for 6 minutes more.

313. Steak Total

Servings: 4
Cooking Time: 30 Minutes
Ingredients:
- 2 lb. rib eye steak
- 1 tbsp. olive oil
- 1 tbsp. steak rub

Directions:
1. Set the Air Fryer to 400°F and allow to warm for 4 minutes.
2. Massage the olive oil and steak rub into both sides of the steak.
3. Put the steak in the fryer's basket and cook for 14 minutes. Turn the steak over and cook on the other side for another 7 minutes.
4. Serve hot.

314. Crispy Roast Garlic-salt Pork

Servings:4
Cooking Time: 45 Minutes
Ingredients:
- 1 teaspoon Chinese five spice powder
- 1 teaspoon white pepper
- 2 pounds pork belly
- 2 teaspoons garlic salt

Directions:
1. Preheat the air fryer to 390°F.
2. Mix all the spices in a bowl to create the dry rub.
3. Score the skin of the pork belly with a knife and season the entire pork with the spice rub.
4. Place in the air fryer basket and cook for 40 to 45 minutes until the skin is crispy.
5. Chop before serving.

315. Simple Lamb Bbq With Herbed Salt

Servings:8
Cooking Time: 1 Hour 20 Minutes
Ingredients:
- 2 ½ tablespoons herb salt
- 2 tablespoons olive oil
- 4 pounds boneless leg of lamb, cut into 2-inch chunks

Directions:
1. Preheat the air fryer to 390°F.
2. Place the grill pan accessory in the air fryer.
3. Season the meat with the herb salt and brush with olive oil.
4. Grill the meat for 20 minutes per batch.
5. Make sure to flip the meat every 10 minutes for even cooking.

316. Pork Belly Marinated In Onion-coconut Cream

Servings:3
Cooking Time: 25 Minutes
Ingredients:
- ½ pork belly, sliced to thin strips
- 1 onion, diced
- 1 tablespoon butter
- 4 tablespoons coconut cream
- Salt and pepper to taste

Directions:
1. Place all ingredients in a mixing bowl and allow to marinate in the fridge for 2 hours.
2. Preheat the air fryer for 5 minutes.
3. Place the pork strips in the air fryer and bake for 25 minutes at 350°F.

317. Italian Pork

Servings: 2
Cooking Time: 50 Minutes
Ingredients:
- 8 oz pork loin
- 1 tablespoon sesame oil
- ½ teaspoon salt
- 1 teaspoon Italian herbs

Directions:
1. In the shallow bowl mix up Italian herbs, salt, and sesame oil. Then brush the pork loin with the Italian herbs mixture and wrap in the foil. Preheat the air fryer to 350F. Put the wrapped pork loin in the air fryer and cook it for 50 minutes. When the time is over, remove the meat from the air fryer and discard the foil. Slice the pork loin into the servings.

318. Salty Lamb Chops

Servings: 4
Cooking Time: 8 Minutes
Ingredients:
- 1-pound lamb chops
- 1 egg, beaten
- ½ teaspoon salt
- ½ cup coconut flour
- Cooking spray

Directions:
1. Chop the lamb chops into small pieces (popcorn) and sprinkle with salt. Then add a beaten egg and stir the meat well. After this, add coconut flour and shake the lamb popcorn until all meat pieces are coated. Preheat the air fryer to 380F. Put the lamb popcorn in the air fryer and spray it with cooking spray. Cook the lamb popcorn for 4 minutes.

Then shake the meat well and cook it for 4 minutes more.

319. Roasted Lamb

Servings:4
Cooking Time:1 Hour 30 Minutes
Ingredients:
- 2½ pounds half lamb leg roast, slits carved
- 2 garlic cloves, sliced into smaller slithers
- 1 tablespoon dried rosemary
- 1 tablespoon olive oil
- Cracked Himalayan rock salt and cracked peppercorns, to taste

Directions:
1. Preheat the Air fryer to 400 °F and grease an Air fryer basket.
2. Insert the garlic slithers in the slits and brush with rosemary, oil, salt, and black pepper.
3. Arrange the lamb in the Air fryer basket and cook for about 15 minutes.
4. Set the Air fryer to 350 °F on the Roast mode and cook for 1 hour and 15 minutes.
5. Dish out the lamb chops and serve hot.

320. Easy Corn Dog Bites

Servings:2
Cooking Time: 10 Minutes
Ingredients:
- ½ cup all-purpose flour
- 1 ½ cup crushed cornflakes
- 2 large beef hot dogs, cut in half crosswise
- 2 large eggs, beaten
- Salt and pepper to taste

Directions:

1. Preheat the air fryer to 330°F.
2. Skewer the hot dogs using the metal skewers included in the double layer rack accessory.
3. In a mixing bowl, combine the flour and eggs to form a batter. Season with salt and pepper to taste. Add water if too dry.
4. Dip the skewered hot dogs in the batter and dredge in cornflakes.
5. Place on the double layer rack accessory and cook for 10 minutes.

321. Charred Onions 'n Steak Cube Bbq

Servings:3
Cooking Time: 40 Minutes
Ingredients:
- 1 cup red onions, cut into wedges
- 1 tablespoon dry mustard
- 1 tablespoon olive oil
- 1-pound boneless beef sirloin, cut into cubes
- Salt and pepper to taste

Directions:
1. Preheat the air fryer to 390°F.
2. Place the grill pan accessory in the air fryer.
3. Toss all ingredients in a bowl and mix until everything is coated with the seasonings.
4. Place on the grill pan and cook for 40 minutes.
5. Halfway through the cooking time, give a stir to cook evenly.

322. Air Fried Steak

Servings: 2
Cooking Time: 10 Minutes

Ingredients:
- 2 sirloin steaks
- 2 tsp olive oil
- 2 tbsp steak seasoning
- Pepper
- Salt

Directions:
1. Preheat the air fryer to 350 F.
2. Coat steak with olive oil and season with steak seasoning, pepper, and salt.
3. Spray air fryer basket with cooking spray and place steak in the air fryer basket.
4. Cook for 10 minutes. Turn halfway through.
5. Slice and serve.

323. Grilled Prosciutto Wrapped Fig

Servings:2
Cooking Time: 8 Minutes
Ingredients:
- 2 whole figs, sliced in quarters
- 8 prosciutto slices
- Pepper and salt to taste

Directions:
1. Wrap a prosciutto slice around one slice of fid and then thread into skewer. Repeat process for remaining Ingredients. Place on skewer rack in air fryer.
2. For 8 minutes, cook on 390°F. Halfway through cooking time, turnover skewers.
3. Serve and enjoy.

324. Roasted Ribeye Steak With Rum

Servings:4
Cooking Time: 50 Minutes
Ingredients:
- ½ cup rum
- 2 pounds bone-in ribeye steak
- 2 tablespoons extra virgin olive oil
- Salt and black pepper to taste

Directions:
1. Place all Ingredients in a Ziploc bag and allow to marinate in the fridge for at least 2 hours.
2. Preheat the air fryer to 390°F.
3. Place the grill pan accessory in the air fryer.
4. Grill for 25 minutes per piece.
5. Halfway through the cooking time, flip the meat for even grilling.

325. Champagne-vinegar Marinated Skirt Steak

Servings:2
Cooking Time: 40 Minutes
Ingredients:
- ¼ cup Dijon mustard
- 1 tablespoon rosemary leaves
- 1-pound skirt steak, trimmed
- 2 tablespoons champagne vinegar
- Salt and pepper to taste

Directions:
1. Place all ingredients in a Ziploc bag and marinate in the fridge for 2 hours.
2. Preheat the air fryer to 390°F.
3. Place the grill pan accessory in the air fryer.
4. Grill the skirt steak for 20 minutes per batch.

5. Flip the beef halfway through the cooking time.

326. Easy Rib Eye Steak

Servings:4
Cooking Time:14 Minutes
Ingredients:
- 2 lbs. rib eye steak
- 1 tablespoon olive oil
- 1 tablespoon steak rubo

Directions:
1. Preheat the Air fryer to 400 °F and grease an Air fryer basket.
2. Rub the steak generously with steak rub and coat with olive oil.
3. Transfer the steak in the Air fryer basket and cook for about 14 minutes, flipping once in between.
4. Dish out the steak and cut into desired size slices to serve.

327. Beef And Tomato Sauce

Servings: 4
Cooking Time: 15 Minutes
Ingredients:
- 1-pound beef loin tri-tip
- 1 tablespoon keto tomato sauce
- 1 teaspoon avocado oil

Directions:
1. Pierce the beef loin tri-tip with a fork to get many small cuts. In the shallow bowl mix up tomato sauce and avocado oil. Brush the beef loin with the BBQ sauce mixture from each side and transfer in the air fryer. Cook the meat at 400F for 15 minutes. When the beef loin is cooked, remove it from the air fryer and let it rest for 5 minutes. Slice the meat into the servings.

328. Pork And Garlic Sauce

Servings: 4
Cooking Time: 25 Minutes
Ingredients:
- 1 pound pork tenderloin, sliced
- A pinch of salt and black pepper
- 4 tablespoons butter, melted
- 2 teaspoons garlic, minced
- 1 teaspoon sweet paprika

Directions:
1. Heat up a pan that fits the air fryer with the butter over medium heat, add all the ingredients except the pork medallions, whisk well and simmer for 4-5 minutes. Add the pork, toss, put the pan in your air fryer and cook at 380 degrees F for 20 minutes. Divide between plates and serve with a side salad.

329. Corned Beef

Servings: 5
Cooking Time: 4 Minutes
Ingredients:
- 5 wonton wraps
- 8 oz corned beef, cooked
- 1 egg, beaten
- 3 oz Swiss cheese, shredded
- 1 teaspoon sunflower oil

Directions:
1. Shred the corned beef with the help of the fork and mix it up with Swiss cheese. Then put the corned beef mixture on the wonton wraps and roll them into rolls. Dip every corned beef roll in the beaten egg. Preheat the air fryer to 400F. Put the wonton rolls in the air fryer in one layer and sprinkle with sunflower oil. Cook the meal for 2 minutes from each side or until the rolls are golden brown.

330. Ham Pinwheels

Servings:4
Cooking Time:11 Minutes
Ingredients:
- 1 puff pastry sheet
- 10 ham slices
- 1 cup Gruyere cheese, shredded plus more for sprinkling
- 4 teaspoons Dijon mustard

Directions:
1. Preheat the Air fryer to 375 °F and grease an Air fryer basket.
2. Place the puff pastry onto a smooth surface and spread evenly with the mustard.
3. Top with the ham and ¾ cup cheese and roll the puff pastry.
4. Wrap the roll in plastic wrap and freeze for about 30 minutes.
5. Remove from the freezer and slice into ½-inch rounds.
6. Arrange the pinwheels in the Air fryer basket and cook for about 8 minutes.
7. Top with remaining cheese and cook for 3 more minutes.
8. Dish out in a platter and serve warm.

331. Simple New York Strip Steak

Servings:2
Cooking Time:10 Minutes
Ingredients:
- 1 (9½-ounces) New York strip steak
- 1 teaspoon olive oil
- Crushed red pepper flakes, to taste

- Salt and black pepper, to taste

Directions:

1. Preheat the Air fryer to 400 °F and grease an Air fryer basket.
2. Rub the steak generously with red pepper flakes, salt and black pepper and coat with olive oil.
3. Transfer the steak in the Air fryer basket and cook for about 10 minutes, flipping once in between.
4. Dish out the steak and cut into desired size slices to serve.

332. Mustard Pork

Servings: 4
Cooking Time: 30 Minutes

Ingredients:

- 1 pound pork tenderloin, trimmed
- A pinch of salt and black pepper
- 2 tablespoons olive oil
- 3 tablespoons mustard
- 2 tablespoons balsamic vinegar

Directions:

1. In a bowl, mix the pork tenderloin with the rest of the ingredients and rub well. Put the roast in your air fryer's basket and cook at 380 degrees F for 30 minutes. Slice the roast, divide between plates and serve.

333. Cheddar Cheese'n Bacon Stuffed Pastry Pie

Servings:3
Cooking Time: 18 Minutes

Ingredients:

- 1/2 cup bacon, cooked
- 1/2 cup cheddar cheese, shredded
- 1/2 cup sausage crumbles, cooked

- 5 eggs
- one box puff pastry sheets

Directions:

1. Scramble the eggs and cook.
2. Lightly grease baking pan of air fryer with cooking spray.
3. Evenly spread half of the puff sheets on bottom of pan.
4. Spread eggs, cooked sausage, crumbled bacon, and cheddar cheese.
5. Top with remaining puff pastry and gently push down with a fork.
6. Cover top of baking pan with foil.
7. For 8 minutes, cook on 330°F. Remove foil and continue cooking for another 5 minutes or until tops of puff pastry is golden brown.
8. Serve and enjoy.

334. Salted 'n Peppered Scored Beef Chuck

Servings:6
Cooking Time: 1 Hour And 30 Minutes

Ingredients:

- 2 ounces black peppercorns
- 2 tablespoons olive oil
- 3 pounds beef chuck roll, scored with knife
- 3 tablespoons salt

Directions:

1. Preheat the air fryer to 390°F.
2. Place the grill pan accessory in the air fryer.
3. Season the beef chuck roll with black peppercorns and salt.
4. Brush with olive oil and cover top with foil.
5. Grill for 1 hour and 30 minutes.
6. Flip the beef every 30 minutes for even grilling on all sides.

335. Simple Beef

Servings: 1
Cooking Time: 25 Minutes
Ingredients:
- 1 thin beef schnitzel
- 1 egg, beaten
- ½ cup friendly bread crumbs
- 2 tbsp. olive oil
- Pepper and salt to taste

Directions:
1. Pre-heat the Air Fryer to 350°F.
2. In a shallow dish, combine the bread crumbs, oil, pepper, and salt.
3. In a second shallow dish, place the beaten egg.
4. Dredge the schnitzel in the egg before rolling it in the bread crumbs.
5. Put the coated schnitzel in the fryer basket and air fry for 12 minutes.

336. Hot Paprika Beef

Servings: 4
Cooking Time: 20 Minutes
Ingredients:
- 1 tablespoon hot paprika
- 4 beef steaks
- Salt and black pepper to the taste
- 1 tablespoon butter, melted

Directions:
1. In a bowl, mix the beef with the rest of the ingredients, rub well, transfer the steaks to your air fryer's basket and cook at 390 degrees F for 10 minutes on each side. Divide the steaks between plates and serve with a side salad.

337. Garlicky Buttered Chops

Servings:4
Cooking Time: 30 Minutes
Ingredients:
- 1 tablespoons butter, melted
- 2 teaspoons chopped parsley
- 2 teaspoons grated garlic
- 4 pork chops
- Salt and pepper to taste

Directions:
1. Preheat the air fryer to 330°F.
2. Place the grill pan accessory in the air fryer.
3. Season the pork chops with the remaining Ingredients.
4. Place on the grill pan and cook for 30 minutes.
5. Flip the pork chops halfway through the cooking time.

338. Garlic Lamb Roast

Servings:6
Cooking Time: 1½ Hours
Ingredients:
- 2¾ pounds half lamb leg roast
- 3 garlic cloves, cut into thin slices
- 2 tablespoons extra-virgin olive oil
- 1 tablespoon dried rosemary, crushed
- Salt and ground black pepper, as required

Directions:
1. In a small bowl, mix together the oil, rosemary, salt, and black pepper.
2. With the tip of a sharp knife, make deep slits on the top of lamb roast fat.
3. Insert the garlic slices into the slits.
4. Coat the lamb roast evenly with oil mixture.

5. Set the temperature of air fryer to 390 degrees F. Grease an air fryer basket.
6. Arrange lamb into the prepared air fryer basket in a single layer.
7. Air Fry for about 15 minutes and then another 1¼ hours at 320 degrees F.
8. Remove from air fryer and transfer the roast onto a platter.
9. With a piece of foil, cover the roast for about 10 minutes before slicing.
10. Cut the roast into desired size slices and serve.

339. Marinated Beef

Servings: 4
Cooking Time: 35 Minutes
Ingredients:
- 2 tablespoons olive oil
- 3 garlic cloves, minced
- Salt and black pepper to the taste
- 4 medium beef steaks
- 1 cup balsamic vinegar

Directions:
1. In a bowl, mix steaks with the rest of the ingredients, and toss. Transfer the steaks to your air fryer's basket and cook at 390 degrees F for 35 minutes, flipping them halfway. Divide between plates and serve with a side salad.

340. Mustard Beef Mix

Servings: 7
Cooking Time: 30 Minutes
Ingredients:
- 2-pound beef ribs, boneless
- 1 tablespoon Dijon mustard
- 1 tablespoon sunflower oil
- 1 teaspoon ground paprika
- 1 teaspoon cayenne pepper

Directions:
1. In the shallow bowl mix up Dijon mustard and sunflower oil. Then sprinkle the beef ribs with ground paprika and cayenne pepper. After this, brush the meat with Dijon mustard mixture and leave for 10 minutes to marinate. Meanwhile, preheat the air fryer to 400F. Put the beef ribs in the air fryer to and cook them for 10 minutes. Then flip the ribs on another side and reduce the air fryer heat to 325F. Cook the ribs for 20 minutes more.

341. Veal Rolls

Servings:4
Cooking Time:15 Minutes
Ingredients:
- 4 (6-ounce) veal cutlets
- 2 tablespoons fresh sage leaves
- 4 cured ham slices
- 1 tablespoon unsalted butter, melted
- Salt and black pepper, to taste

Directions:
1. Preheat the Air fryer to 390 °F and grease an Air fryer basket.
2. Season the veal cutlets with salt and roll them up tightly.
3. Wrap 1 ham slice around each roll and coat with 1 tablespoon of the butter.
4. Top rolls with the sage leaves and transfer into the Air fryer basket.
5. Cook for about 10 minutes, flipping once in between and set the Air fryer to 300 °F.
6. Cook for about 5 more minutes and dish out to serve hot.

342. Rib Eye Steak Seasoned With Italian Herb

Servings:4
Cooking Time: 45 Minutes
Ingredients:
- 1 packet Italian herb mix
- 1 tablespoon olive oil
- 2 pounds bone-in rib eye steak
- Salt and pepper to taste

Directions:
1. Preheat the air fryer to 390°F.
2. Place the grill pan accessory in the air fryer.
3. Season the steak with salt, pepper, Italian herb mix, and olive oil. Cover top with foil.
4. Grill for 45 minutes and flip the steak halfway through the cooking time.

343. Japanese Miso Steak

Servings: 4
Cooking Time: 15 Minutes + Marinating Time
Ingredients:
- 1 ¼ pounds flank steak
- 1 ½ tablespoons sake
- 1 tablespoon brown miso paste
- 2 garlic cloves, pressed
- 1 tablespoon olive oil

Directions:
1. Place all the ingredients in a sealable food bag; shake until completely coated and place in your refrigerator for at least 1 hour.
2. Then, spritz the steak with a non-stick cooking spray; make sure to coat on all sides. Place the steak in the Air Fryer baking pan.

3. Set your Air Fryer to cook at 400 degrees F. Roast for 12 minutes, flipping twice. Serve immediately.

344. Skirt Steak Bbq Recipe From Korea

Servings:1
Cooking Time: 30 Minutes
Ingredients:
- 1 skirt steak, halved
- 3 tablespoons gochujang sauce
- 3 tablespoons olive oil
- 3 tablespoons rice vinegar
- Salt and pepper to taste

Directions:
1. Preheat the air fryer to 390°F.
2. Place the grill pan accessory in the air fryer.
3. Rub all spices and seasonings on the skirt steak.
4. Place on the grill and cook for 15 minutes per batch.
5. Flip the steak halfway through the cooking time.
6. Serve with more gochujang or kimchi.

345. Smoked Pork

Servings: 5
Cooking Time: 20 Minutes
Ingredients:
- 1-pound pork shoulder
- 1 tablespoon liquid smoke
- 1 tablespoon olive oil
- 1 teaspoon salt

Directions:
1. Mix up liquid smoke, salt, and olive oil in the shallow bowl. Then carefully brush the pork shoulder with the liquid smoke mixture from each side. Make

the small cuts in the meat. Preheat the air fryer to 390F. Put the pork shoulder in the air fryer basket and cook the meat for 10 minutes. After this, flip the meat on another side and cook it for 10 minutes more. Let the cooked pork shoulder rest for 10-15 minutes. Shred it with the help of 2 forks.

346. Spicy And Saucy Pork Sirloin

Servings: 3
Cooking Time: 55 Minutes
Ingredients:
- 2 teaspoons peanut oil
- 1 ½ pounds pork sirloin
- Coarse sea salt and ground black pepper, to taste
- 1 tablespoon smoked paprika
- 1/4 cup prepared salsa sauce

Directions:
1. Start by preheating your Air Fryer to 360 degrees F.
2. Drizzle the oil all over the pork sirloin. Sprinkle with salt, black pepper, and paprika.
3. Cook for 50 minutes in the preheated Air Fryer.
4. Remove the roast from the Air Fryer and shred with two forks. Mix in the salsa sauce. Enjoy!

347. Beefy Steak Topped With Chimichurri Sauce

Servings:6
Cooking Time: 60 Minutes
Ingredients:
- 1 cup commercial chimichurri

- 3 pounds steak
- Salt and pepper to taste

Directions:
1. Place all ingredients in a Ziploc bag and marinate in the fridge for 2 hours.
2. Preheat the air fryer to 390°F.
3. Place the grill pan accessory in the air fryer.
4. Grill the skirt steak for 20 minutes per batch.
5. Flip the steak every 10 minutes for even grilling.

348. Wrapped Pork

Servings: 2
Cooking Time: 16 Minutes
Ingredients:
- 8 oz pork tenderloin
- 4 bacon slices
- ½ teaspoon salt
- 1 teaspoon olive oil
- ½ teaspoon chili powder

Directions:
1. Sprinkle the pork tenderloin with salt and chili powder. Then wrap it in the bacon slices and sprinkle with olive oil. Secure the bacon with toothpicks if needed. After this, preheat the air fryer to 375F. Put the wrapped pork tenderloin in the air fryer and cook it for 7 minutes. After this, carefully flip the meat on another side and cook it for 9 minutes more. When the meat is cooked, remove the toothpicks from it (if the toothpicks were used) and slice the meat.

349. Cajun Sweet-sour Grilled Pork

Servings:3
Cooking Time: 12 Minutes
Ingredients:
- ¼ cup brown sugar
- 1/4 cup cider vinegar
- 1-lb pork loin, sliced into 1-inch cubes
- 2 tablespoons Cajun seasoning
- 3 tablespoons brown sugar

Directions:
1. In a shallow dish, mix well pork loin, 3 tablespoons brown sugar, and Cajun seasoning. Toss well to coat. Marinate in the ref for 3 hours.
2. In a medium bowl mix well, brown sugar and vinegar for basting.
3. Thread pork pieces in skewers. Baste with sauce and place on skewer rack in air fryer.
4. For 12 minutes, cook on 360°F. Halfway through cooking time, turnover skewers and baste with sauce. If needed, cook in batches.
5. Serve and enjoy.

350. Fantastic Leg Of Lamb

Servings:4
Cooking Time:1 Hour 15 Minutes
Ingredients:
- 2 pounds (3 ounce) leg of lamb
- 2 fresh rosemary sprigs
- 2 fresh thyme sprigs
- 2 tablespoons olive oil
- Salt and black pepper, to taste

Directions:
1. Preheat the Air fryer to 300 °F and grease an Air fryer basket.
2. Sprinkle the leg of lamb with oil, salt and black pepper and wrap with herb sprigs.
3. Arrange the leg of lamb in the Air fryer basket and cook for about 75 minutes.
4. Dish out and serve warm.

VEGAN & VEGETARIAN RECIPES

351. Caribbean Fried Peppers With Tofu

Servings: 2
Cooking Time: 20 Minutes
Ingredients:
- 2 bell peppers, peeled and cut into slices
- 6 ounces firm tofu, cut into cubes
- 2 tablespoons avocado oil
- 2 teaspoons Caribbean Sorrel Rum Spice Mix

Directions:
1. Toss the bell peppers and tofu with the avocado oil and spice mix.
2. Cook in the preheated Air Fryer at 400 degrees F for 10 minutes, shaking the cooking basket halfway through the cooking time.
3. Adjust the seasonings to taste and enjoy!

352. Cheesy Dinner Rolls

Servings:2
Cooking Time: 5 Minutes
Ingredients:
- 2 dinner rolls
- ½ cup Parmesan cheese, grated
- 2 tablespoons unsalted butter, melted
- ½ teaspoon garlic bread seasoning mix

Directions:
1. Cut the dinner rolls into cross style, but not the all way through.
2. Stuff the slits evenly with cheese.
3. Coat the tops of each roll with butter and then, sprinkle with the seasoning mix.
4. Set the temperature of air fryer to 355 degrees F. Grease an air fryer basket.

5. Arrange dinner rolls into the prepared air fryer basket.
6. Air fry for about 5 minutes or until cheese melts completely.
7. Remove from the air fryer and serve hot.

353. Traditional Jacket Potatoes

Servings:4
Cooking Time: 30 Minutes
Ingredients:
- 2 garlic cloves, minced
- Salt and pepper to taste
- 1 tsp rosemary
- 1 tsp butter

Directions:
1. Wash the potatoes thoroughly under water. Preheat your air fryer to 360 F, and prick the potatoes with a fork. Place them into your air fryer's cooking basket and cook for 25 minutes. Cut the potatoes in half and top with butter and rosemary; season with salt and pepper. Serve immediately.

354. Healthy Apple-licious Chips

Servings:1
Cooking Time: 6 Minutes
Ingredients:
- ½ teaspoon ground cumin
- 1 apple, cored and sliced thinly
- 1 tablespoon sugar
- A pinch of salt
Directions:

1. Place all ingredients in a bowl and toss to coat everything.
2. Put the grill pan accessory in the air fryer and place the sliced apples on the grill pan.
3. Close the air fryer and cook for 6 minutes at 390ºF.

355. Cottage Cheese And Potatoes

Servings:5
Cooking Time: 30 Minutes
Ingredients:
- 1 bunch asparagus, trimmed
- ¼ cup fresh cream
- ¼ cup cottage cheese, cubed
- 1 tbsp whole-grain mustard

Directions:
1. Preheat the air fryer to 400 F and place the potatoes in the basket; cook for 25 minutes. Boil salted water in a pot over medium heat. Add asparagus and cook for 3 minutes until tender.
2. In a bowl, mix cooked potatoes, cottage cheese, cream, asparagus and mustard. Toss well and season with salt and black pepper. Transfer the mixture to the potato skin shells and serve.

356. Almond Asparagus

Servings:3
Cooking Time:6 Minutes
Ingredients:
- 1 pound asparagus
- 1/3 cup almonds, sliced
- 2 tablespoons olive oil
- 2 tablespoons balsamic vinegar
- Salt and black pepper, to taste
Directions:

1. Preheat the Air fryer to 400 ºF and grease an Air fryer basket.
2. Mix asparagus, oil, vinegar, salt, and black pepper in a bowl and toss to coat well.
3. Arrange asparagus into the Air fryer basket and sprinkle with the almond slices.
4. Cook for about 6 minutes and dish out to serve hot.

357. Salted Beet Chips

Servings:2
Cooking Time:6 Minutes
Ingredients:
- 1 tablespoon cooking oil
- 1-pound beets, peeled and sliced
- Salt and pepper to taste
Directions:
1. Place all Ingredients in a bowl and toss to coat everything.
2. Place the sliced beets in the double layer rack.
3. Place the rack with the beets in the air fryer.
4. Close the air fryer and cook for 6 minutes at 390ºF.

358. Honey Glazed Carrots

Servings:4
Cooking Time: 12 Minutes
Ingredients:
- 3 cups carrots, peeled and cut into large chunks
- 1 tablespoon olive oil
- 1 tablespoon honey
- 1 tablespoon fresh thyme, finely chopped

- Salt and ground black pepper, as required

Directions:

1. Set the temperature of air fryer to 390 degrees F. Grease an air fryer basket.
2. In a bowl, mix well carrot, oil, honey, thyme, salt, and black pepper.
3. Arrange carrot chunks into the prepared air fryer basket in a single layer.
4. Air fry for about 12 minutes.
5. Remove from air fryer and transfer the carrot chunks onto serving plates.
6. Serve hot.

359. Scrumptiously Healthy Chips

Servings:2
Cooking Time: 10 Minutes
Ingredients:

- 1 bunch kale
- 1 teaspoon garlic powder
- 2 tablespoons almond flour
- 2 tablespoons olive oil
- Salt and pepper to taste

Directions:

1. Preheat the air fryer for 5 minutes.
2. In a bowl, combine all ingredients until the kale leaves are coated with the other ingredients.
3. Place in a fryer basket and cook for 10 minutes until crispy.

360. Okra With Green Beans

Servings:2
Cooking Time:20 Minutes
Ingredients:

- ½ (10-ounces) bag frozen cut okra
- ½ (10-ounces) bag frozen cut green beans

- ¼ cup nutritional yeast
- 3 tablespoons balsamic vinegar
- Salt and black pepper, to taste

Directions:

1. Preheat the Air fryer to 400 °F and grease an Air fryer basket.
2. Mix the okra, green beans, nutritional yeast, vinegar, salt, and black pepper in a bowl and toss to coat well.
3. Arrange the okra mixture into the Air fryer basket and cook for about 20 minutes.
4. Dish out in a serving dish and serve hot.

361. Curly Vegan Fries

Servings:2
Cooking Time: 20 Minutes
Ingredients:

- 1 tbsp tomato ketchup
- 2 tbsp olive oil
- Salt and pepper to taste
- 2 tbsp coconut oil

Directions:

1. Preheat your air fryer to 360 F and use a spiralizer to spiralize the potatoes. In a bowl, mix oil, coconut oil, salt and pepper. Cover the potatoes with the oil mixture. Place the potatoes in the cooking basket and cook for 15 minutes. Serve with ketchup and enjoy!

362. Broccoli With Cauliflower

Servings:4
Cooking Time:20 Minutes
Ingredients:

- 1½ cups broccoli, cut into 1-inch pieces
- 1½ cups cauliflower, cut into 1-inch pieces
- 1 tablespoon olive oil

- Salt, as required

Directions:

1. Preheat the Air fryer to 375 °F and grease an Air fryer basket.
2. Mix the vegetables, olive oil, and salt in a bowl and toss to coat well.
3. Arrange the veggie mixture in the Air fryer basket and cook for about 20 minutes, tossing once in between.
4. Dish out in a bowl and serve hot.

363. Sesame Seeds Bok Choy(2)

Servings:4
Cooking Time:6 Minutes

Ingredients:

- 4 bunches spinach leaves
- 2 teaspoons sesame seeds
- 1 teaspoon garlic powder
- 1 teaspoon ginger powder
- Salt, to taste

Directions:

1. Preheat the Air fryer to 325 °F and grease an Air fryer basket.
2. Arrange the spinach leaves into the Air fryer basket and season with salt, garlic powder and ginger powder.
3. Cook for about 6 minutes, shaking once in between and dish out onto serving plates.
4. Top with sesame seeds and serve hot.

364. Prawn Toast

Servings:2
Cooking Time: 12 Minutes

Ingredients:

- 1 large spring onion, finely sliced
- 3 white bread slices
- ½ cup sweet corn

- 1 egg white, whisked
- 1 tbsp black sesame seeds

Directions:

1. In a bowl, place prawns, corn, spring onion and the sesame seeds. Add the whisked egg and mix the ingredients. Spread the mixture over the bread slices. Place in the prawns in the air fryer's basket and sprinkle oil. Fry the prawns until golden, for 8-10 minutes at 370 F. Serve with ketchup or chili sauce.

365. Sesame Seeds Bok Choy

Servings:4
Cooking Time: 6 Minutes

Ingredients:

- 4 bunches baby bok choy, bottoms removed and leaves separated
- Olive oil cooking spray
- 1 teaspoon garlic powder
- 1 teaspoon sesame seeds

Directions:

1. Set the temperature of air fryer to 325 degrees F.
2. Arrange bok choy leaves into the air fryer basket in a single layer.
3. Spray with the cooking spray and sprinkle with garlic powder.
4. Air fry for about 5-6 minutes, shaking after every 2 minutes.
5. Remove from air fryer and transfer the bok choy onto serving plates.
6. Garnish with sesame seeds and serve hot.

366. Baked Polenta With Chili-cheese

Servings:3

Cooking Time: 10 Minutes
Ingredients:
- 1 commercial polenta roll, sliced
- 1 cup cheddar cheese sauce
- 1 tablespoon chili powder

Directions:
1. Place the baking dish accessory in the air fryer.
2. Arrange the polenta slices in the baking dish.
3. Add the chili powder and cheddar cheese sauce.
4. Close the air fryer and cook for 10 minutes at 390°F.

367. Stuffed Eggplant

Servings: 2
Cooking Time: 35 Minutes
Ingredients:
- large eggplant
- ¼ medium yellow onion, diced
- 2 tbsp. red bell pepper, diced
- 1 cup spinach
- ¼ cup artichoke hearts, chopped

Directions:
1. Cut the eggplant lengthwise into slices and spoon out the flesh, leaving a shell about a half-inch thick. Chop it up and set aside.
2. Set a skillet over a medium heat and spritz with cooking spray. Cook the onions for about three to five minutes to soften. Then add the pepper, spinach, artichokes, and the flesh of eggplant. Fry for a further five minutes, then remove from the heat.
3. Scoop this mixture in equal parts into the eggplant shells and place each one in the fryer.

4. Cook for twenty minutes at 320°F until the eggplant shells are soft. Serve warm.

368. Cheesy Bbq Tater Tot

Servings:6
Cooking Time: 20 Minutes
Ingredients:
- ½ cup shredded Cheddar
- 12 slices bacon
- 1-lb frozen tater tots, defrosted
- 2 tbsp chives
- Ranch dressing, for serving

Directions:
1. Thread one end of bacon in a skewer, followed by one tater, snuggly thread the bacon around tater like a snake, and then another tater, and then snake the bacon again until you reach the end. Repeat with the rest of the Ingredients.
2. For 10 minutes, cook on 360°F. Halfway through cooking time, turnover skewers. If needed cook in batches.
3. Place skewers on a serving platter and sprinkle cheese and chives on top.
4. Serve and enjoy with ranch dressing on the side.

369. Low-calorie Beets Dish

Servings:2
Cooking Time: 20 Minutes
Ingredients:
- ⅓ cup balsamic vinegar
- 1 tbsp olive oil
- 1 tbsp honey
- Salt and pepper to taste
- 2 springs rosemary

Directions:
1. In a bowl, mix rosemary, pepper, salt, vinegar and honey. Cover beets with

the prepared sauce and then coat with oil. Preheat your air fryer to 400 F, and cook the beets in the air fryer for 10 minutes. Pour the balsamic vinegar in a pan over medium heat; bring to a boil and cook until reduced by half. Drizzle the beets with balsamic glaze, to serve.

370. Cheese Pizza With Broccoli Crust

Servings: 1
Cooking Time: 30 Minutes
Ingredients:
- 3 cups broccoli rice, steamed
- ½ cup parmesan cheese, grated
- 1 egg
- 3 tbsp. low-carb Alfredo sauce
- ½ cup parmesan cheese, grated

Directions:
1. Drain the broccoli rice and combine with the parmesan cheese and egg in a bowl, mixing well.
2. Cut a piece of parchment paper roughly the size of the base of the fryer's basket. Spoon four equal-sized amounts of the broccoli mixture onto the paper and press each portion into the shape of a pizza crust. You may have to complete this part in two batches. Transfer the parchment to the fryer.
3. Cook at 370°F for five minutes. When the crust is firm, flip it over and cook for an additional two minutes.
4. Add the Alfredo sauce and mozzarella cheese on top of the crusts and cook for an additional seven minutes. The crusts are ready when the sauce and cheese have melted. Serve hot.

371. Surprising Quinoa Eggplant Rolls

Servings:3
Cooking Time: 15 Minutes
Ingredients:
- Marinara sauce for dipping
- ½ cup cheese, grated
- 2 tbsp milk
- 1 whole egg, beaten
- 2 cups breadcrumbs

Directions:
1. Preheat air fryer to 400 F. In a bowl, mix beaten egg and milk. In another bowl, mix crumbs and cheese until crumbly. Place eggplant slices in the egg mixture, followed by a dip in the crumb mixture. Place eggplant slices in the cooking basket and cook for 5 minutes. Serve with marinara sauce.

372. Wine Infused Mushrooms

Servings:6
Cooking Time: 32 Minutes
Ingredients:
- 1 tablespoon butter
- 2 teaspoons Herbs de Provence
- ½ teaspoon garlic powder
- 2 pounds fresh mushrooms, quartered
- 2 tablespoons white vermouth*

Directions:
1. Set the temperature of air fryer to 320 degrees F.
2. In an air fryer pan, mix together the butter, Herbs de Provence, and garlic powder and air fry for about 2 minutes.
3. Stir in the mushrooms and air fry for about 25 minutes.
4. Stir in the vermouth and air fry for 5 more minutes.

5. Remove from air fryer and transfer the mushrooms onto serving plates.
6. Serve hot.

373. Paprika Brussels Sprout Chips

Servings: 2
Cooking Time: 20 Minutes
Ingredients:
- 10 Brussels sprouts
- 1 teaspoon canola oil
- 1 teaspoon coarse sea salt
- 1 teaspoon paprika

Directions:
1. Toss all ingredients in the lightly greased Air Fryer basket.
2. Bake at 380 degrees F for 15 minutes, shaking the basket halfway through the cooking time to ensure even cooking.
3. Serve and enjoy!

374. Brussels Sprouts With Balsamic Oil

Servings:4
Cooking Time: 15 Minutes
Ingredients:
- ¼ teaspoon salt
- 1 tablespoon balsamic vinegar
- 2 cups Brussels sprouts, halved
- 2 tablespoons olive oil

Directions:
1. Preheat the air fryer for 5 minutes.
2. Mix all ingredients in a bowl until the zucchini fries are well coated.
3. Place in the air fryer basket.
4. Close and cook for 15 minutes for 350°F.

375. Polenta Fries

Servings:4
Cooking Time: 80 Minutes
Ingredients:
- 2 cups milk
- 1 cup instant polenta
- Salt and black pepper
- Cooking spray
- fresh thyme, chopped

Directions:
1. Line a tray with paper. Pour water and milk into a saucepan and let it simmer. Keep whisking as you pour in the polenta. Continue to whisk until polenta thickens and bubbles; season to taste.
2. Add polenta into the lined tray and spread out. Refrigerate for 45 minutes. Slice the cold, set polenta into batons and spray with oil. Arrange polenta chips into the air fryer basket and cook for 16 minutes at 380 F, turning once halfway through. Make sure the fries are golden and crispy.

376. Sweet Potato French Fries

Servings:4
Cooking Time: 30 Minutes
Ingredients:
- ½ tsp garlic powder
- ½ tsp chili powder
- ¼ tsp cumin
- 3 tbsp olive oil
- 3 sweet potatoes, cut into thick strips

Directions:
1. In a bowl, mix salt, garlic powder, chili powder, and cumin, and whisk in oil. Coat the strips well in this mixture and arrange them on the air fryer's basket.

Cook for 20 minutes at 380 F until crispy. Serve.

377. Tender Butternut Squash Fry

Servings:2
Cooking Time: 10 Minutes
Ingredients:
- 1 tablespoon cooking oil
- 1-pound butternut squash, seeded and sliced
- Salt and pepper to taste

Directions:
1. Place the grill pan accessory in the air fryer.
2. In a bowl, place all Ingredients and toss to coat and season the squash.
3. Place in the grill pan.
4. Close the air fryer and cook for 10 minutes at 330°F.

378. Bell Peppers Cups

Servings:4
Cooking Time:8 Minutes
Ingredients:
- 8 mini red bell peppers, tops and seeds removed
- 1 teaspoon fresh parsley, chopped
- ¾ cup feta cheese, crumbled
- ½ tablespoon olive oil
- Freshly ground black pepper, to taste

Directions:
1. Preheat the Air fryer to 390 °F and grease an Air fryer basket.
2. Mix feta cheese, parsley, olive oil and black pepper in a bowl.
3. Stuff the bell peppers with feta cheese mixture and arrange in the Air fryer basket.

4. Cook for about 8 minutes and dish out to serve hot.

379. Crispy Brussels Sprout Chips

Servings: 2
Cooking Time: 20 Minutes
Ingredients:
- 10 Brussels sprouts, separated into leaves
- 1 teaspoon canola oil
- 1 teaspoon coarse sea salt
- 1 teaspoon paprika

Directions:
1. Toss all ingredients in the lightly greased Air Fryer basket.
2. Bake at 380 degrees F for 15 minutes, shaking the basket halfway through the cooking time to ensure even cooking.
3. Serve and enjoy!

380. Broccoli Salad

Servings: 2
Cooking Time: 15 Minutes
Ingredients:
- 3 cups fresh broccoli florets
- 2 tbsp. coconut oil, melted
- ¼ cup sliced s
- ½ medium lemon, juiced

Directions:
1. Take a six-inch baking dish and fill with the broccoli florets. Pour the melted coconut oil over the broccoli and add in the sliced s. Toss together. Put the dish in the air fryer.
2. Cook at 380°F for seven minutes, stirring at the halfway point.
3. Place the broccoli in a bowl and drizzle the lemon juice over it.

381. Chili Fried Okra

Servings:4
Cooking Time: 15 Minutes
Ingredients:
- 3 tbsp sour cream
- 2 tbsp flour
- 2 tbsp semolina
- ½ tsp red chili powder
- Salt and black pepper to taste

Directions:
1. Preheat the Air fryer to 400 F. Spray the air fryer basket with cooking spray.
2. In a bowl, pour sour cream. In a separate bowl, mix flour, semolina, chili powder, salt, and pepper. Dip okra in the sour cream, followed by a dip in the flour mixture. Place in your air fryer's basket and cook for 5 minutes. Slide out the basket and shake. Cook for 5 more minutes. Allow to cool and serve.

382. Curried Cauliflower Florets

Servings:4
Cooking Time: 34 Minutes
Ingredients:
- Salt to taste
- 1 ½ tbsp curry powder
- ½ cup olive oil
- ⅓ cup fried pine nuts

Directions:
1. Preheat the air fryer to 390 F, and mix the pine nuts and 1 tsp of olive oil, in a medium bowl. Pour them in the air fryer's basket and cook for 2 minutes; remove to cool.
2. Place the cauliflower on a cutting board. Use a knife to cut them into 1-inch florets. Place them in a large mixing bowl. Add the curry powder, salt, and the remaining olive oil; mix well. Place the cauliflower florets in the fryer's basket in 2 batches, and cook each batch for 10 minutes. Remove the curried florets onto a serving platter, sprinkle with the pine nuts, and toss. Serve the florets with tomato sauce or as a side to a meat dish.

383. Salted Garlic Zucchini Fries

Servings:6
Cooking Time: 15 Minutes
Ingredients:
- ¼ teaspoon garlic powder
- ½ cup almond flour
- 2 large egg whites, beaten
- 3 medium zucchinis, sliced into fry sticks
- Salt and pepper to taste

Directions:
1. Preheat the air fryer for 5 minutes.
2. Mix all ingredients in a bowl until the zucchini fries are well coated.
3. Place in the air fryer basket.
4. Close and cook for 15 minutes for 425°F.

384. Roasted Brussels Sprouts

Servings:4
Cooking Time: 25 Minutes
Ingredients:
- ½ tsp garlic, chopped
- 2 tbsp olive oil
- Salt and black pepper to taste

Directions:

1. Wash the Brussels sprouts thoroughly under cold water and trim off the outer leaves, keeping only the head of the sprouts. In a bowl, mix oil, garlic, salt, and pepper. Add sprouts to this mixture and let rest for 5 minutes. Place the coated sprouts in your air fryer's cooking basket and cook for 15 minutes.

385. Spicy Roasted Cashew Nuts

Servings: 4
Cooking Time: 20 Minutes
Ingredients:
- 1 cup whole cashews
- 1 teaspoon olive oil
- Salt and ground black pepper, to taste
- 1/2 teaspoon smoked paprika
- 1/2 teaspoon ancho chili powder

Directions:
1. Toss all ingredients in the mixing bowl.
2. Line the Air Fryer basket with baking parchment. Spread out the spiced cashews in a single layer in the basket.
3. Roast at 350 degrees F for 6 to 8 minutes, shaking the basket once or twice. Work in batches. Enjoy!

386. Caramelized Brussels Sprout

Servings:4
Cooking Time:35 Minutes
Ingredients:
- 1 pound Brussels sprouts, trimmed and halved
- 4 teaspoons butter, melted
- Salt and black pepper, to taste

Directions:
1. Preheat the Air fryer to 400 F and grease an Air fryer basket.
2. Mix all the ingredients in a bowl and toss to coat well.
3. Arrange the Brussels sprouts in the Air fryer basket and cook for about 35 minutes.
4. Dish out and serve warm.

387. Cinnamon Sugar Tortilla Chips

Servings: 4
Cooking Time: 20 Minutes
Ingredients:
- 4 (10-inch) flour tortillas
- 1/4 cup vegan margarine, melted
- 1 ½ tablespoons ground cinnamon
- 1/4 cup caster sugar

Directions:
1. Slice each tortilla into eight slices. Brush the tortilla pieces with the melted margarine.
2. In a mixing bowl, thoroughly combine the cinnamon and sugar. Toss the cinnamon mixture with the tortillas.
3. Transfer to the cooking basket and cook at 360 degrees F for 8 minutes or until lightly golden. Work in batches.
4. They will crisp up as they cool. Serve and enjoy!

388. Pepper-pineapple With Butter-sugar Glaze

Servings:2
Cooking Time: 10 Minutes
Ingredients:

- 1 medium-sized pineapple, peeled and sliced
- 1 red bell pepper, seeded and julienned
- 1 teaspoon brown sugar
- 2 teaspoons melted butter
- Salt to taste

Directions:
1. Preheat the air fryer to 390°F.
2. Place the grill pan accessory in the air fryer.
3. Mix all ingredients in a Ziploc bag and give a good shake.
4. Dump onto the grill pan and cook for 10 minutes making sure that you flip the pineapples every 5 minutes.

389. Cabbage Steaks

Servings:3
Cooking Time: 25 Minutes
Ingredients:
- 1 tbsp garlic stir-in paste
- 1 tsp salt
- 2 tbsp olive oil
- ½ tsp black pepper
- 2 tsp fennel seeds

Directions:
1. Preheat the air fryer to 350 F, and slice the cabbage into 1 ½-inch slice. In a small bowl, combine all the other ingredients; brush cabbage with the mixture. Arrange the cabbage steaks in the air fryer and cook for 15 minutes.

390. Rosemary Olive-oil Over Shrooms N Asparagus

Servings:6
Cooking Time: 15 Minutes
Ingredients:

- ½ pound fresh mushroom, quartered
- 1 bunch fresh asparagus, trimmed and cleaned
- 2 sprigs of fresh rosemary, minced
- 2 teaspoon olive oil
- salt and pepper to taste

Directions:
1. Preheat the air fryer to 400°F.
2. Place the asparagus and mushrooms in a bowl and pour the rest of the ingredients.
3. Toss to coat the asparagus and mushrooms.
4. Place inside the air fryer and cook for 15 minutes.

391. Sesame Seeds Bok Choy(1)

Servings:4
Cooking Time:6 Minutes
Ingredients:
- 4 bunches baby bok choy, bottoms removed and leaves separated
- 1 teaspoon sesame seeds
- Olive oil cooking spray
- 1 teaspoon garlic powder

Directions:
1. Preheat the Air fryer to 325 F and grease an Air fryer basket.
2. Arrange the bok choy leaves into the Air fryer basket and spray with the cooking spray.
3. Sprinkle with garlic powder and cook for about 6 minutes, shaking twice in between.
4. Dish out in the bok choy onto serving plates and serve garnished with sesame seeds.

392. Sweet And Sour Brussel Sprouts

Servings: 2
Cooking Time: 10 Minutes
Ingredients:
- 2 cups Brussels sprouts, trimmed and halved lengthwise
- 1 tablespoon balsamic vinegar
- 1 tablespoon maple syrup
- Salt, as required

Directions:
1. Preheat the Air fryer to 400 °F and grease an Air fryer basket.
2. Mix all the ingredients in a bowl and toss to coat well.
3. Arrange the Brussel sprouts in the Air fryer basket and cook for about 10 minutes, shaking once halfway through.
4. Dish out in a bowl and serve hot.

393. Green Bean Casserole

Servings: 2
Cooking Time: 10 Minutes
Ingredients:
- tbsp. butter, melted
- 1 cup green beans
- 6 oz. cheddar cheese, shredded
- 7 oz. parmesan cheese, shredded
- ¼ cup heavy cream

Directions:
1. Pre-heat your fryer at 400°F.
2. Take a baking dish small enough to fit inside the fryer and cover the bottom with melted butter. Throw in the green beans, cheddar cheese, and any seasoning as desired, then give it a stir. Add the parmesan on top and finally the heavy cream.

3. Cook in the fryer for six minutes. Allow to cool before serving.

394. Garlic-roasted Brussels Sprouts With Mustard

Servings: 3
Cooking Time: 20 Minutes
Ingredients:
- 1 pound Brussels sprouts, halved
- 2 tablespoons olive oil
- Sea salt and freshly ground black pepper, to taste
- 2 garlic cloves, minced
- 1 tablespoon Dijon mustard

Directions:
1. Toss the Brussels sprouts with the olive oil, salt, black pepper, and garlic.
2. Roast in the preheated Air Fryer at 380 degrees F for 15 minutes, shaking the basket occasionally.
3. Serve with Dijon mustard and enjoy!

395. Pineapple Appetizer Ribs

Servings: 4
Cooking Time: 30 Minutes
Ingredients:
- 7 oz salad dressing
- 5 oz can pineapple juice
- 2 cups water
- garlic salt
- salt and black pepper

Directions:
1. Sprinkle the ribs with salt and pepper, and place them in a saucepan. Pour water and cook the ribs for 12 minutes on high heat. Drain the ribs and arrange them in the fryer; sprinkle with garlic salt. Cook for 15 minutes at 390 F.

Prepare the sauce by combining the salad dressing and the pineapple juice. Serve the ribs drizzled with the sauce.

396. Sautéed Bacon With Spinach

Servings:2
Cooking Time:9 Minutes
Ingredients:
- 3 meatless bacon slices, chopped
- 1 onion, chopped
- 4-ounce fresh spinach
- 2 tablespoons olive oil
- 1 garlic clove, minced

Directions:
1. Preheat the Air fryer to 340 °F and grease an Air fryer pan.
2. Put olive oil and garlic in the Air fryer pan and place in the Air fryer basket.
3. Cook for about 2 minutes and add bacon and onions.
4. Cook for about 3 minutes and stir in the spinach.
5. Cook for about 4 minutes and dish out in a bowl to serve.

397. Mushrooms Marinated In Garlic Coco-aminos

Servings:8
Cooking Time: 20 Minutes
Ingredients:
- ¼ cup coconut aminos
- 2 cloves of garlic, minced
- 2 pounds mushrooms, sliced
- 3 tablespoons olive oil

Directions:
1. Place all ingredients in a dish and mix until well-combined.

2. Allow to marinate for 2 hours in the fridge.
3. Preheat the air fryer for 5 minutes.
4. Place the mushrooms in a heat-proof dish that will fit in the air fryer.
5. Cook for 20 minutes at 350°F.

398. Rice Flour Crusted Tofu

Servings:3
Cooking Time: 28 Minutes
Ingredients:
- 1 (14-ounces) block firm tofu, pressed and cubed into ½-inch size
- 2 tablespoons cornstarch
- ¼ cup rice flour
- Salt and ground black pepper, as required
- 2 tablespoons olive oil

Directions:
1. In a bowl, mix together cornstarch, rice flour, salt, and black pepper.
2. Coat the tofu evenly with flour mixture.
3. Drizzle the tofu with oil.
4. Set the temperature of air fryer to 360 degrees F. Grease an air fryer basket.
5. Arrange tofu cubes into the prepared air fryer basket in a single layer.
6. Air fry for about 14 minutes per side.
7. Remove from air fryer and transfer the tofu onto serving plates.
8. Serve warm.

399. Sautéed Green Beans

Servings:2
Cooking Time:10 Minutes
Ingredients:
- 8 ounces fresh green beans, trimmed and cut in half
- 1 teaspoon sesame oil

- 1 tablespoon soy sauce

Directions:

1. Preheat the Air fryer to 390 °F and grease an Air fryer basket.
2. Mix green beans, soy sauce, and sesame oil in a bowl and toss to coat well.
3. Arrange green beans into the Air fryer basket and cook for about 10 minutes, tossing once in between.
4. Dish out onto serving plates and serve hot.

400. Parmesan Asparagus

Servings:3
Cooking Time:10 Minutes
Ingredients:

- 1 pound fresh asparagus, trimmed
- 1 tablespoon Parmesan cheese, grated
- 1 tablespoon butter, melted
- 1 teaspoon garlic powder
- Salt and black pepper, to taste

Directions:

1. Preheat the Air fryer to 400 °F and grease an Air fryer basket.
2. Mix the asparagus, cheese, butter, garlic powder, salt, and black pepper in a bowl and toss to coat well.
3. Arrange the asparagus into the Air fryer basket and cook for about 10 minutes.
4. Dish out in a serving plate and serve hot.

401. Crispy Marinated Tofu

Servings:3
Cooking Time: 20 Minutes
Ingredients:

- 1 (14-ounces) block firm tofu, pressed and cut into 1-inch cubes
- 2 tablespoons low sodium soy sauce
- 2 teaspoons sesame oil, toasted

- 1 teaspoon seasoned rice vinegar
- 1 tablespoon cornstarch

Directions:

1. In a bowl, mix well tofu, soy sauce, sesame oil, and vinegar.
2. Set aside to marinate for about 25-30 minutes.
3. Coat the tofu cubes evenly with cornstarch.
4. Set the temperature of air fryer to 370 degrees F. Grease an air fryer basket.
5. Arrange tofu pieces into the prepared air fryer basket in a single layer.
6. Air fry for about 20 minutes, shaking once halfway through.
7. Remove from air fryer and transfer the tofu onto serving plates.
8. Serve warm.

402. Crispy Nachos

Servings:2
Cooking Time: 20 Minutes
Ingredients:

- 1 cup all-purpose flour
- 1 tbsp butter
- ½ tsp chili powder
- 3 tbsp water
- Salt to taste

Directions:

1. Add a small amount of water to the sweet corn and grind until you obtain a very fine paste. In a large bowl, add the flour, salt, chili powder, butter and mix very well; add corn and stir well.
2. Start to knead with your palm until you obtain a stiff dough. Preheat the air fryer to 350 F.
3. Meanwhile, dust a little bit of flour and spread the dough with a rolling pin. Make it around ½ inch thick. Cut it in

any shape you want and fry the shapes in the air fryer for around 10 minutes. Serve with guacamole salsa.

403. Roasted Rosemary Squash

Servings:2
Cooking Time: 30 Minutes
Ingredients:
- 1 tbsp dried rosemary
- Cooking spray
- Salt to season

Directions:
1. Place the butternut squash on a cutting board and peel it; cut it in half and remove the seeds. Cut the pulp into wedges and season with salt.
2. Preheat air fryer to 350 F, spray the squash with cooking spray and sprinkle with rosemary. Grease the fryer's basket with cooking spray and place the wedges inside. Slide the fryer basket back in and cook for 20 minutes, flipping once halfway through. Serve with maple syrup and goat cheese.

404. Crisped Tofu With Paprika

Servings:4
Cooking Time: 15 Minutes
Ingredients:
- ¼ cup cornstarch
- 1 block extra firm tofu, pressed to remove excess water and cut into cubes
- 1 tablespoon smoked paprika
- salt and pepper to taste

Directions:
1. Line the air fryer basket with aluminum foil and brush with oil.
2. Preheat the air fryer to 370°F.

3. Mix all ingredients in a bowl. Toss to combine.
4. Place in the air fryer basket and cook for 12 minutes.

405. Herbed Potatoes

Servings:4
Cooking Time:15 Minutes
Ingredients:
- 6 small potatoes, chopped
- 2 tablespoons fresh parsley, chopped
- 3 tablespoons olive oil
- 2 teaspoons mixed dried herbs
- Salt and black pepper, to taste

Directions:
1. Preheat the Air fryer to 360 °F and grease an Air fryer basket.
2. Mix the potatoes, oil, herbs, salt and black pepper in a bowl.
3. Arrange the chopped potatoes into the Air fryer basket and cook for about 15 minutes, tossing once in between.
4. Dish out the potatoes onto serving plates and serve garnished with parsley.

406. Spaghetti Squash

Servings: 2
Cooking Time: 45 Minutes
Ingredients:
- spaghetti squash
- 1 tsp. olive oil
- Salt and pepper
- 4 tbsp. heavy cream
- 1 tsp. butter

Directions:
1. Pre-heat your fryer at 360°F.
2. Cut and de-seed the spaghetti squash. Brush with the olive oil and season with salt and pepper to taste.

3. Put the squash inside the fryer, placing it cut-side-down. Cook for thirty minutes. Halfway through cooking, fluff the spaghetti inside the squash with a fork.

4. When the squash is ready, fluff the spaghetti some more, then pour some heavy cream and butter over it and give it a good stir. Serve with the low-carb tomato sauce of your choice.

407. Poblano & Tomato Stuffed Squash

Servings:3
Cooking Time: 50 Minutes
Ingredients:
- 6 grape tomatoes, halved
- 1 poblano pepper, cut into strips
- ¼ cup grated mozzarella, optional
- 2 tsp olive oil divided
- Salt and pepper, to taste

Directions:
1. Preheat the air fryer to 350 F. Trim the ends and cut the squash lengthwise. You will only need one half for this recipe Scoop the flash out, so you make room for the filling. Brush 1 tsp of oil over the squash.
2. Place in the air fryer and roast for 30 minutes. Combine the remaining olive oil with tomatoes and poblanos, season with salt and pepper. Place the peppers and tomatoes into the squash. Cook for 15 more minutes. If using mozzarella, add it on top of the squash, two minutes before the end.

408. Caramelized Carrots

Servings:3

Cooking Time:15 Minutes
Ingredients:
- 1 small bag baby carrots
- ½ cup butter, melted
- ½ cup brown sugar

Directions:
1. Preheat the Air fryer to 400 F and grease an Air fryer basket.
2. Mix the butter and brown sugar in a bowl.
3. Add the carrots and toss to coat well.
4. Arrange the carrots in the Air fryer basket and cook for about 15 minutes.
5. Dish out and serve warm.

409. Easy Glazed Carrots

Servings:4
Cooking Time:12 Minutes
Ingredients:
- 3 cups carrots, peeled and cut into large chunks
- 1 tablespoon olive oil
- 1 tablespoon honey
- Salt and black pepper, to taste

Directions:
1. Preheat the Air fryer to 390 F and grease an Air fryer basket.
2. Mix all the ingredients in a bowl and toss to coat well.
3. Transfer into the Air fryer basket and cook for about 12 minutes.
4. Dish out and serve hot.

410. Parmesan Artichokes

Servings: 4
Cooking Time: 35 Minutes
Ingredients:
- 2 medium artichokes, trimmed and quartered, with the centers removed

- 2 tbsp. coconut oil, melted
- 1 egg, beaten
- ½ cup parmesan cheese, grated
- ¼ cup blanched, finely ground flour

Directions:
1. Place the artichokes in a bowl with the coconut oil and toss to coat, then dip the artichokes into a bowl of beaten egg.
2. In a separate bowl, mix together the parmesan cheese and the flour. Combine with the pieces of artichoke, making sure to coat each piece well. Transfer the artichoke to the fryer.
3. Cook at 400°F for ten minutes, shaking occasionally throughout the cooking time. Serve hot.

411. Cheesy Kale

Servings: 2
Cooking Time: 15 Minutes
Ingredients:
- lb. kale
- 8 oz. parmesan cheese, shredded
- 1 onion, diced
- 1 tsp. butter
- 1 cup heavy cream

Directions:
1. Dice up the kale, discarding any hard stems. In a baking dish small enough to fit inside the fryer, combine the kale with the parmesan, onion, butter and cream.
2. Pre-heat the fryer at 250°F.
3. Set the baking dish in the fryer and cook for twelve minutes. Make sure to give it a good stir before serving.

412. Crispy Ham Rolls

Servings:3

Cooking Time: 17 Minutes
Ingredients:
- 3 packages Pepperidge farm rolls
- 1 tbsp softened butter
- 1 tsp mustard seeds
- 1 tsp poppy seeds
- 1 small chopped onion

Directions:
1. Mix butter, mustard, onion and poppy seeds. Spread the mixture on top of the rolls. Cover with the chopped ham. Roll up and arrange them on the basket of the air fryer; cook at 350 F for 15 minutes.

413. Chili Bean Burritos

Servings:6
Cooking Time: 30 Minutes
Ingredients:
- 1 cup grated cheddar cheese
- 1 can (8 oz) beans
- 1 tsp seasoning, any kind

Directions:
1. Preheat the air fryer to 350 F, and mix the beans with the seasoning. Divide the bean mixture between the tortillas and top with cheddar cheese. Roll the burritos and arrange them on a lined baking dish.Place in the air fryer and cook for 5 minutes, or to your liking.

414. Simple Brown Carrot Roast With Cumin

Servings:6
Cooking Time: 15 Minutes
Ingredients:
- 1 tbsp olive oil
- 1 tsp cumin seeds

- A handful of fresh coriander

Directions:

1. Preheat the fryer to 350 F, and in a bowl, mix oil, carrots, and cumin seeds. Gently stir to coat the carrots well. Place the carrots in your air fryer basket and cook for 12 minutes. Scatter fresh coriander over the carrots.

415. Crispy Shawarma Broccoli

Servings: 4
Cooking Time: 25 Minutes
Ingredients:

- 1 pound broccoli, steamed and drained
- 2 tablespoons canola oil
- 1 teaspoon cayenne pepper
- 1 teaspoon sea salt
- 1 tablespoon Shawarma spice blend

Directions:

1. Toss all ingredients in a mixing bowl.
2. Roast in the preheated Air Fryer at 380 degrees F for 10 minutes, shaking the basket halfway through the cooking time.
3. Work in batches. Bon appétit!

416. Skewered Corn In Air Fryer

Servings:2
Cooking Time: 25 Minutes
Ingredients:

- 1-pound apricot, halved
- 2 ears of corn
- 2 medium green peppers, cut into large chunks
- 2 teaspoons prepared mustard
- Salt and pepper to taste

Directions:

1. Preheat the air fryer to 330°F.
2. Place the grill pan accessory in the air fryer.
3. On the double layer rack with the skewer accessories, skewer the corn, green peppers, and apricot. Season with salt and pepper to taste.
4. Place skewered corn on the double layer rack and cook for 25 minutes.
5. Once cooked, brush with prepared mustard.

417. Roasted Brussels Sprouts & Pine Nuts

Servings:6
Cooking Time: 20 Minutes
Ingredients:

- 1 tbsp olive oil
- 1 ¾ oz raisins, soaked
- Juice of 1 orange
- salt to taste
- 1 ¾ oz toasted pine nuts

Directions:

1. Preheat your air fryer to 392 F. In a bowl, pop the sprouts with oil and salt and stir to combine well. Add the sprouts to the air fryer and roast for 15 minutes. Mix with toasted pine nuts and soaked raisins. Drizzle with orange juice to serve.

418. Roasted Cauliflower

Servings: 2
Cooking Time: 20 Minutes
Ingredients:

- medium head cauliflower
- 2 tbsp. salted butter, melted
- 1 medium lemon
- 1 tsp. dried parsley

- ½ tsp. garlic powder

Directions:

1. Having removed the leaves from the cauliflower head, brush it with the melted butter. Grate the rind of the lemon over it and then drizzle some juice. Finally add the parsley and garlic powder on top.
2. Transfer the cauliflower to the basket of the fryer.
3. Cook for fifteen minutes at 350°F, checking regularly to ensure it doesn't overcook. The cauliflower is ready when it is hot and fork tender.
4. Take care when removing it from the fryer, cut up and serve.

419. Mozzarella Cabbage With Blue Cheese

Servings:4
Cooking Time: 25 Minutes
Ingredients:

- 2 cups Parmesan cheese, chopped
- 4 tbsp melted butter
- Salt and pepper to taste
- ½ cup blue cheese sauce

Directions:

1. Preheat your air fryer to 380 F, and cover cabbage wedges with melted butter; coat with mozzarella. Place the coated cabbage in the cooking basket and cook for 20 minutes. Serve with blue cheese.

420. Mushroom Loaf

Servings: 2
Cooking Time: 20 Minutes
Ingredients:

- 2 cups mushrooms, chopped

- ½ cups cheddar cheese, shredded
- ¾ cup flour
- 2 tbsp. butter, melted
- 2 eggs

Directions:

1. In a food processor, pulse together the mushrooms, cheese, flour, melted butter, and eggs, along with some salt and pepper if desired, until a uniform consistency is achieved.
2. Transfer into a silicone loaf pan, spreading and levelling with a palette knife.
3. Pre-heat the fryer at 375°F and put the rack inside.
4. Set the loaf pan on the rack and cook for fifteen minutes.
5. Take care when removing the pan from the fryer and leave it to cool. Then slice and serve.

421. Spinach & Feta Crescent Triangles

Servings:4
Cooking Time: 20 Minutes
Ingredients:

- 1 cup steamed spinach
- 1 cup crumbled feta cheese
- ¼ tsp garlic powder
- 1 tsp chopped oregano
- ¼ tsp salt

Directions:

1. Preheat the air fryer to 350 F, and roll the dough onto a lightly floured flat surface. Combine the feta, spinach, oregano, salt, and garlic powder together in a bowl. Cut the dough into 4 equal pieces.
2. Divide the spinach/feta mixture between the dough pieces. Fold the

dough and secure with a fork. Place onto a lined baking dish, and then in the air fryer. Cook for 12 minutes, until lightly browned.

422. Easy Fried Tomatoes

Servings:3
Cooking Time: 15 Minutes
Ingredients:
- ¼ tbsp creole seasoning
- Salt and pepper to taste
- ¼ cup flour
- ½ cup buttermilk
- breadcrumbs as needed

Directions:
1. Add flour to one bowl and buttermilk to another. Season tomatoes with salt and pepper. Make a mix of creole seasoning and breadcrumbs. Cover tomato slices with flour, dip in buttermilk and then into the breadcrumbs. Cook the tomato slices in your air fryer for 5 minutes at 400 F. Serve.

423. Feisty Baby Carrots

Servings:4
Cooking Time: 20 Minutes
Ingredients:
- 1 tsp dried dill
- 1 tbsp olive oil
- 1 tbsp honey
- Salt and pepper to taste

Directions:
1. Preheat air fryer to 350 F. In a bowl, mix oil, carrots and honey; stir to coat. Season with dill, pepper and salt. Place the prepared carrots in your air fryer's cooking basket and cook for 12 minutes.

424. Melted Cheese 'n Almonds On Tomato

Servings:3
Cooking Time: 20 Minutes
Ingredients:
- ¼ cup toasted almonds
- 1 yellow red bell pepper, chopped
- 3 large tomatoes
- 4 ounces Monterey Jack cheese
- Salt and pepper to taste

Directions:
1. Preheat the air fryer to 330°F.
2. Place the grill pan accessory in the air fryer.
3. Slice the tops of the tomatoes and remove the seeds to create hollow "cups."
4. In a mixing bowl, combine the cheese, bell pepper, and almonds. Season with salt and pepper to taste.
5. Stuff the tomatoes with the cheese filling.
6. Place the stuffed tomatoes on the grill pan and cook for 15 to 20 minutes.

425. Lemony Green Beans

Servings:3
Cooking Time:12 Minutes
Ingredients:
- 1 pound green beans, trimmed and halved
- 1 teaspoon butter, melted
- 1 tablespoon fresh lemon juice
- ¼ teaspoon garlic powder

Directions:
1. Preheat the Air fryer to 400 °F and grease an Air fryer basket.
2. Mix all the ingredients in a bowl and toss to coat well.

3. Arrange the green beans into the Air fryer basket and cook for about 12 minutes.
4. Dish out in a serving plate and serve hot.

426. Eggplant Caviar

Servings:3
Cooking Time: 20 Minutes
Ingredients:
- ½ red onion, chopped and blended
- 2 tbsp balsamic vinegar
- 1 tbsp olive oil
- salt

Directions:
1. Arrange the eggplants in the basket and cook them for 15 minutes at 380 F. Remove them and let them cool. Then cut the eggplants in half, lengthwise, and empty their insides with a spoon.
2. Blend the onion in a blender. Put the inside of the eggplants in the blender and process everything. Add the vinegar, olive oil and salt, then blend again. Serve cool with bread and tomato sauce or ketchup.

427. Avocado Rolls

Servings:5
Cooking Time: 15 Minutes
Ingredients:
- 10 egg roll wrappers
- 1 tomato, diced
- ¼ tsp pepper
- ½ tsp salt

Directions:
1. Place all filling ingredients in a bowl; mash with a fork until somewhat smooth. There should be chunks left. Divide the feeling between the egg

wrappers. Wet your finger and brush along the edges, so the wrappers can seal well. Roll and seal the wrappers.
2. Arrange them on a baking sheet lined dish, and place in the air fryer. Cook at 350 F for 5 minutes. Serve with sweet chili dipping and enjoy.

428. Garden Fresh Green Beans

Servings:4
Cooking Time:12 Minutes
Ingredients:
- 1 pound green beans, washed and trimmed
- 1 teaspoon butter, melted
- 1 tablespoon fresh lemon juice
- ¼ teaspoon garlic powder
- Salt and freshly ground pepper, to taste

Directions:
1. Preheat the Air fryer to 400 °F and grease an Air fryer basket.
2. Put all the ingredients in a large bowl and transfer into the Air fryer basket.
3. Cook for about 8 minutes and dish out in a bowl to serve warm.

429. Red Wine Infused Mushrooms

Servings:6
Cooking Time:30 Minutes
Ingredients:
- 1 tablespoon butter
- 2 pounds fresh mushrooms, quartered
- 2 teaspoons Herbs de Provence
- ½ teaspoon garlic powder
- 2 tablespoons red wine

Directions:

1. Preheat the Air fryer to 325 °F and grease an Air fryer pan.
2. Mix the butter, Herbs de Provence, and garlic powder in the Air fryer pan and toss to coat well.
3. Cook for about 2 minutes and stir in the mushrooms and red wine.
4. Cook for about 28 minutes and dish out in a platter to serve hot.

430. Air-fried Cauliflower

Servings:4
Cooking Time: 20 Minutes
Ingredients:
- 2 tbsp olive oil
- ½ tsp salt
- ¼ tsp freshly ground black pepper
Directions:
1. In a bowl, toss cauliflower, oil, salt, and black pepper, until the florets are well-coated. Arrange the florets in the air fryer and cook for 8 minutes at 360 F; work in batches if needed. Serve the crispy cauliflower in lettuce wraps with chicken, cheese or mushrooms.

431. Elegant Garlic Mushroom

Servings:3
Cooking Time: 20 Minutes
Ingredients:
- 2 tbsp vermouth
- ½ tsp garlic powder
- 1 tbsp olive oil
- 2 tsp herbs
- 1 tbsp duck fat
Directions:
1. Preheat your air fryer to 350 F, add duck fat, garlic powder and herbs in a blender, and process. Pour the mixture over the mushrooms and cover with vermouth. Place the mushrooms in the cooking basket and cook for 10 minutes. Top with more vermouth and cook for 5 more minutes.

432. Crispy Air-fried Tofu

Servings:4
Cooking Time: 25 Minutes
Ingredients:
- 2 tbsp olive oil
- ½ cup flour
- ½ cup crushed cornflakes
- Salt and black pepper to taste
- Cooking spray
Directions:
1. Sprinkle oil over tofu and massage gently until well-coated. On a plate, mix flour, cornflakes, salt, and black pepper. Dip each strip into the mixture to coat, spray with oil and arrange the strips in your air fryer lined with baking paper. Cook for 14 minutes at 360 F, turning once halfway through.

433. Easy Fry Portobello Mushroom

Servings:2
Cooking Time: 10 Minutes
Ingredients:
- 1 tablespoon cooking oil
- 1-pound Portobello mushroom, sliced
- Salt and pepper to taste
Directions:
1. Place the grill pan accessory in the air fryer.
2. In a bowl, place all Ingredients and toss to coat and season the mushrooms.
3. Place in the grill pan.
4. Close the air fryer and cook for 10 minutes at 330°F.

434. Hasselback Potatoes

Servings:4
Cooking Time:30 Minutes
Ingredients:
- 4 potatoes
- 2 tablespoons Parmesan cheese, shredded
- 1 tablespoon fresh chives, chopped
- 2 tablespoons olive oil

Directions:
1. Preheat the Air fryer to 355 F and grease an Air fryer basket.
2. Cut slits along each potato about ¼-inch apart with a sharp knife, making sure slices should stay connected at the bottom.
3. Coat the potatoes with olive oil and arrange into the Air fryer basket.
4. Cook for about 30 minutes and dish out in a platter.
5. Top with chives and Parmesan cheese to serve.

435. Croissant Rolls

Servings:8
Cooking Time: 6 Minutes
Ingredients:
- 1 (8-ounces) can croissant rolls
- 4 tablespoons butter, melted

Directions:
1. Set the temperature of air fryer to 320 degrees F. Grease an air fryer basket.
2. Arrange croissant rolls into the prepared air fryer basket.
3. Air fry for about 4 minutes.
4. Flip the side and air fry for 1-2 more minutes.
5. Remove from the air fryer and transfer onto a platter.

6. Drizzle with the melted butter and serve hot.

436. Indian Plantain Chips

Servings: 2
Cooking Time: 30 Minutes
Ingredients:
- 1 pound plantain, thinly sliced
- 1 tablespoon turmeric
- 2 tablespoons coconut oil

Directions:
1. Fill a large enough cup with water and add the turmeric to the water.
2. Soak the plantain slices in the turmeric water for 15 minutes. Brush with coconut oil and transfer to the Air Fryer basket.
3. Cook in the preheated Air Fryer at 400 degrees F for 10 minutes, shaking the cooking basket halfway through the cooking time.
4. Serve at room temperature. Enjoy!

437. Perfectly Roasted Mushrooms

Servings:4
Cooking Time:32 Minutes
Ingredients:
- 1 tablespoon butter
- 2 pounds mushrooms, quartered
- 2 tablespoons white vermouth
- 2 teaspoons herbs de Provence
- ½ teaspoon garlic powder

Directions:
1. Preheat the Air fryer to 320 °F and grease an Air fryer pan.
2. Mix herbs de Provence, garlic powder and butter in the Air fryer pan and transfer into the Air fryer basket.

3. Cook for about 2 minutes and stir in the mushrooms.
4. Cook for about 25 minutes and add white vermouth.
5. Cook for 5 more minutes and dish out to serve warm.

438. Simple Air Fried Ravioli

Servings:6
Cooking Time: 15 Minutes
Ingredients:
- 2 cup Italian breadcrumbs
- ¼ cup Parmesan cheese
- 1 cup buttermilk
- 1 tsp olive oil
- ¼ tsp garlic powder

Directions:
1. Preheat the air fryer to 390 F, and in a small bowl, combine the breadcrumbs, Parmesan cheese, garlic powder, and olive oil. Dip the ravioli in the buttermilk and then coat them with the breadcrumb mixture.
2. Line a baking sheet with parchment paper and arrange the ravioli on it. Place in the air fryer and cook for 5 minutes. Serve the air-fried ravioli with marinara jar sauce.

439. Broccoli & Parmesan Dish

Servings:4
Cooking Time: 25 Minutes

Ingredients:
- 1 tbsp olive oil
- 1 lemon, Juiced
- Salt and pepper to taste
- 1-ounce Parmesan cheese, grated

Directions:
1. In a bowl, mix all ingredients. Add the mixture to your air fryer and cook for 20 minutes at 360 F. Serve.

440. Turmeric Crispy Chickpeas

Servings:4
Cooking Time: 22 Minutes
Ingredients:
- 1 tbsp butter, melted
- ½ tsp dried rosemary
- ¼ tsp turmeric
- Salt to taste

Directions:
1. Preheat the Air fryer to 380 F.
2. In a bowl, combine together chickpeas, butter, rosemary, turmeric, and salt; toss to coat. Place the prepared chickpeas in your Air Fryer's cooking basket and cook for 6 minutes. Slide out the basket and shake; cook for another 6 minutes until crispy.

SNACKS & APPETIZERS RECIPES

441. Homemade Mayonnaise

Servings: 4
Cooking Time: 30 Minutes
Ingredients:
- 1 large egg
- Juice from 1 lemon.
- 1 tsp dry mustard
- ½ tsp black pepper
- 1 cup avocado oil

Directions:
1. Combine the egg and lemon juice in a container and let sit for 20 minutes.
2. Add the dry mustard, pepper, and avocado oil.
3. Insert an electric whisk into the container.
4. Blend for 30 seconds.
5. Transfer to a sealed container and store in your refrigerator.

442. Creamy Cheddar Eggs

Servings:8
Cooking Time: 16 Minutes
Ingredients:
- 4 eggs
- 2 oz pork rinds
- ¼ cup Cheddar cheese, shredded
- 1 tablespoon heavy cream
- 1 teaspoon fresh dill, chopped

Directions:
1. Place the eggs in the air fryer and cook them at 255F for 16 minutes. Then cool the eggs in the cold water and peel. Cut every egg into the halves and remove the egg yolks. Transfer the egg yolks in the mixing bowl. Add shredded cheese, heavy cream, and fresh dill. Stir the mixture with the help of the fork until smooth and add pork rinds. Mix it up. Fill the egg whites with the egg yolk mixture.

443. Parmesan Green Beans Sticks

Servings: 4
Cooking Time: 12 Minutes
Ingredients:
- 12 ounces green beans, trimmed
- 1 cup parmesan, grated
- 1 egg, whisked
- A pinch of salt and black pepper
- ¼ teaspoon sweet paprika

Directions:
1. In a bowl, mix the parmesan with salt, pepper and the paprika and stir. Put the egg in a separate bowl, Dredge the green beans in egg and then in the parmesan mix. Arrange the green beans in your air fryer's basket and cook at 380 degrees F for 12 minutes. Serve as a snack.

444. Fried Green Tomatoes

Servings: 2
Cooking Time: 10 Minutes
Ingredients:
- 2 medium green tomatoes
- 1 egg
- ¼ cup blanched finely ground flour
- 1/3 cup parmesan cheese, grated

Directions:
1. Slice the tomatoes about a half-inch thick.

2. Crack the egg into a bowl and beat it with a whisk. In a separate bowl, mix together the flour and parmesan cheese.
3. Dredge the tomato slices in egg, then dip them into the flour-cheese mixture to coat. Place each slice into the fryer basket. They may need to be cooked in multiple batches.
4. Cook at 400°F for seven minutes, turning them halfway through the cooking time, and then serve warm.

445. Roasted Peppers

Servings: 4
Cooking Time: 40 Minutes
Ingredients:
- 12 medium bell peppers
- 1 sweet onion, small
- 1 tbsp. Maggi sauce
- 1 tbsp. extra virgin olive oil

Directions:
1. 1 Warm up the olive oil and Maggi sauce in Air Fryer at 320°F.
2. 2 Peel the onion, slice it into 1-inch pieces, and add it to the Air Fryer.
3. 3 Wash and de-stem the peppers. Slice them into 1-inch pieces and remove all the seeds, with water if necessary [ensuring to dry the peppers afterwards].
4. 4 Place the peppers in the Air Fryer.
5. 5 Cook for about 25 minutes, or longer if desired. Serve hot.

446. Sweet Corn And Bell Pepper Sandwich With Barbecue Sauce

Servings:2
Cooking Time:23 Minutes

Ingredients:
- 2 tablespoons butter, softened
- 1 cup sweet corn kernels
- 1 roasted green bell pepper, chopped
- 4 bread slices, trimmed and cut horizontally
- ¼ cup barbecue sauce

Directions:
1. Preheat the Air fryer to 355 F and grease an Air fryer basket.
2. Heat butter in a skillet on medium heat and add corn.
3. Sauté for about 2 minutes and dish out in a bowl.
4. Add bell pepper and barbecue sauce to the corn.
5. Spread corn mixture on one side of 2 bread slices and top with remaining slices.
6. Dish out and serve warm.

447. Chocolate Bacon Bites

Servings: 4
Cooking Time: 10 Minutes
Ingredients:
- 4 bacon slices, halved
- 1 cup dark chocolate, melted
- A pinch of pink salt

Directions:
1. Dip each bacon slice in some chocolate, sprinkle pink salt over them, put them in your air fryer's basket and cook at 350 degrees F for 10 minutes. Serve as a snack.

448. Rutabaga Fries

Servings: 8
Cooking Time: 18 Minutes
Ingredients:

- 1 lb rutabaga, cut into fries shape
- 2 tsp olive oil
- 1 tsp garlic powder
- 1/2 tsp chili pepper
- 1/2 tsp salt

Directions:
1. Add all ingredients into the large mixing bowl and toss to coat.
2. Preheat the air fryer to 365 F.
3. Transfer rutabaga fries into the air fryer basket and cook for 18 minutes. Shake 2-3 times.
4. Serve and enjoy.

449. Blue Cheesy Potato Wedges

Servings: 4
Cooking Time: 20 Minutes
Ingredients:
- 2 Yukon Gold potatoes, peeled and cut into wedges
- 2 tablespoons ranch seasoning
- Kosher salt, to taste
- 1/2 cup blue cheese, crumbled

Directions:
1. Sprinkle the potato wedges with the ranch seasoning and salt. Grease generously the Air Fryer basket.
2. Place the potatoes in the cooking basket.
3. Roast in the preheated Air Fryer at 400 degrees for 12 minutes. Top with the cheese and roast an additional 3 minutes or until cheese begins to melt. Bon appétit!

450. Coconut Radish Chips

Servings: 4
Cooking Time: 15 Minutes

Ingredients:
- 16 ounces radishes, thinly sliced
- A pinch of salt and black pepper
- 2 tablespoons coconut oil, melted

Directions:
1. In a bowl, mix the radish slices with salt, pepper and the oil, toss well, place them in your air fryer's basket and cook at 400 degrees F for 15 minutes, flipping them halfway. Serve as a snack.

451. Bacon Butter

Servings:5
Cooking Time: 2 Minutes
Ingredients:
- ½ cup butter
- 3 oz bacon, chopped

Directions:
1. Preheat the air fryer to 400F and put the bacon inside. Cook it for 8 minutes. Stir the bacon every 2 minutes. Meanwhile, soften the butter in the oven and put it in the butter mold. Add cooked bacon and churn the butter. Refrigerate the butter for 30 minutes.

452. Hot Cheesy Dip

Servings: 6
Cooking Time: 12 Minutes
Ingredients:
- 12 ounces coconut cream
- 2 teaspoons keto hot sauce
- 8 ounces cheddar cheese, grated

Directions:
1. In ramekin, mix the cream with hot sauce and cheese and whisk. Put the ramekin in the fryer and cook at 390 degrees F for 12 minutes. Whisk, divide into bowls and serve as a dip.

453. Brussels Sprout Crisps

Servings: 4
Cooking Time: 20 Minutes
Ingredients:
- 1 pound Brussels sprouts, ends and yellow leaves removed and halved lengthwise
- Salt and black pepper, to taste
- 1 tablespoon toasted sesame oil
- 1 teaspoon fennel seeds
- Chopped fresh parsley, for garnish

Directions:
1. Place the Brussels sprouts, salt, pepper, sesame oil, and fennel seeds in a resealable plastic bag. Seal the bag and shake to coat.
2. Air-fry at 380 degrees F for 15 minutes or until tender. Make sure to flip them over halfway through the cooking time.
3. Serve sprinkled with fresh parsley. Bon appétit!

454. Parmesan & Garlic Cauliflower

Servings: 4
Cooking Time: 40 Minutes
Ingredients:
- 3/4 cup cauliflower florets
- 2 tbsp butter
- 1 clove garlic, sliced thinly
- 2 tbsp shredded parmesan
- 1 pinch of salt

Directions:
1. Preheat your fryer to 350°F/175°C.
2. On a low heat, melt the butter with the garlic for 5-10 minutes.
3. Strain the garlic in a sieve.

4. Add the cauliflower, parmesan and salt.
5. Bake for 20 minutes or until golden.

455. Bbq Lil Smokies

Servings: 6
Cooking Time: 20 Minutes
Ingredients:
- 1 pound beef cocktail wieners
- 10 ounces barbecue sauce, no sugar added

Directions:
1. Start by preheating your Air Fryer to 380 degrees F.
2. Prick holes into your sausages using a fork and transfer them to the baking pan.
3. Cook for 13 minutes. Spoon the barbecue sauce into the pan and cook an additional 2 minutes.
4. Serve with toothpicks. Bon appétit!

456. Crispy Crackling Bites

Servings: 10
Cooking Time: 50 Minutes
Ingredients:
- 1 pound pork rind raw, scored by the butcher
- 1 tablespoon sea salt
- 2 tablespoons smoked paprika

Directions:
1. Sprinkle and rub salt on the skin side of the pork rind. Allow it to sit for 30 minutes.
2. Roast at 380 degrees F for 8 minutes; turn them over and cook for a further 8 minutes or until blistered.
3. Sprinkle the smoked paprika all over the pork crackling and serve. Bon appétit!

457. Brussels Sprouts

Servings: 2
Cooking Time: 15 Minutes
Ingredients:
- 2 cups Brussels sprouts, sliced in half
- 1 tbsp. balsamic vinegar
- 1 tbsp. olive oil
- ¼ tsp. salt

Directions:
1. Toss all of the ingredients together in a bowl, coating the Brussels sprouts well.
2. Place the sprouts in the Air Fryer basket and air fry at 400°F for 10 minutes, shaking the basket at the halfway point.

458. Sprouts Wraps

Servings: 12
Cooking Time: 20 Minutes
Ingredients:
- 12 bacon strips
- 12 Brussels sprouts
- A drizzle of olive oil

Directions:
1. Wrap each Brussels sprouts in a bacon strip, brush them with some oil, put them in your air fryer's basket and cook at 350 degrees F for 20 minutes. Serve as an appetizer.

459. Zucchini Rolls

Servings: 2 – 4
Cooking Time: 15 Minutes
Ingredients:
- 3 zucchinis, sliced thinly lengthwise with a mandolin or very sharp knife
- 1 tbsp. olive oil
- 1 cup goat cheese
- ¼ tsp. black pepper

Directions:
1. Preheat your Air Fryer to 390°F.
2. Coat each zucchini strip with a light brushing of olive oil.
3. Combine the sea salt, black pepper and goat cheese.
4. Scoop a small, equal amount of the goat cheese onto the center of each strip of zucchini. Roll up the strips and secure with a toothpick.
5. Transfer to the Air Fryer and cook for 5 minutes until the cheese is warm and the zucchini slightly crispy. If desired, add some tomato sauce on top.

460. Bacon-wrapped Brie

Servings: 1
Cooking Time: 15 Minutes
Ingredients:
- 4 slices sugar-free bacon
- 8 oz. brie cheese

Directions:
1. On a cutting board, lay out the slices of bacon across each other in a star shape (two Xs overlaid). Then place the entire round of brie in the center of this star.
2. Lift each slice of bacon to wrap it over the brie and use toothpicks to hold everything in place. Cut up a piece of parchment paper to fit in your fryer's basket and place it inside, followed by the wrapped brie, setting it in the center of the sheet of parchment.
3. Cook at 400°F for seven minutes. Turn the brie over and cook for a further three minutes.
4. It is ready once the bacon is crispy and cheese is melted on the inside.
5. Slice up the brie and enjoy hot.

461. Curried Sweet Potato Fries

Servings: 3
Cooking Time: 20 Minutes
Ingredients:

- 2 small sweet potatoes, peel and cut into fries shape
- 1/4 tsp coriander
- 1/2 tsp curry powder
- 2 tbsp olive oil
- 1/4 tsp sea salt

Directions:

1. Add all ingredients into the large mixing bowl and toss well.
2. Spray air fryer basket with cooking spray.
3. Transfer sweet potato fries in the air fryer basket.
4. Cook for 20 minutes at 370 F. Shake halfway through.
5. Serve and enjoy.

462. Cheesy Garlic Bread

Servings: 2
Cooking Time: 20 Minutes
Ingredients:

- 1 friendly baguette
- 4 tsp. butter, melted
- 3 chopped garlic cloves
- 5 tsp. sundried tomato pesto
- 1 cup mozzarella cheese, grated

Directions:

1. 1 Cut your baguette into 5 thick round slices.
2. 2 Add the garlic cloves to the melted butter and brush onto each slice of bread.
3. 3 Spread a teaspoon of sun dried tomato pesto onto each slice.
4. 4 Top each slice with the grated mozzarella.
5. 5 Transfer the bread slices to the Air Fryer and cook them at 180°F for 6 – 8 minutes.
6. 6 Top with some freshly chopped basil leaves, chili flakes and oregano if desired.

463. Cheese Rounds

Servings:4
Cooking Time: 6 Minutes
Ingredients:

- 1 cup Cheddar cheese, shredded

Directions:

1. Preheat the air fryer to 400F. Then line the air fryer basket with baking paper. Sprinkle the cheese on the baking paper in the shape of small rounds. Cook them for 6 minutes or until the cheese is melted and starts to be crispy.

464. Potato Chips

Servings: 4
Cooking Time: 45 Minutes
Ingredients:

- 2 large potatoes, peel and sliced
- 1 tbsp. rosemary
- 3.5 oz. sour cream
- ¼ tsp. salt

Directions:

1. Place the potato slices in water and allow to absorb for 30 minutes.
2. Drain the potato slices and transfer to a large bowl. Toss with the rosemary, sour cream, and salt.
3. Pre-heat the Air Fryer to 320°F

4. Put the coated potato slices in the fryer's basket and cook for 35 minutes. Serve hot.

465. Avocado Fries

Servings: 4
Cooking Time: 20 Minutes
Ingredients:
- ½ cup panko
- ½ tsp. salt
- 1 whole avocado
- 1 oz. aquafaba

Directions:
1. In a shallow bowl, stir together the panko and salt.
2. In a separate shallow bowl, add the aquafaba.
3. Dip the avocado slices into the aquafaba, before coating each one in the panko.
4. Place the slices in your Air Fryer basket, taking care not to overlap any. Air fry for 10 minutes at 390°F.

466. Cheesy Polenta Sticks

Servings:4
Cooking Time:6 Minutes
Ingredients:
- 2½ cups cooked polenta
- ¼ cup Parmesan cheese
- 1 tablespoon olive oil
- Salt, to taste

Directions:
1. Preheat the Air fryer to 350 and grease a baking dish with olive oil.
2. Place polenta in the baking dish and refrigerate, covered for about 1 hour.
3. Remove from the refrigerator and cut into desired sized slices.

4. Place polenta sticks into the Air fryer and season with salt.
5. Top with Parmesan cheese and cook for about 6 minutes.
6. Dish out and serve warm.

467. Pickled Bacon Bowls

Servings: 4
Cooking Time: 20 Minutes
Ingredients:
- 4 dill pickle spears, sliced in half and quartered
- 8 bacon slices, halved
- 1 cup avocado mayonnaise

Directions:
1. Wrap each pickle spear in a bacon slice, put them in your air fryer's basket and cook at 400 degrees F for 20 minutes. Divide into bowls and serve as a snack with the mayonnaise.

468. Sweet Potato Fries

Servings: 5
Cooking Time: 35 Minutes
Ingredients:
- 2 large sweet potatoes
- 1 tbsp. extra virgin olive oil

Directions:
1. 1 Wash the sweet potatoes. Dry and peel them before chopping them into shoestring fries. In a bowl, toss the fries with the olive oil to coat well.
2. 2 Set your Air Fryer to 320°F and briefly allow to warm. Put the sweet potatoes in the Air Fryer basket and fry for 15 minutes, stirring them at the halfway point.
3. 3 Once done, toss again to make sure no fries are sticking to each other.

4. 4 Turn the heat to 350°F and cook for a further 10 minutes, again giving them a good stir halfway through the cooking time.
5. 5 Serve your fries straightaway.

469. Brussels Sprouts With Feta Cheese

Servings: 4
Cooking Time: 20 Minutes
Ingredients:
- 3/4 pound Brussels sprouts, trimmed and cut off the ends
- 1 teaspoon kosher salt
- 1 tablespoon lemon zest
- Non-stick cooking spray
- 1 cup feta cheese, cubed

Directions:
1. Firstly, peel the Brussels sprouts using a small paring knife. Toss the leaves with salt and lemon zest; spritz them with a cooking spray, coating all sides.
2. Bake at 380 degrees for 8 minutes; shake the cooking basket halfway through the cooking time and cook for 7 more minutes.
3. Make sure to work in batches so everything can cook evenly. Taste and adjust the seasonings. Serve with feta cheese. Bon appétit!

470. Kale Chips

Servings: 2
Cooking Time: 15 Minutes
Ingredients:
- 1 head kale
- 1 tbsp. olive oil
- 1 tsp. soy sauce

Directions:

1. De-stem the head of kale and shred each leaf into a 1 ½" piece. Wash and dry well.
2. Toss the kale with the olive oil and soy sauce to coat it completely.
3. Transfer to the Air Fryer and cook at 390°F for 2 to 3 minutes, giving the leaves a good toss at the halfway mark.

471. Aromatic Kale Chips

Servings: 4
Cooking Time: 5 Minutes
Ingredients:
- 2 ½ tablespoons olive oil
- 1 ½ teaspoons garlic powder
- 1 bunch of kale, torn into small pieces
- 2 tablespoons lemon juice
- 1 1/2 teaspoons seasoned salt

Directions:
1. Toss your kale with the other ingredients.
2. Cook at 195 degrees F for 4 to 5 minutes, tossing kale halfway through.
3. Serve with your favorite dipping sauce.

472. Spicy Dip

Servings: 6
Cooking Time: 5 Minutes
Ingredients:
- 12 oz hot peppers, chopped
- 1 1/2 cups apple cider vinegar
- Pepper
- Salt

Directions:
1. Add all ingredients into the air fryer baking dish and stir well.
2. Place dish in the air fryer and cook at 380 F for 5 minutes.

3. Transfer pepper mixture into the blender and blend until smooth.
4. Serve and enjoy.

473. Sage Radish Chips

Servings:6
Cooking Time: 35 Minutes
Ingredients:
- 2 cups radish, sliced
- ½ teaspoon sage
- 2 teaspoons avocado oil
- ½ teaspoon salt

Directions:
1. In the mixing bowl mix up radish, sage, avocado oil, and salt. Preheat the air fryer to 320F. Put the sliced radish in the air fryer basket and cook it for 35 minutes. Shake the vegetables every 10 minutes.

474. Buffalo Cauliflower Wings

Servings:4
Cooking Time: 14 Minutes
Ingredients:
- 1 cauliflower head, cut into florets
- 1 tbsp butter, melted
- 1/2 cup buffalo sauce
- Pepper
- Salt

Directions:
1. Spray air fryer basket with cooking spray.
2. In a bowl, mix together buffalo sauce, butter, pepper, and salt.
3. Add cauliflower florets into the air fryer basket and cook at 400 F for 7 minutes.
4. Transfer cauliflower florets into the buffalo sauce mixture and toss well.

5. Again, add cauliflower florets into the air fryer basket and cook for 7 minutes more at 400 F.
6. Serve and enjoy.

475. Quick And Easy Popcorn

Servings: 4
Cooking Time: 20 Minutes
Ingredients:
- 2 tablespoons dried corn kernels
- 1 teaspoon safflower oil
- Kosher salt, to taste
- 1 teaspoon red pepper flakes, crushed

Directions:
1. Add the dried corn kernels to the Air Fryer basket; brush with safflower oil.
2. Cook at 395 degrees F for 15 minutes, shaking the basket every 5 minutes.
3. Sprinkle with salt and red pepper flakes. Bon appétit!

476. Green Beans & S

Servings: 4
Cooking Time: 15 Minutes
Ingredients:
- 1 lb fresh green beans, trimmed
- 2 tbsp butter
- ¼ cup sliced s
- 2 tsp lemon pepper

Directions:
1. Steam the green beans for 8 minutes, until tender, then drain.
2. On a medium heat, melt the butter in a skillet.
3. Sauté the s until browned.
4. Sprinkle with salt and pepper.
5. Mix in the green beans.

477. Sugar Snap Bacon

Servings: 4
Cooking Time: 10 Minutes
Ingredients:
- 3 cups sugar snap peas
- ½ tbsp lemon juice
- 2 tbsp bacon fat
- 2 tsp garlic
- ½ tsp red pepper flakes

Directions:
1. In a skillet, cook the bacon fat until it begins to smoke.
2. Add the garlic and cook for 2 minutes.
3. Add the sugar peas and lemon juice.
4. Cook for 2-3 minutes.
5. Remove and sprinkle with red pepper flakes and lemon zest.
6. Serve!

478. Crust-less Meaty Pizza

Servings: 1
Cooking Time: 15 Minutes
Ingredients:
- ½ cup mozzarella cheese, shredded
- 2 slices sugar-free bacon, cooked and crumbled
- ¼ cup ground sausage, cooked
- 7 slices pepperoni
- 1 tbsp. parmesan cheese, grated

Directions:
1. Spread the mozzarella across the bottom of a six-inch cake pan. Throw on the bacon, sausage, and pepperoni, then add a sprinkle of the parmesan cheese on top. Place the pan inside your air fryer.
2. Cook at 400°F for five minutes. The cheese is ready once brown in color and bubbly. Take care when removing the pan from the fryer and serve.

479. Pickled Chips

Servings:4
Cooking Time: 10 Minutes
Ingredients:
- 1 cup pickles, sliced
- 2 eggs, beaten
- ½ cup coconut flakes
- 1 teaspoon dried cilantro
- ¼ cup Provolone cheese, grated

Directions:
1. Mix up coconut flakes, dried cilantro, and Provolone cheese. Then dip the sliced pickles in the egg and coat in coconut flakes mixture. Preheat the air fryer to 400F. Arrange the pickles in the air fryer in one layer and cook them for 5 minutes. Then flip the pickles on another side and cook for another 5 minutes.

480. Bacon-wrapped Sausage Skewers

Servings: 2
Cooking Time: 8 Minutes
Ingredients:
- 5 Italian chicken sausages
- 10 slices bacon

Directions:
1. Preheat your air fryer to 370°F/190°C.
2. Cut the sausage into four pieces.
3. Slice the bacon in half.
4. Wrap the bacon over the sausage.
5. Skewer the sausage.
6. Fry for 4-5 minutes until browned.

481. Banana Chips

Servings: 3
Cooking Time: 20 Minutes
Ingredients:
- 2 large raw bananas, peel and sliced
- ½ tsp. red chili powder
- 1 tsp. olive oil
- ¼ tsp. turmeric powder
- 1 tsp. salt

Directions:
1. Put some water in a bowl along with the turmeric powder and salt.
2. Place the sliced bananas in the bowl and allow to soak for 10 minutes.
3. Dump the contents into a sieve to strain the banana slices before drying them with a paper towel.
4. Pre-heat the Air Fryer to 350°F.
5. Put the banana slices in a bowl and coat them with the olive oil, chili powder and salt.
6. Transfer the chips to the fryer basket and air fry for 15 minutes.

482. Tortilla Chips

Servings: 2
Cooking Time: 5 Minutes
Ingredients:
- 8 corn tortillas
- Salt to taste
- 1 tbsp. olive oil

Directions:
1. 1 Pre-heat your Air Fryer to 390°F.
2. 2 Slice the corn tortillas into triangles. Coat with a light brushing of olive oil.
3. 3 Put the tortilla pieces in the wire basket and air fry for 3 minutes. You may need to do this in multiple batches.
4. 4 Season with salt before serving.

483. Fried Mushrooms

Servings: 4
Cooking Time: 40 Minutes
Ingredients:
- 2 lb. button mushrooms
- 3 tbsp. white or French vermouth [optional]
- 1 tbsp. coconut oil
- 2 tsp. herbs of your choice
- ½ tsp. garlic powder

Directions:
1. 1 Wash and dry the mushrooms. Slice them into quarters.
2. 2 Pre-heat your Air Fryer at 320°F and add the coconut oil, garlic powder, and herbs to the basket.
3. 3 Briefly cook the ingredients for 2 minutes and give them a stir. Put the mushrooms in the air fryer and cook for 25 minutes, stirring occasionally throughout.
4. 4 Pour in the white vermouth and mix. Cook for an additional 5 minutes.
5. 5 Serve hot.

484. Classic Deviled Eggs

Servings: 3
Cooking Time: 20 Minutes
Ingredients:
- 5 eggs
- 2 tablespoons mayonnaise
- 2 tablespoons sweet pickle relish
- Sea salt, to taste
- 1/2 teaspoon mixed peppercorns, crushed

Directions:

1. Place the wire rack in the Air Fryer basket; lower the eggs onto the wire rack.
2. Cook at 270 degrees F for 15 minutes.
3. Transfer them to an ice-cold water bath to stop the cooking. Peel the eggs under cold running water; slice them into halves.
4. Mash the egg yolks with the mayo, sweet pickle relish, and salt; spoon yolk mixture into egg whites. Arrange on a nice serving platter and garnish with the mixed peppercorns. Bon appétit!

485. Granny's Green Beans

Servings: 4
Cooking Time: 10 Minutes
Ingredients:
- 1 lb green beans, trimmed
- 1 cup butter
- 2 cloves garlic, minced
- 1 cup toasted pine nuts

Directions:
1. Boil a pot of water.
2. Add the green beans and cook until tender for 5 minutes.
3. Heat the butter in a large skillet over a high heat. Add the garlic and pine nuts and sauté for 2 minutes or until the pine nuts are lightly browned.
4. Transfer the green beans to the skillet and turn until coated.
5. Serve!

486. Crispy & Healthy Kale Chips

Servings: 2
Cooking Time: 5 Minutes
Ingredients:

- 1 bunch of kale, remove stem and cut into pieces
- 1/2 tsp garlic powder
- 1 tsp olive oil
- 1/2 tsp salt

Directions:
1. Preheat the air fryer to 370 F.
2. Add all ingredients into the large bowl and toss well.
3. Transfer kale mixture into the air fryer basket and cook for 3 minutes.
4. Shake basket well and cook for 2 minutes more.
5. Serve and enjoy.

487. Crispy Kale Chips

Servings:4
Cooking Time:3 Minutes
Ingredients:

- 1 head fresh kale, stems and ribs removed and cut into 1½ inch pieces
- 1 tablespoon olive oil
- 1 teaspoon soy sauce

Directions:
1. Preheat the Air fryer to 380 F and grease an Air fryer basket.
2. Mix together all the ingredients in a bowl until well combined.
3. Arrange the kale in the Air fryer basket and cook for about 3 minutes, flipping in between.
4. Dish out and serve warm.

488. Crunchy Bacon Bites

Servings:4
Cooking Time: 10 Minutes
Ingredients:
- 4 bacon strips, cut into small pieces
- 1/2 cup pork rinds, crushed

- 1/4 cup hot sauce

Directions:
1. Add bacon pieces in a bowl.
2. Add hot sauce and toss well.
3. Add crushed pork rinds and toss until bacon pieces are well coated.
4. Transfer bacon pieces in air fryer basket and cook at 350 F for 10 minutes.
5. Serve and enjoy.

489. Parmesan Zucchini Bites

Servings: 6
Cooking Time: 10 Minutes
Ingredients:
- 1 egg, lightly beaten
- 4 zucchinis, grated and squeeze out all liquid
- 1 cup shredded coconut
- 1 tsp Italian seasoning
- 1/2 cup parmesan cheese, grated

Directions:
1. Add all ingredients into the bowl and mix until well combined.
2. Spray air fryer basket with cooking spray.
3. Make small balls from zucchini mixture and place into the air fryer basket and cook at 400 F for 10 minutes.
4. Serve and enjoy.

490. Mozzarella Snack

Servings: 8
Cooking Time: 5 Minutes
Ingredients:
- 2 cups mozzarella, shredded
- ¾ cup almond flour
- 2 teaspoons psyllium husk powder
- ¼ teaspoon sweet paprika

Directions:

1. Put the mozzarella in a bowl, melt it in the microwave for 2 minutes, add all the other ingredients quickly and stir really until you obtain a dough. Divide the dough into 2 balls, roll them on 2 baking sheets and cut into triangles. Arrange the tortillas in your air fryer's basket and bake at 370 degrees F for 5 minutes. Transfer to bowls and serve as a snack.

491. Air Fry Bacon

Servings:11
Cooking Time: 10 Minutes
Ingredients:
- 11 bacon slices

Directions:
1. Place half bacon slices in air fryer basket.
2. Cook at 400 F for 10 minutes.
3. Cook remaining half bacon slices using same steps.
4. Serve and enjoy.

492. Fruit Pastries

Servings:8
Cooking Time: 20 Minutes
Ingredients:
- ½ of apple, peeled, cored and chopped
- 1 teaspoon fresh orange zest, finely grated
- ½ tablespoon white sugar
- ½ teaspoon ground cinnamon
- 7.05 ounces prepared frozen puff pastry

Directions:
1. In a bowl, mix together all the ingredients except puff pastry.
2. Cut the pastry in 16 squares.
3. Using a teaspoon, place apple mixture in the center of each square.

4. Fold each square into a triangle and slightly press the edges with your wet fingers.
5. Then, using a fork, firmly press the edges.
6. Set the temperature of Air Fryer to 390 degrees F.
7. Add the pastries into an Air Fryer basket in a single layer in 2 batches.
8. Air Fry for about 10 minutes.
9. Enjoy!

493. Zesty Cilantro Roasted Cauliflower

Servings: 2
Cooking Time: 10 Minutes
Ingredients:
- 2 cups cauliflower florets, chopped
- 2 tbsp. coconut oil, melted
- 2 ½ tsp. taco seasoning mix
- 1 medium lime
- 2 tbsp. cilantro, chopped

Directions:
1. Mix the cauliflower with the melted coconut oil and the taco seasoning, ensuring to coat the florets all over.
2. Cook at 350°F for seven minutes, shaking the basket a few times through the cooking time. Then transfer the cauliflower to a bowl.
3. Squeeze the lime juice over the cauliflower and season with the cilantro. Toss once more to coat and enjoy.

494. Roasted Peanuts

Servings:10
Cooking Time: 14 Minutes
Ingredients:

- 2½ cups raw peanuts
- 1 tablespoon olive oil
- Salt, as required

Directions:
1. Set the temperature of Air Fryer to 320 degrees F.
2. Add the peanuts in an Air Fryer basket in a single layer.
3. Air Fry for about 9 minutes, tossing twice.
4. Remove the peanuts from Air Fryer basket and transfer into a bowl.
5. Add the oil, and salt and toss to coat well.
6. Return the nuts mixture into Air Fryer basket.
7. Air Fry for about 5 minutes.
8. Once done, transfer the hot nuts in a glass or steel bowl and serve.

495. Shrimp Kabobs

Servings: 2
Cooking Time: 8 Minutes
Ingredients:
- 1 cup shrimp
- 1 lime juice
- 1 garlic clove, minced
- 1/4 tsp pepper
- 1/8 tsp salt

Directions:
1. Preheat the air fryer to 350 F.
2. Add shrimp, lime juice, garlic, pepper, and salt into the bowl and toss well.
3. Thread shrimp onto the soaked wooden skewers and place into the air fryer basket.
4. Cook for 8 minutes. Turn halfway through.
5. Serve and enjoy.

496. Pepperoni Chips

Servings: 6
Cooking Time: 8 Minutes
Ingredients:
- 6 oz pepperoni slices

Directions:
1. Place one batch of pepperoni slices in the air fryer basket.
2. Cook for 8 minutes at 360 F.
3. Cook remaining pepperoni slices using same steps.
4. Serve and enjoy.

497. Chocolate Cookie Dough Balls

Servings:6
Cooking Time: 20 Minutes
Ingredients:
- 16½ ounces store-bought chilled chocolate chip cookie dough
- ¼ cup butter, melted
- ½ cup chocolate cookie crumbs
- 2 tablespoons sugar

Directions:
1. Cut the cookie dough into 12 equal-sized pieces and then, shape each into a ball.
2. Add the melted butter in a shallow dish.
3. In another dish, mix together the cookie crumbs, and sugar.
4. Dip each cookie ball in the melted butter and then evenly coat with the cookie crumbs.
5. In the bottom of a baking sheet, place the coated cookie balls and freeze for at least 2 hours.
6. Preheat the air fryer to 350 degrees F.
7. Line the air fryer basket with a piece of foil.
8. Place the cookies balls in an Air Fryer basket in a single layer in 2 batches.
9. Air Fry for about 10 minutes.
10. Enjoy!

498. Cabbage Chips

Servings: 6
Cooking Time: 30 Minutes
Ingredients:
- 1 large cabbage head, tear cabbage leaves into pieces
- 2 tbsp olive oil
- 1/4 cup parmesan cheese, grated
- Pepper
- Salt

Directions:
1. Preheat the air fryer to 250 F.
2. Add all ingredients into the large mixing bowl and toss well.
3. Spray air fryer basket with cooking spray.
4. Divide cabbage in batches.
5. Add one cabbage chips batch in air fryer basket and cook for 25-30 minutes at 250 F or until chips are crispy and lightly golden brown.
6. Serve and enjoy.

499. Simple Banana Chips

Servings:8
Cooking Time:10 Minutes
Ingredients:
- 2 raw bananas, peeled and sliced
- 2 tablespoons olive oil
- Salt and black pepper, to taste

Directions:
1. Preheat the Air fryer to 355 F and grease an Air fryer basket.

2. Drizzle banana slices evenly with olive oil and arrange in the Air fryer basket.
3. Cook for about 10 minutes and season with salt and black pepper.
4. Dish out and serve warm.

500. Roasted Carrots

Servings: 2
Cooking Time: 20 Minutes
Ingredients:
- 1 tbsp. olive oil
- 3 cups baby carrots or carrots, cut into large chunks
- 1 tbsp. honey
- Salt and pepper to taste

Directions:
1. In a bowl, coat the carrots with the honey and olive oil before sprinkling on some salt and pepper.
2. Place into the Air Fryer and cook at 390°F for 12 minutes. Serve hot.

501. Smoked Almonds

Servings: 6
Cooking Time: 6 Minutes
Ingredients:
- 1 cup almonds
- 1/4 tsp cumin
- 1 tsp chili powder
- 1/4 tsp smoked paprika
- 2 tsp olive oil

Directions:
1. Add almond into the bowl and remaining ingredients and toss to coat.
2. Transfer almonds into the air fryer basket and cook at 320 F for 6 minutes. Shake halfway through.
3. Serve and enjoy.

502. Cucumber Sushi

Servings:10
Cooking Time: 10 Minutes
Ingredients:
- 10 bacon slices
- 2 tablespoons cream cheese
- 1 cucumber

Directions:
1. Place the bacon slices in the air fryer in one layer and cook for 10 minutes at 400F. Meanwhile, cut the cucumber into small wedges. When the bacon is cooked, cool it to the room temperature and spread with cream cheese. Then place the cucumber wedges over the cream cheese and roll the bacon into the sushi.

503. Parmigiana Tomato Chips

Servings: 4
Cooking Time: 15 Minutes
Ingredients:
- 4 Roma tomatoes, sliced
- 2 tablespoons olive oil
- Sea salt and white pepper, to taste
- 1 teaspoon Italian seasoning mix
- 1/2 cup Parmesan cheese, grated

Directions:
1. Start by preheating your Air Fryer to 350 degrees F. Generously grease the Air Fryer basket with nonstick cooking oil.
2. Toss the sliced tomatoes with the remaining ingredients. Transfer them to the cooking basket without overlapping.
3. Cook in the preheated Air Fryer for 5 minutes. Shake the cooking basket and

cook an additional 5 minutes. Work in batches.

4. Serve with Mediterranean aioli for dipping, if desired. Bon appétit!

504. Bacon Jalapeno Poppers

Servings: 10
Cooking Time: 8 Minutes
Ingredients:

- 10 jalapeno peppers, cut in half and remove seeds
- 1/3 cup cream cheese, softened
- 5 bacon strips, cut in half

Directions:

1. Preheat the air fryer to 370 F.
2. Stuff cream cheese into each jalapeno half.
3. Wrap each jalapeno half with half bacon strip and place in the air fryer basket.
4. Cook for 6-8 minutes.
5. Serve and enjoy.

505. Steak Nuggets

Servings: 4
Cooking Time: 15 Minutes
Ingredients:

- 1 lb beef steak, cut into chunks
- 1 large egg, lightly beaten
- 1/2 cup pork rind, crushed
- 1/2 cup parmesan cheese, grated
- 1/2 tsp salt

Directions:

1. Add egg in a small bowl.
2. In a shallow bowl, mix together pork rind, cheese, and salt.
3. Dip each steak chunk in egg then coat with pork rind mixture and place on a plate. Place in refrigerator for 30 minutes.

4. Spray air fryer basket with cooking spray.
5. Preheat the air fryer to 400 F.
6. Place steak nuggets in air fryer basket and cook for 15-18 minutes or until cooked. Shake after every 4 minutes.
7. Serve and enjoy.

506. Crunchy Roasted Pepitas

Servings: 4
Cooking Time: 20 Minutes
Ingredients:

- 2 cups fresh pumpkin seeds with shells
- 1 tablespoon olive oil
- 1 teaspoon sea salt
- 1 teaspoon ground coriander
- 1 teaspoon cayenne pepper

Directions:

1. Toss the pumpkin seeds with the olive oil.
2. Spread in an even layer in the Air Fryer basket; roast the seeds at 350 degrees F for 15 minutes, shaking the basket every 5 minutes.
3. Immediately toss the seeds with the salt, coriander, salt, and cayenne pepper. Enjoy!

507. Crispy Shrimps

Servings:2
Cooking Time:8 Minutes
Ingredients:

- 1 egg
- ¼ pound nacho chips, crushed
- 10 shrimps, peeled and deveined
- 1 tablespoon olive oil
- Salt and black pepper, to taste

Directions:

1. Preheat the Air fryer to 365 F and grease an Air fryer basket.
2. Crack egg in a shallow dish and beat well.
3. Place the nacho chips in another shallow dish.
4. Season the shrimps with salt and black pepper, coat into egg and then roll into nacho chips.
5. Place the coated shrimps into the Air fryer basket and cook for about 8 minutes.
6. Dish out and serve warm.

508. Homemade Apple Chips

Servings: 4
Cooking Time: 20 Minutes
Ingredients:
- 2 cooking apples, cored and thinly sliced
- 1 teaspoon peanut oil
- 1/4 teaspoon ground cloves
- 1/4 teaspoon ground cinnamon
- 1 tablespoon smooth peanut butter

Directions:
1. Toss the apple slices with the peanut oil.
2. Bake at 350 degrees F for 5 minutes; shake the basket to ensure even cooking and continue to cook an additional 5 minutes.
3. Spread each apple slice with a little peanut butter and sprinkle with ground cloves and cinnamon. Bon appétit!

509. Amazing Blooming Onion

Servings: 4
Cooking Time: 40 Minutes
Ingredients:
- 4 medium/small onions
- 1 tbsp. olive oil

- 4 dollops of butter

Directions:
1. 1 Peel the onion. Cut off the top and bottom.
2. 2 To make it bloom, cut as deeply as possible without slicing through it completely. 4 cuts [i.e. 8 segments] should do it.
3. 3 Place the onions in a bowl of salted water and allow to absorb for 4 hours to help eliminate the sharp taste and induce the blooming process.
4. 4 Pre-heat your Air Fryer to 355°F.
5. 5 Transfer the onions to the Air Fryer. Pour over a light drizzle of olive oil and place a dollop of butter on top of each onion.
6. 6 Cook or roast for 30 minutes. Remove the outer layer before serving if it is too brown.

510. Flax Cheese Chips

Servings: 2
Cooking Time: 20 Minutes
Ingredients:
- 1 ½ cup cheddar cheese
- 4 tbsp ground flaxseed meal
- Seasonings of your choice

Directions:
1. Preheat your fryer to 425°F/220°C.
2. Spoon 2 tablespoons of cheddar cheese into a mound, onto a non-stick pad.
3. Spread out a pinch of flax seed on each chip.
4. Season and bake for 10-15 minutes.

511. Ranch Kale Chips

Servings: 4
Cooking Time: 5 Minutes

Ingredients:
- 4 cups kale, stemmed
- 1 tbsp nutritional yeast flakes
- 2 tsp ranch seasoning
- 2 tbsp olive oil
- 1/4 tsp salt

Directions:
1. Add all ingredients into the large mixing bowl and toss well.
2. Spray air fryer basket with cooking spray.
3. Add kale in air fryer basket and cook for 4-5 minutes at 370 F. Shake halfway through.
4. Serve and enjoy.

512. Glazed Carrot Chips With Cheese

Servings: 3
Cooking Time: 20 Minutes
Ingredients:
- 3 carrots, sliced into sticks
- 1 tablespoon coconut oil
- 1/3 cup Romano cheese, preferably freshly grated
- 2 teaspoons granulated garlic
- Sea salt and ground black pepper, to taste

Directions:
1. Toss all ingredients in a mixing bowl until the carrots are coated on all sides.
2. Cook at 380 degrees F for 15 minutes, shaking the basket halfway through the cooking time.
3. Serve with your favorite dipping sauce. Bon appétit!

513. Parmesan Turnip Slices

Servings: 8
Cooking Time: 10 Minutes
Ingredients:
- 1 lb turnip, peel and cut into slices
- 1 tbsp olive oil
- 3 oz parmesan cheese, shredded
- 1 tsp garlic powder
- 1 tsp salt

Directions:
1. Preheat the air fryer to 360 F.
2. Add all ingredients into the mixing bowl and toss to coat.
3. Transfer turnip slices into the air fryer basket and cook for 10 minutes.
4. Serve and enjoy.

514. Polenta Sticks

Servings:4
Cooking Time: 6 Minutes
Ingredients:
- 2½ cups cooked polenta
- Salt, as required
- ¼ cup Parmesan cheese, shredded

Directions:
1. Add the polenta evenly into a greased baking dish and with the back of a spoon, smooth the top surface.
2. Cover the baking dish and refrigerate for about 1 hour or until set.
3. Remove from the refrigerator and cut down the polenta into the desired size slices.
4. Set the temperature of Air Fryer to 350 degrees F. Grease a baking dish.
5. Arrange the polenta sticks into the prepared baking dish in a single layer and sprinkle with salt.

6. Place the baking dish into an Air Fryer basket.
7. Air Fry for about 5-6 minutes.
8. Top with the cheese and serve.

515. Curly's Cauliflower

Servings: 4
Cooking Time: 30 Minutes
Ingredients:
- 4 cups bite-sized cauliflower florets
- 1 cup friendly bread crumbs, mixed with 1 tsp. salt
- ¼ cup melted butter [vegan/other]
- ¼ cup buffalo sauce [vegan/other]
- Mayo [vegan/other] or creamy dressing for dipping

Directions:
1. 1 In a bowl, combine the butter and buffalo sauce to create a creamy paste.
2. 2 Completely cover each floret with the sauce.
3. 3 Coat the florets with the bread crumb mixture. Cook the florets in the Air Fryer for approximately 15 minutes at 350°F, shaking the basket occasionally.
4. 4 Serve with a raw vegetable salad, mayo or creamy dressing.

516. Italian Dip

Servings: 8
Cooking Time: 12 Minutes
Ingredients:
- 8 oz cream cheese, softened
- 1 cup mozzarella cheese, shredded
- 1/2 cup roasted red peppers
- 1/3 cup basil pesto
- 1/4 cup parmesan cheese, grated

Directions:

1. Add parmesan cheese and cream cheese into the food processor and process until smooth.
2. Transfer cheese mixture into the air fryer pan and spread evenly.
3. Pour basil pesto on top of cheese layer.
4. Sprinkle roasted pepper on top of basil pesto layer.
5. Sprinkle mozzarella cheese on top of pepper layer and place dish in air fryer basket.
6. Cook dip at 250 F for 12 minutes.
7. Serve and enjoy.

517. Buffalo Cauliflower

Servings: 1
Cooking Time: 10 Minutes
Ingredients:
- ½ packet dry ranch seasoning
- 2 tbsp. salted butter, melted
- Cauliflower florets
- ¼ cup buffalo sauce

Directions:
1. In a bowl, combine the dry ranch seasoning and butter. Toss with the cauliflower florets to coat and transfer them to the fryer.
2. Cook at 400°F for five minutes, shaking the basket occasionally to ensure the florets cook evenly.
3. Remove the cauliflower from the fryer, pour the buffalo sauce over it, and enjoy.

518. Paprika Chips

Servings: 4
Cooking Time: 5 Minutes
Ingredients:
- 8 ounces cheddar cheese, shredded

- 1 teaspoon sweet paprika

Directions:

1. Divide the cheese in small heaps in a pan that fits the air fryer, sprinkle the paprika on top, introduce the pan in the machine and cook at 400 degrees F for 5 minutes. Cool the chips down and serve them.

519. Radish Chips

Servings: 1
Cooking Time: 15 Minutes

Ingredients:

- 2 cups water
- 1 lb. radishes
- ½ tsp. garlic powder
- ¼ tsp. onion powder
- 2 tbsp. coconut oil, melted

Directions:

1. Boil the water over the stove.
2. In the meantime, prepare the radish chips. Slice off the tops and bottoms and, using a mandolin, shave into thin slices of equal size. Alternatively, this step can be completed using your food processor if it has a slicing blade.
3. Put the radish chips in the pot of boiling water and allow to cook for five minutes, ensuring they become translucent. Take care when removing from the water and place them on a paper towel to dry.
4. Add the radish chips, garlic powder, onion powder, and melted coconut oil into a bowl and toss to coat. Transfer the chips to your fryer.
5. Cook at 320°F for five minutes, occasionally giving the basket a good shake to ensure even cooking. The

chips are done when cooked through and crispy. Serve immediately.

520. Bbq Chicken Wings

Servings: 4
Cooking Time: 15 Minutes

Ingredients:

- 1 lb chicken wings
- 1/2 cup BBQ sauce, sugar-free
- 1/4 tsp garlic powder
- Pepper

Directions:

1. Preheat the air fryer to 400 F.
2. Season chicken wings with garlic powder and pepper and place into the air fryer basket.
3. Cook chicken wings for 15 minutes. Shake basket 3-4 times while cooking.
4. Transfer cooked chicken wings in a large mixing bowl. Pour BBQ sauce over chicken wings and toss to coat.
5. Serve and enjoy.

521. Seasoned Crab Sticks

Servings:4
Cooking Time:12 Minutes

Ingredients:

- 1 packet crab sticks, shred into small pieces
- 2 teaspoon sesame oil
- Cajun seasoning, to taste

Directions:

1. Preheat the Air fryer to 320 F and grease an Air fryer basket.
2. Drizzle crab stick pieces with sesame oil and arrange in the Air fryer basket.
3. Cook for about 12 minutes and serve, sprinkled with Cajun seasoning.

522. Roasted Almonds

Servings: 8
Cooking Time: 8 Minutes
Ingredients:
- 2 cups almonds
- 1/4 tsp pepper
- 1 tsp paprika
- 1 tbsp garlic powder
- 1 tbsp soy sauce

Directions:
1. Add pepper, paprika, garlic powder, and soy sauce in a bowl and stir well.
2. Add almonds and stir to coat.
3. Spray air fryer basket with cooking spray.
4. Add almonds in air fryer basket and cook for 6-8 minutes at 320 F. Shake basket after every 2 minutes.
5. Serve and enjoy.

523. Sesame Tortilla Chips

Servings:4
Cooking Time: 4 Minutes
Ingredients:
- 4 low carb tortillas
- ½ teaspoon salt
- 1 teaspoon sesame oil

Directions:
1. Cut the tortillas into the strips. Preheat the air fryer to 365F. Place the tortilla strips in the air fryer basket and sprinkle with sesame oil. Cook them for 3 minutes. Then give a shake to the chips and sprinkle with salt. Cook the chips for 1 minute more.

524. Spinach With Bacon & Shallots

Servings: 4
Cooking Time: 30 Minutes
Ingredients:
- 16 oz raw spinach
- ½ cup chopped white onion
- ½ cup chopped shallot
- ½ pound raw bacon slices
- 2 tbsp butter

Directions:
1. Slice the bacon strips into small narrow pieces.
2. In a skillet, heat the butter and add the chopped onion, shallots and bacon.
3. Sauté for 15-20 minutes or until the onions start to caramelize and the bacon is cooked.
4. Add the spinach and sauté on a medium heat. Stir frequently to ensure the leaves touch the skillet while cooking.
5. Cover and steam for around 5 minutes, stir and continue until wilted.
6. Serve!

525. Mozzarella Sticks

Servings: 4
Cooking Time: 60 Minutes
Ingredients:
- 6 x 1-oz. mozzarella string cheese sticks
- 1 tsp. dried parsley
- ½ oz. pork rinds, finely ground
- ½ cup parmesan cheese, grated
- 2 eggs

Directions:
1. Halve the mozzarella sticks and freeze for forty-five minutes. Optionally you can leave them longer and place in a

Ziploc bag to prevent them from becoming freezer burned.

2. In a small bowl, combine the dried parsley, pork rinds, and parmesan cheese.

3. In a separate bowl, beat the eggs with a fork.

4. Take a frozen mozzarella stick and dip it into the eggs, then into the pork rind mixture, making sure to coat it all over. Proceed with the rest of the cheese sticks, placing each coated stick in the basket of your air fryer.

5. Cook at 400°F for ten minutes, until they are golden brown.

6. Serve hot, with some homemade marinara sauce if desired.

526. Bacon-wrapped Jalapeno Popper

Servings: 4
Cooking Time: 20 Minutes
Ingredients:

- 6 jalapenos
- 1/3 cup medium cheddar cheese, shredded
- ¼ tsp. garlic powder
- 3 oz. full-fat cream cheese
- 12 slices sugar-free bacon

Directions:

1. Prepare the jalapenos by slicing off the tops and halving each one lengthwise. Take care when removing the seeds and membranes, wearing gloves if necessary.

2. In a microwavable bowl, combine the cheddar cheese, garlic powder, and cream cheese. Microwave for half a minute and mix again, before spoon equal parts of this mixture into each of the jalapeno halves.

3. Take a slice of bacon and wrap it around one of the jalapeno halves, covering it entirely. Place it in the basket of your fryer. Repeat with the rest of the bacon and jalapenos.

4. Cook at 400°F for twelve minutes, flipping the peppers halfway through in order to ensure the bacon gets crispy. Make sure not to let any of the contents spill out of the jalapeno halves when turning them.

5. Eat the peppers hot or at room temperature.

527. Roasted Parsnip

Servings: 5
Cooking Time: 55 Minutes
Ingredients:

- 2 lb. parsnips [about 6 large parsnips]
- 2 tbsp. maple syrup
- 1 tbsp. coconut oil
- 1 tbsp. parsley, dried flakes

Directions:

1. 1 Melt the duck fat or coconut oil in your Air Fryer for 2 minutes at 320°F.

2. 2 Rinse the parsnips to clean them and dry them. Chop into 1-inch cubes. Transfer to the fryer.

3. 3 Cook the parsnip cubes in the fat/oil for 35 minutes, tossing them regularly.

4. 4 Season the parsnips with parsley and maple syrup and allow to cook for another 5 minutes or longer to achieve a soft texture throughout. Serve straightaway.

528. Air Fried Chicken Tenders

Servings:4
Cooking Time:10 Minutes
Ingredients:

- 12 oz chicken breasts, cut into tenders
- 1 egg white
- 1/8 cup flour
- ½ cup panko bread crumbs
- Salt and black pepper, to taste

Directions:

1. Preheat the Air fryer to 350 F and grease an Air fryer basket.
2. Season the chicken tenders with salt and black pepper.
3. Coat the chicken tenders with flour, then dip in egg whites and then dredge in the panko bread crumbs.
4. Arrange in the Air fryer basket and cook for about 10 minutes.
5. Dish out in a platter and serve warm.

529. Fried Queso Blanco

Servings: 4
Cooking Time: 170 Minutes
Ingredients:

- 5 oz queso blanco
- 1 ½ tbsp olive oil
- 3 oz cheese
- 2 oz olives
- 1 pinch red pepper flakes

Directions:

1. Cube some cheese and freeze it for 1-2 hours.
2. Pour the oil in a skillet and heat to boil over a medium temperature.

3. Add the cheese cubes and heat till brown.
4. Combine the cheese together using a spatula and flatten.
5. Cook the cheese on both sides, flipping regularly.
6. While flipping, fold the cheese into itself to form crispy layers.
7. Use a spatula to roll it into a block.
8. Remove it from the pan, allow it to cool, cut it into small cubes, and serve.

530. Mini Pepper Poppers

Servings: 4
Cooking Time: 10 Minutes
Ingredients:

- 8 mini sweet peppers
- ¼ cup pepper jack cheese, shredded
- 4 slices sugar-free bacon, cooked and crumbled
- 4 oz. full-fat cream cheese, softened

Directions:

1. Prepare the peppers by cutting off the tops and halving them lengthwise. Then take out the membrane and the seeds.
2. In a small bowl, combine the pepper jack cheese, bacon, and cream cheese, making sure to incorporate everything well
3. Spoon equal-sized portions of the cheese-bacon mixture into each of the pepper halves.
4. Place the peppers inside your fryer and cook for eight minutes at 400°F. Take care when removing them from the fryer and enjoy warm.

DESSERTS RECIPES

531. Grape Stew

Servings: 4
Cooking Time: 14 Minutes
Ingredients:
- 1 pound red grapes
- Juice and zest of 1 lemon
- 26 ounces grape juice

Directions:
1. In a pan that fits your air fryer, add all ingredients and toss.
2. Place the pan in the fryer and cook at 320 degrees F for 14 minutes.
3. Divide into cups, refrigerate, and serve cold.

532. Chocolate Pudding

Servings: 1
Cooking Time: 50 Minutes
Ingredients:
- 3 tbsp chia seeds
- 1 cup unsweetened milk
- 1 scoop cocoa powder
- ¼ cup fresh raspberries
- ½ tsp honey

Directions:
1. Mix together all of the ingredients in a large bowl.
2. Let rest for 15 minutes but stir halfway through.
3. Stir again and refrigerate for 30 minutes. Garnish with raspberries.
4. Serve!

533. White Chocolate Chip Cookies

Servings:8

Cooking Time: 30 Minutes
Ingredients:
- 3 oz brown sugar
- 2 oz white chocolate chips
- 1 tbsp honey
- 1 ½ tbsp milk
- 4 oz butter

Directions:
1. Preheat the air fryer to 350 F, and beat the butter and sugar until fluffy. Beat in the honey, milk, and flour. Gently fold in the chocolate cookies. Drop spoonfuls of the mixture onto a prepared cookie sheet. Cook for 18 minutes.

534. Air Fried Doughnuts

Servings:4
Cooking Time: 25 Minutes
Ingredients:
- 1 tsp baking powder
- ½ cup milk
- 2 ½ tbsp butter
- 1 egg
- 2 oz brown sugar

Directions:
1. Preheat the air fryer to 350 F, and beat the butter with the sugar, until smooth. Beat in eggs, and milk. In a bowl, combine the flour with the baking powder. Gently fold the flour into the butter mixture.
2. Form donut shapes and cut off the center with cookie cutters. Arrange on a lined baking sheet and cook in the fryer for 15 minutes. Serve with whipped cream or icing.

535. Orange Marmalade

Servings: 4
Cooking Time: 20 Minutes
Ingredients:
- 4 oranges, peeled and chopped
- 3 cups sugar
- 1½ cups water

Directions:
1. In a pan that fits your air fryer, mix the oranges with the sugar and the water; stir.
2. Place the pan in the fryer and cook at 340 degrees F for 20 minutes.
3. Stir well, divide into cups, refrigerate, and serve cold.

536. Toasted Coconut Flakes

Servings: 1
Cooking Time: 5 Minutes
Ingredients:
- 1 cup unsweetened coconut flakes
- 2 tsp. coconut oil, melted
- ¼ cup granular erythritol
- Salt

Directions:
1. In a large bowl, combine the coconut flakes, oil, granular erythritol, and a pinch of salt, ensuring that the flakes are coated completely.
2. Place the coconut flakes in your fryer and cook at 300°F for three minutes, giving the basket a good shake a few times throughout the cooking time. Fry until golden and serve.

537. Vanilla Bean Dream

Servings: 1
Cooking Time: 35 Minutes

Ingredients:
- ½ cup extra virgin coconut oil, softened
- ½ cup coconut butter, softened
- Juice of 1 lemon
- Seeds from ½ a vanilla bean

Directions:
1. Whisk the ingredients in an easy-to-pour cup.
2. Pour into a lined cupcake or loaf pan.
3. Refrigerate for 20 minutes. Top with lemon zest.
4. Serve!

538. Apple Crumble

Servings:4
Cooking Time: 25 Minutes
Ingredients:
- 1 (14-ounces) can apple pie filling
- ¼ cup butter, softened
- 9 tablespoons self-rising flour
- 7 tablespoons caster sugar
- Pinch of salt

Directions:
1. Set the temperature of air fryer to 320 degrees F. Lightly, grease a baking dish.
2. Place apple pie filling evenly into the prepared baking dish.
3. In a medium bowl, add the remaining ingredients and mix until a crumbly mixture forms.
4. Spread the mixture evenly over apple pie filling.
5. Arrange the baking dish in an air fryer basket.
6. Air fry for about 25 minutes.
7. Remove the baking dish from air fryer and place onto a wire rack to cool for about 10 minutes.
8. Serve warm.

539. Coconut Berry Pudding

Servings: 6
Cooking Time: 15 Minutes
Ingredients:
- 2 cups coconut cream
- 1 lime zest, grated
- 3 tbsp erythritol
- ¼ cup blueberries
- 1/3 cup blackberries

Directions:
1. Add all ingredients into the blender and blend until well combined.
2. Spray 6 ramekins with cooking spray.
3. Pour blended mixture into the ramekins and place in the air fryer.
4. Cook at 340 F for 15 minutes.
5. Serve and enjoy.

540. Macaroon Bites

Servings: 2
Cooking Time: 30 Minutes
Ingredients:
- 4 egg whites
- ½ tsp vanilla
- ½ tsp EZ-Sweet (or equivalent of 1 cup artificial sweetener)
- 4½ tsp water
- 1 cup unsweetened coconut

Directions:
1. Preheat your fryer to 375°F/190°C.
2. Combine the egg whites, liquids and coconut.
3. Put into the fryer and reduce the heat to 325°F/160°C.
4. Bake for 15 minutes.
5. Serve!

541. Apple Pastry Pouch

Servings:2
Cooking Time: 25 Minutes
Ingredients:
- 1 tablespoon brown sugar
- 2 tablespoons raisins
- 2 small apples, peeled and cored
- 2 puff pastry sheets
- 2 tablespoons butter, melted

Directions:
1. In a bowl, mix together the sugar and raisins.
2. Fill the core of each apple with raisins mixture.
3. Place one apple in the center of each pastry sheet and fold dough to cover the apple completely.
4. Then, pinch the edges to seal.
5. Coat each apple evenly with butter.
6. Set the temperature of air fryer to 355 degrees F. Lightly, grease an air fryer basket.
7. Arrange apple pouches into the prepared air fryer basket in a single layer.
8. Air fry for about 25 minutes.
9. Remove from air fryer and transfer the apple pouches onto a platter.
10. Serve warm.

542. Easy Mug Brownie

Servings: 1
Cooking Time: 10 Minutes
Ingredients:
- 1 scoop chocolate protein powder
- 1 tbsp cocoa powder
- 1/2 tsp baking powder
- 1/4 cup unsweetened almond milk

Directions:

1. Add baking powder, protein powder, and cocoa powder in a mug and mix well.
2. Add milk in a mug and stir well.
3. Place the mug in the air fryer and cook at 390 F for 10 minutes.
4. Serve and enjoy.

543. Brownies Muffins

Servings:12
Cooking Time:10 Minutes
Ingredients:
- 1 package Betty Crocker fudge brownie mix
- ¼ cup walnuts, chopped
- 1 egg
- 2 teaspoons water
- 1/3 cup vegetable oil

Directions:
1. Preheat the Air fryer to 300 °F and grease 12 muffin molds lightly.
2. Mix all the ingredients in a bowl and divide evenly into the muffin molds.
3. Arrange the molds in the Air Fryer basket and cook for about 10 minutes.
4. Dish out and invert the muffins onto wire rack to completely cool before serving.

544. Berry Cookies

Servings: 4
Cooking Time: 9 Minutes
Ingredients:
- 2 teaspoons butter, softened
- 1 tablespoon Splenda
- 1 egg yolk
- ½ cup almond flour
- 1 oz strawberry, chopped, mashed

Directions:

1. In the mixing bowl mix up butter, Splenda, egg yolk, and almond flour. Knead the non-sticky dough. Then make the small balls from the dough. Use your finger to make small holes in every ball. Then fill the balls with mashed strawberries. Preheat the air fryer to 360F. Line the air fryer basket with baking paper and put the cookies inside. Cook them for 9 minutes.

545. Baked Plum Cream

Servings: 4
Cooking Time: 20 Minutes
Ingredients:
- 1 pound plums, pitted and chopped
- ¼ cup swerve
- 1 tablespoon lemon juice
- 1 and ½ cups heavy cream

Directions:
1. In a bowl, mix all the ingredients and whisk really well. Divide this into 4 ramekins, put them in the air fryer and cook at 340 degrees F for 20 minutes. Serve cold.

546. Butter Plums

Servings: 4
Cooking Time: 20 Minutes
Ingredients:
- 2 teaspoons cinnamon powder
- 4 plums, halved
- 4 tablespoons butter, melted
- 3 tablespoons swerve

Directions:
1. In a pan that fits your air fryer, mix the plums with the rest of the ingredients, toss, put the pan in the air fryer and

cook at 300 degrees F for 20 minutes. Divide into cups and serve cold.

547. Banana And Rice Pudding

Servings: 6
Cooking Time: 20 Minutes
Ingredients:
- 1 cup brown rice
- 3 cups milk
- 2 bananas, peeled and mashed
- ½ cup maple syrup
- 1 teaspoon vanilla extract

Directions:
1. Place all the ingredients in a pan that fits your air fryer; stir well.
2. Put the pan in the fryer and cook at 360 degrees F for 20 minutes.
3. Stir the pudding, divide into cups, refrigerate, and serve cold.

548. Bacon Cookies

Servings: 2
Cooking Time: 15 Minutes
Ingredients:
- ¼ tsp. ginger
- 1/5 tsp. baking soda
- 2/3 cup peanut butter
- 2 tbsp. Swerve
- 3 slices bacon, cooked and chopped

Directions:
1. In a bowl, mix the ginger, baking soda, peanut butter, and Swerve together, making sure to combine everything well.
2. Stir in the chopped bacon.
3. With clean hands, shape the mixture into a cylinder and cut in six. Press down each slice into a cookie with your palm.

4. Pre-heat your fryer at 350°F.
5. When the fryer is warm, put the cookies inside and cook for seven minutes. Take care when taking them out of the fryer and allow to cool before serving.

549. Delicious Vanilla Custard

Servings: 2
Cooking Time: 20 Minutes
Ingredients:
- 5 eggs
- 2 tbsp swerve
- 1 tsp vanilla
- ½ cup unsweetened almond milk
- ½ cup cream cheese

Directions:
1. Add eggs in a bowl and beat using a hand mixer.
2. Add cream cheese, sweetener, vanilla, and almond milk and beat for 2 minutes more.
3. Spray two ramekins with cooking spray.
4. Pour batter into the prepared ramekins.
5. Preheat the air fryer to 350 F.
6. Place ramekins into the air fryer and cook for 20 minutes.
7. Serve and enjoy.

550. Lemon Berries Stew

Servings: 4
Cooking Time: 20 Minutes
Ingredients:
- 1 pound strawberries, halved
- 4 tablespoons stevia
- 1 tablespoon lemon juice
- 1 and ½ cups water

Directions:
1. In a pan that fits your air fryer, mix all the ingredients, toss, put it in the fryer

and cook at 340 degrees F for 20 minutes. Divide the stew into cups and serve cold.

551. Chocolate Mug Cake

Servings:1
Cooking Time:13 Minutes
Ingredients:
- ¼ cup self-rising flour
- 1 tablespoon cocoa powder
- 3 tablespoons whole milk
- 5 tablespoons caster sugar
- 3 tablespoons coconut oil

Directions:
1. Preheat the Air fryer to 390 °F and grease a large mug lightly.
2. Mix all the ingredients in a shallow mug until well combined.
3. Arrange the mug into the Air fryer basket and cook for about 13 minutes.
4. Dish out and serve warm.

552. Strawberry Jam

Servings: 6
Cooking Time: 25 Minutes
Ingredients:
- Juice of 2 limes
- 4 cups sugar
- 1 pound strawberries, chopped
- 2 cups water

Directions:
1. In a pan that fits your air fryer, mix the strawberries with the sugar, lime juice and the water; stir.
2. Place the pan in the fryer and cook at 340 degrees F for 25 minutes.
3. Blend the mix using an immersion blender, divide into cups, refrigerate, and serve cold.

553. Apple Tart

Servings:2
Cooking Time:25 Minutes
Ingredients:
- 2½-ounce butter, chopped and divided
- 3 ½-ounce flour
- 1 egg yolk
- 1 large apple, peeled, cored and cut into 12 wedges
- 1-ounce sugar

Directions:
1. Preheat the Air fryer to 390 °F and grease a baking pan lightly.
2. Mix half of the butter and flour in a bowl until a soft dough is formed.
3. Roll the dough into 6-inch round on a floured surface.
4. Place the remaining butter and sugar in a baking pan and arrange the apple wedges in a circular pattern.
5. Top with rolled dough and press gently along the edges of the pan.
6. Transfer the baking pan in the Air fryer basket and cook for about 25 minutes.
7. Dish out and serve hot.

554. Nutella And Banana Pastries

Servings:4
Cooking Time:12 Minutes
Ingredients:
- 1 puff pastry sheet, cut into 4 equal squares
- ½ cup Nutella
- 2 bananas, sliced
- 2 tablespoons icing sugar

Directions:

1. Preheat the Air fryer to 375 F and grease an Air fryer basket.
2. Spread Nutella on each pastry square and top with banana slices and icing sugar.
3. Fold each square into a triangle and slightly press the edges with a fork.
4. Arrange the pastries in the Air fryer basket and cook for about 12 minutes.
5. Dish out and serve immediately.

555. Baked Apples

Servings:2
Cooking Time: 35 Minutes
Ingredients:
- 2 tbsp butter, cold
- 3 tbsp sugar
- 3 tbsp crushed walnuts
- 2 tbsp raisins
- 1 tsp cinnamon

Directions:
1. Preheat the Air fryer to 400 F.
2. In a bowl, add butter, sugar, walnuts, raisins and cinnamon; mix with fingers until you obtain a crumble. Arrange the apples in the air fryer. Stuff the apples with the filling mixture. Cook for 30 minutes.

556. Strawberry Cups

Servings: 8
Cooking Time: 10 Minutes
Ingredients:
- 16 strawberries, halved
- 2 tablespoons coconut oil
- 2 cups chocolate chips, melted

Directions:
1. In a pan that fits your air fryer, mix the strawberries with the oil and the melted chocolate chips, toss gently, put the pan in the air fryer and cook at 340 degrees F for 10 minutes. Divide into cups and serve cold.

557. Moon Pie

Servings:4
Cooking Time: 10 Minutes
Ingredients:
- 8 large marshmallows
- 8 squares each of dark, milk and white chocolate

Directions:
1. Arrange the cracker halves on a cutting board. Put 2 marshmallows onto half of the graham cracker halves. Place 2 squares of chocolate onto the cracker with the marshmallows. Put the remaining crackers on top to create 4 sandwiches. Wrap each one in the baking paper so it resembles a parcel. Cook in the fryer for 5 minutes at 340 F.

558. Mock Cherry Pie

Servings:8
Cooking Time: 30 Minutes
Ingredients:
- 21 oz cherry pie filling
- 1 egg yolk
- 1 tbsp milk

Directions:
1. Preheat air fryer to 310 F.
2. Place one pie crust in a pie pan; poke holes into the crust. Cook for 5 minutes.
3. Spread the pie filling over. Cut the other pie crust into strips and arrange the pie-style over the baked crust. Whisk milk and egg yolk, and brush the

mixture over the pie. Return the pie to the fryer and cook for 15 minutes.

559. Chocolate Banana Sandwiches

Servings:2
Cooking Time: 30 Minutes
Ingredients:
- 1 tbsp butter, melted
- 6 oz milk chocolate, broken into chunks
- 1 banana, sliced

Directions:
1. Brush the brioche slices with butter. Spread chocolate and banana on 2 brioche slices. Top with the remaining 2 slices to create 2 sandwiches. Arrange the sandwiches into your air fryer and cook for 14 minutes at 400 F, turning once halfway through. Slice in half and serve with vanilla ice cream.

560. Crème Brûlée

Servings:8
Cooking Time:13 Minutes
Ingredients:
- 10 egg yolks
- 4 cups heavy cream
- 2 tablespoons sugar
- 2 tablespoons vanilla extract

Directions:
1. Preheat the Air fryer to 370 F and grease 8 (6-ounce) ramekins lightly.
2. Mix all the ingredients in a bowl except stevia until well combined.
3. Divide the mixture evenly in the ramekins and transfer into the Air fryer.
4. Cook for about 13 minutes and remove from the Air fryer.

5. Let it cool slightly and refrigerate for about 3 hours to serve.

561. Cocoa Spread

Servings: 4
Cooking Time: 5 Minutes
Ingredients:
- 2 oz walnuts, chopped
- 5 teaspoons coconut oil
- ½ teaspoon vanilla extract
- 1 tablespoon Erythritol
- 1 teaspoon of cocoa powder

Directions:
1. Preheat the air fryer to 350F. Put the walnuts in the mason jar. Add coconut oil, vanilla extract, Erythritol, and cocoa powder. Stir the mixture until smooth with the help of the spoon. Then place the mason jar with Nutella in the preheated air fryer and cook it for 5 minutes. Stir Nutella before serving.

562. Bananas & Ice Cream

Servings: 2
Cooking Time: 25 Minutes
Ingredients:
- 2 large bananas
- 1 tbsp. butter
- 1 tbsp. sugar
- 2 tbsp. friendly bread crumbs
- Vanilla ice cream for serving

Directions:
1. Place the butter in the Air Fryer basket and allow it to melt for 1 minute at 350°F.
2. Combine the sugar and bread crumbs in a bowl.

3. Slice the bananas into 1-inch-round pieces. Drop them into the sugar mixture and coat them well.
4. Place the bananas in the Air Fryer and cook for 10 – 15 minutes.
5. Serve warm, with ice cream on the side if desired.

563. Cheesecake Cups

Servings: 4
Cooking Time: 10 Minutes
Ingredients:
- 8 oz cream cheese, softened
- 2 oz heavy cream
- 1 tsp Sugar Glycerite
- 1 tsp Splenda
- 1 tsp vanilla flavoring (Frontier Organic)

Directions:
1. Combine all the ingredients.
2. Whip until a pudding consistency is achieved.
3. Divide in cups.
4. Refrigerate until served!

564. Chocolate Brownie

Servings: 4
Cooking Time: 16 Minutes
Ingredients:
- 1 cup bananas, overripe
- 1 scoop protein powder
- 2 tbsp unsweetened cocoa powder
- 1/2 cup almond butter, melted

Directions:
1. Preheat the air fryer to 325 F.
2. Spray air fryer baking pan with cooking spray.
3. Add all ingredients into the blender and blend until smooth.

4. Pour batter into the prepared pan and place in the air fryer basket.
5. Cook brownie for 16 minutes.
6. Serve and enjoy.

565. Cranberry Cream Surprise

Servings: 1
Cooking Time: 30 Minutes
Ingredients:
- 1 cup mashed cranberries
- ½ cup Confectioner's Style Swerve
- 2 tsp natural cherry flavoring
- 2 tsp natural rum flavoring
- 1 cup organic heavy cream

Directions:
1. Combine the mashed cranberries, sweetener, cherry and rum flavorings.
2. Cover and refrigerate for 20 minutes.
3. Whip the heavy cream until soft peaks form.
4. Layer the whipped cream and cranberry mixture.
5. Top with fresh cranberries, mint leaves or grated dark chocolate.
6. Serve!

566. Chocolate Candies

Servings: 4
Cooking Time: 2 Minutes
Ingredients:
- 1 oz almonds, crushed
- 1 oz dark chocolate
- 2 tablespoons peanut butter
- 2 tablespoons heavy cream

Directions:
1. Preheat the air fryer to 390F. Chop the dark chocolate and put it in the air fryer mold. Add peanut butter and

heavy cream. Stir the mixture and transfer in the air fryer. Cook it for 2 minutes or until it starts to be melt. Then line the air tray with parchment. Put the crushed almonds on the tray in one layer. Then pour the cooked chocolate mixture over the almonds. Flatten gently if needed and let it cool. Crack the cooked chocolate layer into the candies.

567. Apple Pie Crumble

Servings:4
Cooking Time:25 Minutes
Ingredients:
- 1 (14-ounce) can apple pie
- ¼ cup butter, softened
- 9 tablespoons self-rising flour
- 7 tablespoons caster sugar
- Pinch of salt

Directions:
1. Preheat the Air fryer to 320 F and grease a baking dish.
2. Mix all the ingredients in a bowl until a crumbly mixture is formed.
3. Arrange the apple pie in the baking dish and top with the mixture.
4. Transfer the baking dish into the Air fryer basket and cook for about 25 minutes.
5. Dish out in a platter and serve.

568. Berry Layer Cake

Servings: 1
Cooking Time: 8 Minutes
Ingredients:
- ¼ lemon pound cake
- ¼ cup whipping cream
- ½ tsp Truvia

- 1/8 tsp orange flavor
- 1 cup of mixed berries

Directions:
1. Using a sharp knife, divide the lemon cake into small cubes.
2. Dice the strawberries.
3. Combine the whipping cream, Truvia, and orange flavor.
4. Layer the fruit, cake and cream in a glass.
5. Serve!

569. Banana Chips With Chocolate Glaze

Servings: 2
Cooking Time: 20 Minutes
Ingredients:
- 2 banana, cut into slices
- 1/4 teaspoon lemon zest
- 1 tablespoon agave syrup
- 1 tablespoon cocoa powder
- 1 tablespoon coconut oil, melted

Directions:
1. Toss the bananas with the lemon zest and agave syrup. Transfer your bananas to the parchment-lined cooking basket.
2. Bake in the preheated Air Fryer at 370 degrees F for 12 minutes, turning them over halfway through the cooking time.
3. In the meantime, melt the coconut oil in your microwave; add the cocoa powder and whisk to combine well.
4. Serve the baked banana chips with a few drizzles of the chocolate glaze. Enjoy!

570. Crusty

Servings: 3
Cooking Time: 60 Minutes

Ingredients:
- 2 cups flour
- 4 tsp melted butter
- 2 large eggs
- ½ tsp salt

Directions:
1. Mix together the flour and butter.
2. Add in the eggs and salt and combine well to form a dough ball.
3. Place the dough between two pieces of parchment paper. Roll out to 10" by 16" and ¼ inch thick.
4. Serve!

571. Fiesta Pastries

Servings:8
Cooking Time:20 Minutes
Ingredients:
- ½ of apple, peeled, cored and chopped
- 1 teaspoon fresh orange zest, grated finely
- 7.05-ounce prepared frozen puff pastry, cut into 16 squares
- ½ tablespoon white sugar
- ½ teaspoon ground cinnamon

Directions:
1. Preheat the Air fryer to 390 °F and grease an Air fryer basket.
2. Mix all ingredients in a bowl except puff pastry.
3. Arrange about 1 teaspoon of this mixture in the center of each square.
4. Fold each square into a triangle and slightly press the edges with a fork.
5. Arrange the pastries in the Air fryer basket and cook for about 10 minutes.
6. Dish out and serve immediately.

572. Apple And Cinnamon Sauce

Servings: 6
Cooking Time: 30 Minutes
Ingredients:
- 6 apples, peeled, cored and cut into wedges
- 1 tablespoon cinnamon powder
- 1 cup sugar
- 1 cup red wine

Directions:
1. In a pan that fits your air fryer, place all of the ingredients and toss.
2. Place the pan in the fryer and cook at 320 degrees F for 30 minutes.
3. Divide into cups and serve right away.

573. Raspberry Pudding Surprise

Servings: 1
Cooking Time: 40 Minutes
Ingredients:
- 3 tbsp chia seeds
- ½ cup unsweetened milk
- 1 scoop chocolate protein powder
- ¼ cup raspberries, fresh or frozen
- 1 tsp honey

Directions:
1. Combine the milk, protein powder and chia seeds together.
2. Let rest for 5 minutes before stirring.
3. Refrigerate for 30 minutes.
4. Top with raspberries.
5. Serve!

574. Cream Cups

Servings: 6

Cooking Time: 10 Minutes
Ingredients:
- 2 tablespoons butter, melted
- 8 ounces cream cheese, soft
- 3 tablespoons coconut, shredded and unsweetened
- 3 eggs
- 4 tablespoons swerve

Directions:
1. In a bowl, mix all the ingredients and whisk really well. Divide into small ramekins, put them in the fryer and cook at 320 degrees F and bake for 10 minutes. Serve cold.

575. Cherry Pie

Servings: 8
Cooking Time: 35 Minutes
Ingredients:
- 1 tbsp. milk
- 2 ready-made pie crusts
- 21 oz. cherry pie filling
- 1 egg yolk

Directions:
1. Pre-heat the Air Fryer to 310°F.
2. Coat the inside of a pie pan with a little oil or butter and lay one of the pie crusts inside. Use a fork to pierce a few holes in the pastry.
3. Spread the pie filling evenly over the crust.
4. Slice the other crust into strips and place them on top of the pie filling to make the pie look more homemade.
5. Place in the Air Fryer and cook for 15 minutes.

576. Lemon Curd

Servings:2

Cooking Time: 30 Minutes
Ingredients:
- 3 tbsp sugar
- 1 egg
- 1 egg yolk
- ¾ lemon, juiced

Directions:
1. Add sugar and butter in a medium ramekin and beat evenly. Add egg and yolk slowly while still whisking the fresh yellow color will be attained. Add the lemon juice and mix. Place the bowl in the fryer basket and cook at 250 F for 6 minutes. Increase the temperature again to 320 F and cook for 15 minutes.
2. Remove the bowl onto a flat surface; use a spoon to check for any lumps and remove. Cover the ramekin with a plastic wrap and refrigerate overnight or serve immediately.

577. Lemon Bars Recipe

Servings: 6
Cooking Time:35 Minutes
Ingredients:
- 4 eggs
- 1 cup butter; soft
- 2 ¼ cups flour
- Juice from 2 lemons
- 2 cups sugar

Directions:
1. In a bowl; mix butter with 1/2 cup sugar and 2 cups flour; stir well, press on the bottom of a pan that fits your air fryer, introduce in the fryer and cook at 350 °F, for 10 minutes
2. In another bowl, mix the rest of the sugar with the rest of the flour, eggs and lemon juice, whisk well and spread

over crust. Introduce in the fryer at 350 °F, for 15 minutes more, leave aside to cool down, cut bars and serve them.

578. Apple Wedges

Servings: 4
Cooking Time: 25 Minutes
Ingredients:
- 4 large apples
- 2 tbsp. olive oil
- ½ cup dried apricots, chopped
- 1 – 2 tbsp. sugar
- ½ tsp. ground cinnamon

Directions:
1. Peel the apples and slice them into eight wedges. Throw away the cores.
2. Coat the apple wedges with the oil.
3. Place each wedge in the Air Fryer and cook for 12 - 15 minutes at 350°F.
4. Add in the apricots and allow to cook for a further 3 minutes.
5. Stir together the sugar and cinnamon. Sprinkle this mixture over the cooked apples before serving.

579. Crème Brulee

Servings:3
Cooking Time: 60 Minutes
Ingredients:
- 1 cup milk
- 2 vanilla pods
- 10 egg yolks
- 4 tbsp sugar + extra for topping

Directions:
1. In a pan, add the milk and cream. Cut the vanilla pods open and scrape the seeds into the pan with the vanilla pods also. Place the pan over medium heat on a stovetop until almost boiled while stirring regularly. Turn off the heat. Add the egg yolks to a bowl and beat it. Add the sugar and mix well but not too bubbly.
2. Remove the vanilla pods from the milk mixture; pour the mixture onto the eggs mixture while stirring constantly. Let it sit for 25 minutes. Fill 2 to 3 ramekins with the mixture. Place the ramekins in the fryer basket and cook them at 190 F for 50 minutes. Once ready, remove the ramekins and let sit to cool. Sprinkle the remaining sugar over and use a torch to melt the sugar, so it browns at the top.

580. Grilled Banana Boats

Servings: 3
Cooking Time: 15 Minutes
Ingredients:
- 3 large bananas
- 1 tablespoon ginger snaps
- 2 tablespoons mini chocolate chips
- 3 tablespoons mini marshmallows
- 3 tablespoons crushed vanilla wafers

Directions:
1. In the peel, slice your banana lengthwise; make sure not to slice all the way through the banana. Divide the remaining ingredients between the banana pockets.
2. Place in the Air Fryer grill pan. Cook at 395 degrees F for 7 minutes.
3. Let the banana boats cool for 5 to 6 minutes, and then eat with a spoon. Bon appétit!

581. Cinnamon Apple Chips

Servings: 6
Cooking Time: 8 Minutes
Ingredients:
- 3 Granny Smith apples, wash, core and thinly slice
- 1 tsp ground cinnamon
- Pinch of salt

Directions:
1. Rub apple slices with cinnamon and salt and place into the air fryer basket.
2. Cook at 390 F for 8 minutes. Turn halfway through.
3. Serve and enjoy.

582. Chocolate Peanut Butter Cups

Servings: 2
Cooking Time: 70 Minutes
Ingredients:
- 1 stick unsalted butter
- 1 oz / 1 cube unsweetened chocolate
- 5 packets Sugar in the Raw
- 1 tbsp heavy cream
- 4 tbsp peanut butter

Directions:
1. In a microwave, melt the butter and chocolate.
2. Add the Sugar.
3. Stir in the cream and peanut butter.
4. Line the muffin tins. Fill the muffin cups.
5. Freeze for 60 minutes.
6. Serve!

583. Lemon Mousse

Servings:6
Cooking Time:10 Minutes

Ingredients:
- 12-ounces cream cheese, softened
- ¼ teaspoon salt
- 1 teaspoon lemon liquid stevia
- 1/3 cup fresh lemon juice
- 1½ cups heavy cream

Directions:
1. Preheat the Air fryer to 345 degrees F and grease a large ramekin lightly.
2. Mix all the ingredients in a large bowl until well combined.
3. Pour into the ramekin and transfer into the Air fryer.
4. Cook for about 10 minutes and pour into the serving glasses.
5. Refrigerate to cool for about 3 hours and serve chilled.

584. Air Fried Snickerdoodle Poppers

Servings:6
Cooking Time: 30 Minutes
Ingredients:
- 1 can of Pillsbury Grands Flaky Layers Biscuits
- 1 ½ cups cinnamon sugar
- melted butter, for brushing

Directions:
1. Preheat air fryer to 350 F. Unroll the flaky biscuits; cut them into fourths. Roll each ¼ into a ball. Arrange the balls on a lined baking sheet, and cook in the air fryer for 7 minutes, or until golden.
2. Prepare the Jell-O following the package's instructions. Using an injector, inject some of the vanilla pudding into each ball. Brush the balls with melted butter and then coat them with cinnamon sugar.

585. Sugar Pork Rinds

Servings: 2
Cooking Time: 10 Minutes
Ingredients:
- 2 oz. pork rinds
- 2 tsp. unsalted butter, melted
- ¼ cup powdered erythritol
- ½ tsp. ground cinnamon

Directions:
1. Coat the rinds with the melted butter.
2. In a separate bowl, combine the erythritol and cinnamon and pour over the pork rinds, ensuring the rinds are covered completely and evenly.
3. Transfer the pork rinds into the fryer and cook at 400°F for five minutes.

586. Strawberry Shake

Servings: 1
Cooking Time: 5 Minutes
Ingredients:
- 3/4 cup coconut milk (from the carton)
- ¼ cup heavy cream
- 7 ice cubes
- 2 tbsp sugar-free strawberry Torani syrup
- ¼ tsp Xanthan Gum

Directions:
1. Combine all the ingredients into blender.
2. Blend for 1-2 minutes.
3. Serve!

587. Chocolate Banana Pastries

Servings:4
Cooking Time: 12 Minutes
Ingredients:
- 1 puff pastry sheet
- ½ cup Nutella
- 2 bananas, peeled and sliced

Directions:
1. Cut the pastry sheet into 4 equal-sized squares.
2. Spread Nutella evenly on each square of pastry.
3. Divide the banana slices over Nutella.
4. Fold each square into a triangle and with wet fingers, slightly press the edges.
5. Then with a fork, press the edges firmly.
6. Set the temperature of air fryer to 375 degrees F. Lightly, grease an air fryer basket.
7. Arrange pastries into the prepared air fryer basket in a single layer.
8. Air fry for about 10-12 minutes.
9. Remove from air fryer and transfer the pastries onto a platter.
10. Serve warm.

588. Berry Pudding

Servings: 6
Cooking Time: 15 Minutes
Ingredients:
- 2 cups coconut cream
- 1/3 cup blackberries
- 1/3 cup blueberries
- 3 tablespoons swerve
- Zest of 1 lime, grated

Directions:
1. In a blender, combine all the ingredients and pulse well. Divide this into 6 small ramekins, put them in your air fryer and cook at 340 degrees F for 15 minutes. Serve cold.

589. Crispy Fruit Tacos

Servings:2
Cooking Time:5 Minutes
Ingredients:
- 2 soft shell tortillas
- 4 tablespoons strawberry jelly
- ¼ cup blueberries
- ¼ cup raspberries
- 2 tablespoons powdered sugar

Directions:
1. Preheat the Air fryer to 300 °F and grease an Air fryer basket.
2. Put 2 tablespoons of strawberry jelly over each tortilla and top with blueberries and raspberries.
3. Sprinkle with powdered sugar and transfer into the Air fryer basket.
4. Cook for about 5 minutes until crispy and serve.

590. Chia Pudding

Servings: 1
Cooking Time: 10 Minutes
Ingredients:
- cup chia seeds
- 1 cup unsweetened coconut milk
- 1 tsp. liquid Sugar
- 1 tbsp. coconut oil
- 1 tsp. butter

Directions:
1. Pre-heat the fryer at 360°F.
2. In a bowl, gently combine the chia seeds with the milk and Sugar, before mixing the coconut oil and butter. Spoon seven equal-sized portions into seven ramekins and set these inside the fryer.
3. Cook for four minutes. Take care when removing the ramekins from the fryer

and allow to cool for four minutes before serving.

591. Pineapple Sticks

Servings: 4
Cooking Time: 20 Minutes
Ingredients:
- ½ fresh pineapple, cut into sticks
- ¼ cup desiccated coconut

Directions:
1. Pre-heat the Air Fryer to 400°F.
2. Coat the pineapple sticks in the desiccated coconut and put each one in the Air Fryer basket.
3. Air fry for 10 minutes.

592. Chocolate Apple Chips

Servings: 2
Cooking Time: 15 Minutes
Ingredients:
- 1 large Pink Lady apple, cored and sliced
- 1 tablespoon light brown sugar
- A pinch of kosher salt
- 2 tablespoons lemon juice
- 2 teaspoons cocoa powder

Directions:
1. Toss the apple slices with the other ingredients.
2. Bake at 350 degrees F for 5 minutes; shake the basket to ensure even cooking and continue to cook an additional 5 minutes.
3. Bon appétit!

593. Banana Oatmeal Cookies

Servings: 6
Cooking Time: 20 Minutes

Ingredients:
- 2 cups quick oats
- ¼ cup milk
- 4 ripe bananas, mashed
- ¼ cup coconut, shredded

Directions:
1. Pre-heat the Air Fryer to 350°F.
2. Combine all of the ingredients in a bowl.
3. Scoop equal amounts of the cookie dough onto a baking sheet and put it in the Air Fryer basket.
4. Bake the cookies for 15 minutes.

594. Hot Coconut 'n Cocoa Buns

Servings:8
Cooking Time: 15 Minutes
Ingredients:
- ¼ cup cacao nibs
- 1 cup coconut milk
- 1/3 cup coconut flour
- 3 tablespoons cacao powder
- 4 eggs, beaten

Directions:
1. Preheat the air fryer for 5 minutes.
2. Combine all ingredients in a mixing bowl.
3. Form buns using your hands and place in a baking dish that will fit in the air fryer.
4. Bake for 15 minutes for 375F.
5. Once air fryer turns off, leave the buns in the air fryer until it cools completely.

595. Chocolate And Avocado Cream

Servings: 4
Cooking Time: 20 Minutes

Ingredients:
- 2 avocados, peeled, pitted and mashed
- 3 tablespoons chocolate, melted
- 4 tablespoons erythritol
- 3 tablespoons cream cheese, soft

Directions:
1. In a pan that fits the air fryer, combine all the ingredients, whisk, put the pan in the fryer and cook at 340 degrees F for 20 minutes. Divide into bowls and serve cold.

596. Basic Butter Cookies

Servings:8
Cooking Time:10 Minutes
Ingredients:
- 4-ounce unsalted butter
- 1 cup all-purpose flour
- ¼ teaspoon baking powder
- 1¼-ounce icing sugar

Directions:
1. Preheat the Air fryer to 340 F and grease a baking sheet lightly.
2. Mix butter, icing sugar, flour and baking powder in a large bowl.
3. Mix well until a dough is formed and transfer into the piping bag fitted with a fluted nozzle.
4. Pipe the dough onto a baking sheet and arrange the baking sheet in the Air fryer.
5. Cook for about 10 minutes until golden brown and serve with tea.

597. Coffee Surprise

Servings: 1
Cooking Time: 5 Minutes
Ingredients:
- 2 heaped tbsp flaxseed, ground

- 100ml cooking cream 35% fat
- ½ tsp cocoa powder, dark and unsweetened
- 1 tbsp goji berries
- Freshly brewed coffee

Directions:
1. Mix together the flaxseeds, cream and cocoa and coffee.
2. Season with goji berries.
3. Serve!

598. Blueberry Cookies

Servings: 2
Cooking Time: 30 Minutes
Ingredients:
- 3 oz blueberries
- ½ teaspoon avocado oil

Directions:
1. Put the blueberries in the blender and grind them until smooth. Then line the air fryer basket with baking paper. Brush it with the avocado oil. After this, pour the blended blueberries on the prepared baking paper and flatten it in one layer with the help of the spatula. Cook the blueberry leather for 30 minutes at 300F. Cut into cookies and serve.

599. Choco-coconut Puddin

Servings: 1
Cooking Time: 65 Minutes

Ingredients:
- 1 cup coconut milk
- 2 tbsp cacao powder or organic cocoa
- ½ tsp Sugar powder extract or 2 tbsp honey/maple syrup
- ½ tbsp quality gelatin
- 1 tbsp water

Directions:
1. On a medium heat, combine the coconut milk, cocoa and sweetener.
2. In a separate bowl, mix in the gelatin and water.
3. Add to the pan and stir until fully dissolved.
4. Pour into small dishes and refrigerate for 1 hour.
5. Serve!

600. Lemon Berry Jam

Servings: 12
Cooking Time: 20 Minutes
Ingredients:
- ¼ cup swerve
- 8 ounces strawberries, sliced
- 1 tablespoon lemon juice
- ¼ cup water

Directions:
1. In a pan that fits the air fryer, combine all the ingredients, put the pan in the machine and cook at 380 degrees F for 20 minutes. Divide the mix into cups, cool down and serve.

CPSIA information can be obtained
at www.ICGtesting.com
Printed in the USA
LVHW100542120221
679113LV00025B/889

9 781922 547989